MW01484432

MANAGING STAKEHOLDER EXPECTATIONS FOR PROJECT SUCCESS

A Knowledge Integration Framework and Value Focused Approach

Ori Schibi, PMP

Copyright © 2014 by PM Konnectors

ISBN-13: 978-1-60427-086-0

Printed and bound in the U.S.A. Printed on acid-free paper.

10 9 8 7 6 5 4 3 2 1

Library of Congress Cataloging-in-Publication Data

Schibi, Ori, 1971–
  Managing stakeholder expectations for project success: a knowledge
integration framework and value focused approach / by Ori Schibi.
    p. cm
  Includes index.
  ISBN 978-1-60427-086-0 (hardcover : alk. paper) 1. Project management.
I. Title.
  HD69.P75S35 2013
  658.4'04—dc23

                           2013033269

Phone: (954) 727-9333
Fax: (561) 892-0700
Web: www.jrosspub.com

Dedication

This Book is Dedicated to:

Eva, my wife, my best friend, my love and my everything. It is my greatest fortune to have found someone who enriches every aspect of my life and who has so much grace, kindness, inner and outer beauty and love for me and our beautiful daughters. Eva played an instrumental role in bringing this book to realization with her support, supreme editing capabilities, dedication, knowledge, inquiring mind, and above all, patience.

Our wonderful daughters Kayla and Maya.

And my mother, Hava, who has provided me with love, care, dedication, and everything I ever needed to do anything I put my mind to, with support, advice and unconditional love and commitment.

For all of these, I am most grateful.

Acknowledgments

Special thanks goes out to:

Ron Kerr
Ari Glaziel
Cheryl Lee
Eitan Shibi
Barry Bender
Karen Yepson
Naaman Shibi

For their knowledgeable and thorough review and input.

Table of Contents

Preface...xi
About the Author xvii
Introduction xix

CHAPTER 1   The (Sad) Reality of Project Management 1
The Reality in Quotes.. 1
Not Enough of 5
Instant Gratification..7
The Short History of Project Management 7
Sign of the Times...8
More With Less..10
Give Me a Schedule...12
The Structure of Our Brain and Project Management 15
Culture of Alligators 17

CHAPTER 2   Project Complexity and Readiness Assessment 21
Introduction to the Readiness Assessment..22
What the Readiness Assessment is About 25
Assessment Considerations 26
Assessment Results: How Do You Know When You Are Ready? 29
Introduction to the Project Complexity Assessment 30
What is Complexity?..32
Project Attributes 35
Thoughts on Complexity 37
Kickoff Meeting...37
Kickoff Summary 40
Readiness and Complexity Final Thoughts...40

**CHAPTER 3   Culture and Politics: The Organization's Pillars
and Speed Bumps** 43
What is Politics? 44
Understanding Politics 47

Blood Is Thicker Than Water 51
Let's Talk About Politics: The Interstate Story 51
Emotional Resilience 54
Win-Win..54
Coffee and Value 56
Team Building..57
Is There an "I" in Team?..58
A Different View of Leadership 59
Leadership Styles...60
Conflict...62
Team Development 62
Sources of Conflict..65
Conflict—The Good, The Bad, and The Ugly 71
Conflict Resolution Techniques 73
Escalation 76
Misconceptions About Conflict 77
May Come in Handy..77
Final Political Thoughts 79

CHAPTER 4 Understanding Stakeholders and What They Want 83
Stakeholder Identification..85
Stakeholder Analysis Brick and Mortar.......................................87
Confidential 91
Stakeholders and the Requirements 92
Take It Up a Notch 95
Attitudes 102
Responsibility Assignment Matrix...103
Focus 107
Stakeholder Engagement and Expectations Management 108
Stakeholder Management Plan...110
Evaluate the Process..110
Stakeholder Expectations Management Final Thoughts..................110

CHAPTER 5 Connecting Success and Constraints.................................... 113
Defining Success Through Constraints.......................................115
The Triple Constraint/Competing Demands 117
The Constraints Face-off...117
The Balloon...119
Setting Expectations..124
Success Acceptance and Approval 126
Project Charter 127

Beyond Scope, Time, and Cost 128
Success Factors..129
Enhance the Measurements..130
Let's Put It In Order 132
Final Thoughts About Quality and Success 133

CHAPTER 6   Assumptions: The Project Manager's Best Friends................. 135
What Is an Assumption? 136
Specify and Record Assumptions...136
What Might Happen with Assumptions...139
Assumption Categories..140
Document Assumptions from the Start...141
How to Identify Assumptions...142
Assumption Log 145
Project Assumptions 146
Potential Backlash 147
Assume and Monitor 148
Keep in Mind..149
Final Thoughts on Assumptions..150

CHAPTER 7   Managing Those Things That Make a Difference................... 153
How Do You Manage Your Day? 154
What to Manage 157
Transformational Focus...158
Time Wasted 163
More Transformational Areas of Focus 165
Final Thoughts About Managing What Matters...................................172

CHAPTER 8   Managing Risk Effectively: What's Missing from Current Risk Management Methodologies 173
Characteristics of Risk...174
What to Aim For 175
Risk Methodologies...176
Where to Start...176
Do Not Wait Until the Wheels Fall Off...178
Risk Planning and Approach..178
Risk Register...179
SWOT Analysis 181
SWOT on Steroids..182
Risk Identification 184
The Risk Identification Process...186

Risk Analysis..188
Risk Urgency: Beyond Probability and Impact.................................195
Risk Assessment 196
Next Step: Triggers and Detectability..197
Risk Response Planning 198
Contingency...202
Secondary and Residual Risks...204
Controlling Risk 206
Additional Risk Considerations 208
Final Thoughts on Risk 213

CHAPTER 9   Learn What Quality Means.. 215
Management Responsibility...216
About Quality 218
What Is Quality?...218
Cost of Quality...220
Quality Management Plan 223
Quality Considerations..224
Poka-Yoke..225
Project Health 226
Health Measurements..228
Final Thoughts on Quality..232

CHAPTER 10   Managing Project Change.. 235
Change Control 236
Proactive Project Change Management...237
The Change Control Process...241
Project Change Management Considerations......................................247
Final Thoughts on Change 255

CHAPTER 11   Designing and Managing Project Communications............ 257
Not a 50–50 Effort...259
Changing Project Management..261
Communication Planning...264
Team Contract and Ground Rules..268
More Thoughts on Communication 272
Final Thought: Own the Communications...276

CHAPTER 12   Organizational Influences.. 279
Chapter Structure: 3 in 1 280
Alignment...280

Critical Chain...281
Risk and Change Requests...283
Lessons Learned and Post Implementation Review............................284
Lessons Learned are Not Only About Lessons 285
Post Implementation Review...290
Project Rescue and Recovery...292
What is Recovery About?...294
Tips For Recovery 295
Thoughts on Recovery...297
Organizational Influences Final Thoughts..299

CHAPTER 13   Integration: Putting It All Together 301
Not a Perfect World 302
Doing It Right...304
Integration, for Real..318
Who Is More Important? 319
How to Say No When You Need to (and Still Keep Your Job) 321
Final Thoughts..324
Moving Forward...325

Index 327

Preface

With thousands of project management books out there, it is still hard to find a book that can serve as a "cheat sheet"—a guide project managers (PMs) can reference in order to effectively tackle situations they face. There are many books that offer templates and toolkits, some that deal with concepts, and others that provide insights about the "mechanics" of managing projects (e.g., building a schedule, creating a work breakdown structure).

THE OBJECTIVES OF THIS BOOK

The main objective of this book is to incorporate best practices and concepts into the day-to-day realities of PMs. It provides PMs with the ability to think about the situations they face, identify proper sources of information, assess changing realities, and ask relevant questions that serve as eye openers to those involved. The book incorporates my experience of over 20 years in project management and consulting, teaching and professional development, along with particular emphasis on the Project Management Institute's *A Guide to the Project Management Body of Knowledge* (*PMBOK® Guide*) and some "seasoning" from Accrediting Project Management Group's (APMG) PRINCE2. This book does not regurgitate these concepts, and it does not propose a replacement; it puts the PM in a state of mind to leverage these concepts and methodologies in the context of organizational challenges and project realities.

What Makes this Book Different?

This book offers a new way of managing and dealing with projects. It focuses on communications, understanding stakeholders' needs and managing their expectations, learning about organizational politics, and performing value-adding activities—that is, managing and focusing on those things that matter for project success, rather than doing the same things in the same ways everyone else does. The new way is about leveraging what is already known about project management and utilizing existing methodologies and concepts, so they work for us and benefit the causes for which projects are undertaken.

The Structure of this Book

This book takes you on a journey through ideas and thoughts that may be viewed by some as "common sense" or as things that "should go without saying." In our reality of time and resource constraints, however, they are often left unsaid and consistently do not get sufficient focus or consideration.

Chapter 1, "The (Sad) Reality of Project Management," contains a discussion of the state of project management and the reality that, with half a million project management professionals worldwide, it is not easy to find a PM who can build a credible schedule. You should review how project trade-offs work and what to expect from them in every project, so you can direct your focus toward those things that actually matter for success. It contains observations about some of the "secrets" to project success, as well as a discussion regarding why PMs who are appointed for their technical skills may not achieve the same level of success as their counterparts who are focused on people skills. There is also a benefit to learning about the cultural aspects of organizations that seem to encourage and condone PMs to actively work against each other. While there is no simple way to change this reality, the chapter proposes ways to start an organic movement toward improving collaboration. I call it a "culture of alligators," as PMs, within an organization, treat each other in a similar fashion as alligators fighting over food. This chapter introduces you to the culture of alligators, and the rest of the book deals with how to overcome it.

Chapter 2, "Project Complexity and Readiness Assessment," compares the need for project readiness to our routines of getting ready before leaving for work or the preparation process to boarding a flight to go on vacation. You can use the information about assessing project readiness to establish habits of creating checklists and other measures, which can help you determine how prepared your organization is for undertaking the project. As a result, you can approach your sponsor with valid questions about your findings. The chapter also addresses questions and observation points to quantify the level of complexity the project is expected to bring, so you can better prepare decision makers. With the ability to measure the level of project complexity by applying criteria that allow benchmarking and comparison over time, you will be better prepared for what you may be up against on future projects.

Chapter 3, "Culture and Politics: The Organization's Pillars and Speed Bumps," takes the discussion from Chapter 2 and deals with the fact that culture is one of the toughest things to change in an organization, and politics are here to stay. You can benefit from understanding organizational politics, which is possible if you start small and approach it systematically. While culture and politics are often viewed as hurdles and areas of uncertainty, the chapter reiterates the difficulty in navigating the political landscape of an organization and proposes ways to decipher organizational politics and utilize it for the benefit of our projects. It also reviews leadership styles and presents techniques to identify the one that is most applicable to your individual situation.

Chapter 4, "Understanding Stakeholders and What They Want," points at the shifting focus toward communication and stakeholder expectations management, to illustrate the criticality of these aspects to project success. Stakeholder analysis is one of the first things the PM needs to perform in the project, and this chapter introduces questions and checklists of things to look for when analyzing stakeholders. You will be able to pick up tips and lists of things to look for that, in turn, will draw a clearer picture of how to manage stakeholder expectations, what to expect from them, and how to treat them.

Chapter 5, "Connecting Success and Constraints," provides a first look into what project integration really means and how to create a picture of the project landscape. This will pave the way for you to "do the right thing," rather than drive the project's bus "blindfolded." I have seen too many projects on which the PM was doing a good job managing a project, but it was not the "right" good job (i.e., the PM was not sufficiently aware of all project and related business objectives). The chapter introduces concepts for gathering information and defining success criteria and in turn, tying them to the project constraints.

Chapter 6, "Assumptions: The Project Manager's Best Friends," deals with what all PMs rely on, but no one really likes. Assumptions are not only an important part of life and of projects but also critical to delivering project success, to managing risks, and even to making it possible to take action that will move the project forward. The chapter discusses the general fear PMs have of assumptions, and elaborates on the negative connotations they have. You will learn how to identify, address, track, and act on assumptions and to link them to project success. It proposes ways to track assumptions and to take actions according to the course they take. You can glean the benefit of learning how to avoid paralysis—failing to make a decision in the face of insufficient information. Linking assumptions to risks is an important component to effective assumption management, which is a further aspect discussed in this chapter.

Chapter 7, "Managing Those Things That Make a Difference," is another feature that makes this book unique and valuable. It contrasts the importance of delivering on project objectives and success criteria with being effective at managing them. You will be able to take a look at your own project management style, and learn how to pick your battles and focus on those things that can really make a difference in your project. The chapter illustrates the link between effective management of "back office aspects" of the project (such as quality, risk, communication, and change) and delivering success on the traditional measures of scope, time, and cost, as well as on the project's intended benefits for the organization. It introduces what should be a popular sentiment among PMs: "my dream job as a PM is to come in as the chief PM and bring my deputy along with me," where the chief PM will manage those things that matter, and the deputy will handle those "pesky" deliverables, schedules, and budgets.

Chapter 8, "Managing Risk Effectively: What's Missing from Current Risk Management Methodologies," takes the existing methodologies of risk management and applies them proactively, in such a way that can be suitable for any project. The chapter distinguishes between project risk and business risk and encourages PMs to think about project risks in the context of business risks, for better alignment with organizational objectives. It will trigger you to properly identify risks, and in turn, you will learn how to pick your battles (prioritize risks) based on organizational and project priorities. The chapter includes a breakdown of the process of risk response into all of its components, to align them with project success criteria.

Chapter 9, "Learn What Quality Means," reinforces the importance of quality management planning through a review of several quality concepts that are well known, yet not sufficiently followed. You will be able to pick up ideas for applying these concepts to your projects and make them signature attributes of your project management style. This chapter covers the basics: defining what quality is, how to measure it, and how to build a meaningful quality plan. It also discusses ways to determine project health, introducing multiple measures for checking a project's interim performance that go beyond the traditional focus on deliverables and results.

Chapter 10, "Managing Project Change," deals with one of the most painful aspects of managing projects. While Agile projects have found a way to reduce the impact of scope changes or postpone the changes themselves, most PMs still deal with the realities of requirement and scope changes. The chapter reviews techniques to reduce the number of changes introduced throughout the project, and introduces a simple process that is both effective and formal to enable the proper measure of change impact and risks associated with the change requested. You will learn how to measure whether and when a change is really required, and to question whether a change request should be made for scope changes—only—or for other changing conditions as well. Overall, the chapter offers an approach for PMs to become more proactive about managing project changes. It also proposes a technique to overcome a common problem in managing project change: how to measure the overall impact of a proposed change, taking into consideration all other changes in the pipeline.

Chapter 11, "Designing and Managing Project Communications," extends the stakeholder analysis to design a communication plan that is applicable, relevant, effective, and efficient—to address all stakeholders' needs. You will learn how to trade the appropriate currency and speak the proper language to reach all stake-holders in a timely and effective manner. The chapter discusses the components of a communication plan and introduces aspects that should go without saying, but unfortunately require elaboration in most project realities.

Chapter 12, "Organizational Influences," deals with three distinct matters that share a common denominator: they have a direct impact on the organization and as a result, must be taken into consideration by PMs. The first of the three topics is organizational influences, which peeks into the importance of asking the right questions to ensure alignment between project and organizational goals. The second area includes a review of how to conduct a lessons learned process and a post implementation review as part of the effort to improve organizational capabilities. The third one deals with project rescue and recovery, which discusses recovery efforts for projects that fail to deliver on significant success criteria, or which fail altogether.

Chapter 13, "Integration: Putting It All Together," explains how to apply the concepts introduced throughout the book and their contribution to project success. It takes from the "Integration Knowledge Area" in the *PMBOK® Guide* and introduces a framework of what it really means and what the PM needs to do in order to perform "proper" integration. You will learn how to manage project trade-offs, and what to do to establish an understanding of the trade-offs throughout the project organization. It will result in transparency, focus, and a clear path to managing stakeholders' expectations for project success. The chapter also offers insights into teaching PMs how to say no when they need to, along with a proposed action plan for implementing improvement ideas.

How to Use this Book

The great news is that you do not need to read this book from start to finish in order to benefit from it. You can keep it close by and refer to the relevant chapter as you need them, or familiarize yourself with the contents of the book and revisit areas that need more focus. This book may turn out to be one of your best friends in your projects, as it recognizes simple human behavioral characteristics and applies them against the reality of our projects. You will find in it the context, framework, and supporting information that are the backbone and essence of project work: figuring out what questions to ask, managing stakeholders' expectations, and identifying ways to make it easy for the team to deliver value and benefit to the organization. It may also provide answers to some of the project problems you face. Yet, similar to dealing with a good friend, you should always make sure that whatever advice, ideas, or concepts you take away and incorporate into your projects are relevant, applicable, realistic, and above all, address the specific needs of your project. Do not try to be someone you are not, and do not try to do things that are beyond what you can deliver or your organization can handle.

About the Author

Ori Schibi is President of PM Konnectors, a Toronto-based privately held corporation. With a focus on strategy, change management, project management and business analysis, his company provides a variety of services—ranging from facilitation services, workshops, and training/professional development, to consulting that delivers value to clients through a wide range of innovative business solutions.

Ori is a thought-leader and subject matter expert with over 23 years of experience in driving operational improvements, process efficiencies, software implementations, project recoveries, PMOs and complex programs to stabilize business, create growth and value, and lead sustainable change. His diverse international cross-industry experience and high energy combined with strong leadership skills have resulted in a proven track record of delivering outstanding results and achieving high customer satisfaction. An underlying theme in his work is a unique and innovative approach to value creation through establishing collaborative relations between business and IT departments—bridging gaps, building partnerships, and getting teams to focus on the main goals of creating value and customer satisfaction.

Large- to mid-sized organizations in diverse industries and government agencies around the world have benefited from Ori's innovative approach. He recently performed specialized deliveries for the United Nations in Europe (UNHCR–The High Commissioner for Refugees) to establish practices and develop project management and business analysis efficiencies in their operations.

This published author and speaker is a certified PRINCE2® (Practitioner) and Project Management Professional (PMP®), with an MBA from the prestigious Schulich School of Business at York University.

Last but certainly not least, Ori is a devoted husband and father who lives with his family in Thornhill, Ontario, Canada.

Introduction

My decision to write this book developed out of my frustration with a void in the current literature in the marketplace. I was in search of a guide that recognizes my experience and the fact that I have access to tools and techniques, but that empowers me to take a situation I face and handle it properly. I did not want a prescriptive list of instructions, but rather concepts, questions to ask, and areas to focus on that I can explore in order to leverage my knowledge and experience and maximize the benefits I produce for my bosses.

The book I was looking for was like the algorithm so commonly used by companies, such as Google, Facebook, Amazon, Netflix, and others that collect information about us—our preferences, our activities, and our lifestyles—and in turn, give us choices we are likely to be interested in. Every small questionnaire, activity, search, and comment we make is carefully learned by our service providers, and they introduce us to options that may appeal to us, based on the profile they develop. Initially, it looked impressive when my webmail provider offered diaper advertisements—right around the time my wife and I had our first baby—and when the online bookstore offered me a list of parenting books I might be interested in.

It is clear that a book cannot offer such an interactive experience, yet it should connect with readers on a level that allows each individual reader to take the advice, concepts, ideas, and lists the book offers and apply them to every environment you may encounter in a way that is suitable for that specific situation. In the absence of such a book, I decided to put together my own observations and ideas, so I could access them on later projects. Over time, these notes grew into a book that is intended to provide both new and experienced project managers with valuable concepts that focus on how to really manage projects, how to approach project situations, how to dissect the challenges we face, and what questions we need to ask in order to deliver the project-associated value and benefits.

WHAT THIS BOOK IS NOT ABOUT

This book does not provide templates and tools, as these are available essentially everywhere. While templates can be helpful, by nature they do not trigger us to think about the challenges we face but to produce a shortcut solution to them. A former colleague compared using templates to driving with GPS: we stop thinking about where we're going and just follow the directions given by the voice that tells us where to turn. "Turn right" may look good on the map, but it may end up depositing us in a lake if we do not think about what we are actually doing. Moreover, templates and tools are only as good as our ability to utilize them in our situations, and quite often, the old saying, "a fool with a tool is still a fool," is applicable. From what I have seen in many organizations, in a variety of industries, and all over the world, the extension to this rule also applies: "the sharper the tool, the bloodier the fool." Unfortunately, despite hundreds of thousands of project manager practitioners out there, who hold designations and use many tools, in reality there are still too many projects that can best be described as "bloody."

This book is also not a prescription. It does not provide a step-by-step roadmap for managing projects, simply because it does not deal with the "mechanics" of the project. Many books, approaches, and methodologies exist, which offer us tricks and techniques for building schedules and creating a work breakdown structure or budget. Yet, with a long list of things to do, we no longer think about how to apply these concepts in our situations. Throughout the years, I have noticed that most things we do (in general, but mainly in our projects) have two layers: what we do and how we do it—the content and the context. When I was a child, my two older brothers always told me that I should say to them whatever I wanted, even if it was unpleasant or harsh, as long as it was always done nicely and politely. It was frustrating because what I really wanted was to scream and be rude, but I quickly learned the difference between honey and vinegar: it is not only about what we do but also about how we do it. Consider project management—we can take the most advanced technique to build a schedule, put it into the most sophisticated tool, and it still may not yield the desired result. It will produce a fancy schedule, but not necessarily the right one for us, fulfilling the prediction of "garbage in, garbage out." Without understanding the nature of the resources and the real success criteria of the project, no tool or technique can be effectively utilized.

This book does not reinvent the wheel; it takes the wheels that are already there and leverages them so that each reader can apply them to a specific context and challenge. It is not a guide for the "how" but the "what:" what the project manager needs to know and consider for managing projects successfully. While Chapter 1 deals with the realities of project management, there are underlying tendencies in many projects, which have become almost second nature, that probably serve as contributing factors to the less-than-ideal state of project management as we know it.

THE VORTEX

In the past I started projects full of good intentions about my methodology, approach, and tools to apply, only to find myself—just a few days later—overwhelmed by the pace of events, the number of issues piling up, the political pressures, and the overwhelming volume of distractions. It was as if I was sucked into a vortex of events that dictated the sequence, order, and outcomes, and turned me into a reactive project manager. I was led by the events, was consumed by responding to things as they happened, and had no capacity, time, or context to plan ahead. As a result, my reactions became driven by panic, and in an attempt take shortcuts and achieve short term wins, they started to drift toward not making sense.

Various stakeholders, who sensed this weakness, preyed upon it and pushed for their own agendas, knowing I was not in a position to question or challenge them. The reactive mode became the most influential factor in my management style and prevented me from realizing many insights and building realistic plans. There was nothing proactive in what I was doing, and issues, risks, and stakeholder demands were handled after they surfaced in an attempt to correct things and cut losses. Before long, performance fell below expectations, and the vicious cycle of panic continued to prevail and dictate the coming events. That vortex of events left me focusing on the transactional aspects of the project, which consumed my capacity for putting out fires, while neglecting the management of transformational aspects, which fall under the category of preventive action, that could make a positive difference to the process of managing the project and ultimately, to project success.

MANAGEMENT BY EMERGENCIES

One of the main symptoms of our reactive mode while in the vortex of events is "management by emergencies." With a lack of insight into what is coming, plans that no longer reflect reality, pressures from various stakeholders, and events that manage us (rather than the opposite), the little capacity we have left to manage the project is consumed by emergencies. Some stakeholders quickly pick up on this condition: they realize that using the word "emergency" or "urgent" gets our attention, and with this knowledge, they take over the last remaining capacity we have. By attending to quasi-emergencies, we channel our energy and attention into events and activities that do not add value to the project, and as a result, we neglect to properly manage ongoing needs and events—not to mention real emergencies. Before long, what should have been a routine transaction turns into a real emergency. We now need to go through yet another shift in our priorities and end up in a vicious cycle of managing emergencies, rather than managing the project, and slowly but surely, the project falls behind.

MANAGEMENT BY EXCEPTIONS

The context of this section does not refer to project performance tolerances and the "Management by Exception" proposed by the PRINCE2 methodology for project management, but rather to the exceptions we allow in our projects, such as breaking the rules, extending privileges to certain individuals, thinking in terms of extenuating circumstances, and turning the exception into the new norm. Our lives are made up of many routines and repetitive events and so too, are our projects. The routine/standard events are usually documented by processes or established as best practices, although many of them are simply a result of habits and unwritten rules and practices. As long as we follow these processes, routines, sequences, expectations, and practices, our system seems to hold up, and things tend to fall into place. It is when we start with the exceptions, special approvals, concessions, allowances, and one-time special occasions that things begin to derail.

Take, for example, a project meeting: there is an unwritten expectation that no one should be late so we can start on time, but it is routine for at least one person (often the same one repeatedly) to be late. Every time, there is a different reason, excuse, or exception, but at the end of the day, it hurts the project team and its ability to deliver results. A similar example is when developers or engineers do not follow process and do things they are not supposed to or in a way that is not endorsed. When you ask them why, they always have an excuse or an exception. For them, it may be normal procedure to not follow process or to do things their own way, but most of us would call it a "culture of heroes" or "cowboy programming." There is value in following process and doing things the way they are designed to be done, and failing to do so often leads to inferior results.

One of my roles as a project manager is to ensure processes are in place, that they make sense, and that they are followed—to reduce the chance for variations, errors, and defects. Starting with one small exception inevitably leads to more, to larger ones, and to a culture of exceptions—where stakeholders and team members conduct themselves under the misconception that it is acceptable to not follow the process, and nothing will happen if they do their own things. Beyond performance problems, there are two behavioral problems this leads to: (1) Other team members and stakeholders who follow process start to resent those who don't and get away with it; and (2) Those who get away with their exceptions develop a sense of entitlement, thinking they can keep pushing for more and larger exceptions, which results in inflicting more damage on the project and its relationships. One advantage of having a process is that it establishes a standard way of doing things that can serve as a benchmark. Chapter 11 deals with communications and provides ideas for establishing behavioral norms in the project organization, which can serve as boundaries that define what is acceptable. It makes it easier for team members and stakeholders to realize the acceptable range of conduct, and by defining clear boundaries, it allows leniency, less micromanagement, more self-management, and an enhanced feeling of freedom for the team overall.

LIFE IS NOT AN EXACT SCIENCE

We all have to deal with pressure and stress at work. There is an ever-growing need to do more with less, and as project managers, we are expected to make commitments to targets that may not be fully articulated or clear and at times, even downright unrealistic. Related to these challenges is a systematic lack of decision making, clarity, or support that project managers receive from management or senior stakeholders. Many people tend to think this is done deliberately, at least to an extent; and while there is a lot to be said about the support levels project managers receive from management, we should establish that in the overwhelming majority of situations, this is not the case. Similar to the fact that we, as project managers, are often overwhelmed by the challenges and lack of clarity we face, so too are the senior stakeholders, sponsors, and executives. Because they are focused on their own struggles and battles, they cannot feed us with a silver spoon of information, so they leave us to figure it all out, both empowering and trusting us on a level they probably would not be willing to admit. With this comes responsibility and—one of the most important and challenging aspects of responsibility—is taking ownership of the communication to make sure we are clear in expressing our needs to senior management by applying the concept that "it takes two to tango."

When senior management makes a request that may seem unreasonable, the onus is on us to reach out for more information. The chapters on Politics, Stakeholders, and Communications all deal with how to make communication work, and with how reaching out for more information should include setting expectations and if required, providing senior stakeholders with options that are based on what is available and can be done.

EXPECTATION MANAGEMENT

One of the most challenging requests directed at project managers is to make time, budget, or other commitments very early on in the project, even though little is known at that point. It is often quite obvious that this expectation is unrealistic, yet we cannot respond with only our gut feel, so we need to support our answers with empirical information. It is also our responsibility as project managers to manage stakeholders' expectations, which should begin by establishing estimate accuracy levels: we should set the expectation that it is not possible to provide exact timelines or budget numbers for the entire project up front. Many approaches, such as

Agile, attempt to address this by, for example, shortening the planning horizon and thereby improving the chance for accurate expectations. More often than not, we fall victim to unrealistic expectations for accuracy and yet still try to, somehow, make good on those commitments. While it is pretty clear this is not an efficient process and does not provide effective results, it is not enough to know it: we need to communicate it to the decision makers. The inefficiency is a result of the scramble to come up with accurate estimates, wasting a lot of our capacity and attention on the process, rather than on improving our position to make the right decision. The ineffective part is related to the poor result of this entire process, which often needs to be undone. There is a good reason *A Guide to the Project Management Body of Knowledge (PMBOK® Guide)* offers a level of confidence or accuracy expectations, which become more specific as the planning process progresses, but it is quite clear that the project manager cannot produce specific and accurate estimates at the very start of the project. Even as more information comes to light and more details become apparent, the onus is on the project manager to ensure there is no expectation for exact estimates. After all, project management is not an exact science—if only because we deal with and depend upon people. The goal is not to go back to management with no information or with a request for more time, but rather to try to do the best with what we have and to manage the stakeholders' expectations accordingly.

BUSY VS. PRODUCTIVE

Another sign of the times is that we are all so busy. Meetings, e-mails, emergencies, client calls, plans, reports, deliverables, changes, and personal concerns—not to mention crises, disasters, and problems—mean everyone is busy. We are so busy that we do not have enough time to do our own things. When a colleague asks for help, our first reaction is that we are busy. But what is busy? Or how busy are we, really? There is no argument that we are busy, overworked, and at times, overwhelmed by the volume of things we need to handle. But at the same time, we need to look at how productive we are. If we make the distinction, it can open our eyes to the difference between "busy" and "productive:" busy is about how full our day is, but we also want to check how much value we have produced during the day.

When someone tells me at the end of a busy day how busy they were, I look for the breakdown of the day to get a better look at productivity: "I had six back-to-back meetings and had to address 150 e-mails." Busy it definitely is, but how productive was this person? As we tend to confuse the two words, my goal is to reduce the amount of "busy" and increase the amount of "productive." While most of us can make this simple distinction, some stakeholders tend to confuse the two and think that long meetings and many e-mails indicate productivity. While meetings and e-mails are an important part of our reality, in my projects I try to reduce them without compromising the quality of the work and communication. In return, it gives my stakeholders and resources more time to be productive, perform the work they are supposed to, and by so doing, add more value.

TIME MANAGEMENT

Time management is related to being too busy but not productive enough. Time management is not only about doing things faster but also about managing priorities, so we do those things that are more important first. Try to ask yourself a few questions related to how you manage your time, and it may give you some indication as to whether you need to improve in this area (most of us do!) and if so, how bad things are.

1. At the start of the day, do you have an idea of what you are going to work on during the day?
2. At the end of the day, do you feel like you completed what you intended to do that day?
3. Do you feel that you worked on the tasks with the highest priority during the day? Do you sometimes end up working on a task that does not return the intended value?
4. Do you set aside sufficient (or any) time for planning and scheduling?
5. Do you procrastinate, barely meet deadlines, or often need to ask for extra time? How common is it that you need to work overtime or from home to complete a task?
6. How much time do you actually spend on tasks as compared to the amount of time you thought you would spend on them?
7. Are you distracted by the deadlines of your tasks to the degree that it compromises your performance on them?
8. What are the criteria you apply to help you decide what to work on next? How much control do you have over your priorities? Do you have visibility of the overall task priorities for the project/organization? Do you regularly ask your boss for clarification on priorities, or confirm or discuss the priorities with your boss?
9. How often, and how much of your time, do you spend on interruptions? Do emergencies and other unplanned distractions prevent you from meeting deadlines?
10. When you plan for a task, do you think about risks? Do you allow for contingencies?

This is not a scientific survey, but your answers will give you a good feel for how effective you are at managing your time. If you answered "yes" to most of the questions above, you are probably fairly efficient at managing your time, and you may want to consider where you can make further improvements. Otherwise, the more negative answers you give and the more uncertainty involved in your answers, the more urgent it is for you to focus on improving your time management skills. You can break down your action items into the following focus areas: goal setting, prioritization, scheduling, managing disturbances, and procrastination. Time management is important to help you keep your work and effort under control, and when not managed properly, it is a significant contributor to stress and results in less efficient efforts, more risks, and inferior results. A more tangible way to help you better manage your time is to build an action plan that includes the following:

Better plan your day;
List your tasks in order of priority;
Confirm the intended result with your boss;
Allow sufficient time for tasks;
Learn to say no to less important tasks and interruptions;
Break tasks into smaller, more manageable components (this is what project management is all about!);
Take time to evaluate how you actually manage your time.

Although this book does not directly deal with the art of time management, it provides ample techniques and concepts that will help you get informed, recognize the dynamics in your environments, and in turn, give you a better handle on prioritizing the endless list of things you need to do and better manage your time. In other words, it will help you do more in less time and ensure that what you do is what you need to do.

NO CONFLICT

This book also covers conflict management techniques, their effectiveness, and how sustainable they are. The modern view of conflict no longer refers to it as a bad thing and in fact, sees it as a necessity that can be a source of innovation, team building, and growth—if managed and handled properly. Many people do not like conflict, do not enjoy being part of an environment that is engaged in conflict, and view conflict as an unpleasant thing. In addition, people do not see the value in engaging in conflict; they have a negative view of the overall process of conflict and do not see benefits in its results. All this leads to an ongoing effort to avoid conflict as much as possible and translates into environments that do not deal with differences, do not address issues, and prevent teams and organizations from improving and growing.

The main focus for many people is not to fix problems but to avoid conflict—almost at all costs—and maintain a sense of harmony, even if artificial. This will not stop conflict from taking place, and will probably increase conflict to the degree that the team gets consumed by it. Performance will inevitably suffer. Embracing conflict, handling it consistently and professionally, and making sure that conflict is a legitimate means (if used properly) to pursue our objectives, should result in a positive outcome and empower us to ask ourselves after every conflict whether the team is better off now than it was prior to the conflict. Otherwise, the team dynamic, with all its consequences, moves in the wrong direction.

Web
Added
Value™

This book has free material available for download from the
Web Added Value™ resource center at *www.jrosspub.com*

At J. Ross Publishing we are committed to providing today's professional with practical, hands-on tools that enhance the learning experience and give readers an opportunity to apply what they have learned. That is why we offer free ancillary materials available for download on this book and all participating Web Added Value™ publications. These online resources may include interactive versions of material that appears in the book or supplemental templates, worksheets, models, plans, case studies, proposals, spreadsheets and assessment tools, among other things. Whenever you see the WAV™ symbol in any of our publications, it means bonus materials accompany the book and are available from the Web Added Value Download Resource Center at www.jrosspub.com.

Downloads for *Managing Stakeholder Expectations for Project Success: A Knowledge Integration Framework and Value Focused Approach* consist of:

- Checklists for determining project readiness and complexity
- Pre-kickoff questions for stakeholders with a rating scale and a kickoff meeting checklist
- A stakeholder engagement and expectations management planning checklist with a series of questions for each of the seven categories to focus on
- Stakeholder communication plan components that address what to convey to whom, when, and how
- Quality management plan components
- Risk breakdown structure (RBS) extensions: areas to review for risk within each project category as specified by the RBS

1

The (Sad) Reality of Project Management

This chapter does not deal with any one specific aspect of projects; rather, it provides ideas and solutions for the associated challenges that surround them. Chapter 1 can be viewed as a gateway to the rest of the book, providing context through a discussion of the current state of project management. It articulates many of the challenges that we deal with and points out some of the main flaws in our current way of delivering projects.

THE REALITY IN QUOTES

We begin by introducing a series of quotations or statements commonly uttered by various stakeholders about their projects. These statements are relevant to most project environments, and they appear in relation to each chapter's theme and concepts. The expressions represent situations, challenges, and issues that project managers (PMs) regularly face (either by hearing them or by using them) in project realities. They are commonly used, perhaps too commonly; for the most part, they represent misconceptions, misrepresentations, or misunderstandings of the team, situation, project, or even organization.

Usually these statements also lead PMs and other stakeholders to make the wrong decisions. Some of these quotations may sound silly; others are downright ridiculous; but, due to their "popularity," they all articulate the state of our project realities and may provide some insight into why so many PMs often fall short of delivering on the promises and commitments of their projects.

1

Each expression is followed by a short discussion about what it really means and its potential impact on a project. It is fair to assume that these things are mostly said—not due to ignorance or carelessness—with good intentions, in an attempt to improve things and make stakeholders feel better. At times, it is apparent that these statements combine reality with hope and wishful thinking. The discussion that accompanies each quotation also provides some approaches for dealing with the true meaning behind what was just said and opens the door to becoming better prepared to take appropriate action. Many of these observations will resonate with you and, in addition to the explanation they offer, the book addresses the challenges they introduce and how to overcome these challenges. Some of the quotations are presented in this chapter; others appear at the start of each subsequent chapter they pertain to.

"Whose fault is it?" Not mine. It is human nature to look for someone else to blame when something goes wrong. However, is it really the first thing we need to do? When something breaks down or goes wrong, we first need to try to address it and then fix it. Pointing fingers and blaming others is not constructive and does not add value; it demoralizes the team and, above all, does not solve the problem at hand. Assuming that most project problems are not a result of sabotage, it would be much wiser to channel our already limited resources into finding a solution. Investigating where the problem originated and by whom will have to take place after we fix it so that we can learn from our mistake, move on, and avoid making the same mistake again.

At times, the best candidates for solving a problem or an issue may be those who are "at fault," since they might have the specific knowledge and context to fix it. Removing them from the project will leave us shorthanded, resulting in additional work for those remaining—potentially without the specific expertise to help in the recovery effort. Organizations tend to be quick to remove PMs when things do not progress according to plan. While the PM's leadership skills and ability to drive the project forward are paramount to success, too often it is not clear whether the problem actually is the PM. Replacing the PM may not improve things at all, as we are merely substituting a person. In fact, obtaining a new PM may introduce new risks and cost/time. In addition, it will take even more time to bring the new PM up to speed to the point that this person actually adds value. At the end of the day, there is a chance that the new PM may end up facing the same challenges as the predecessor did, but now the project is further behind and has a new PM who probably lacks experience and expertise.

"This project is a top priority." Many PMs hear this, but before long, it becomes clear that words are cheap, and there are other projects in the organization that are also labeled "top priority." When people hear that their project is a top priority, they should expect to see evidence to support it—for example, relevant resources are allocated to their project in a timely manner. When these conditions are not present, it quickly becomes apparent that the project is not really a top priority, and the onus is on the PM to address this issue and set the stakeholders' expectations that, without the appropriate level of support, the project objectives cannot be delivered as intended.

"I don't have time." Time management is related to one's ability to prioritize what needs to be done. Virtually everyone is pressed for time, and it comes down to figuring out how to manage those things in such a way that the more urgent things get done first. It sounds simple, yet most people simply do not know how to do it. It makes it even more challenging when additional work is delegated onto one's plate with no indication about its priority in relation to other tasks or any additional time to perform it.

"There is no need to conduct stakeholder analysis. I have worked with them before." There is growing recognition of the need to conduct stakeholder analysis and to revisit it several times throughout the project. Even if the PM has previously worked with certain team members and stakeholders before, it does not mean that their dispositions, views, or needs are the same as they used to be. Opinions, circumstances, views, agendas, and drivers change, and even previous allies may turn into foes from one project to another. The main challenge with conducting stakeholder analysis is that PMs do not have the time or capacity for it and as a result, simply do not do it in most cases. The results of the analysis should remain essentially confidential, since there may be sensitive information and views about our colleagues, team members, and other stakeholders. As part of the stakeholder analysis, PMs should also measure each stakeholder's ability to influence the project and their own ability to work with the stakeholders—to reach them, influence them, and change their minds if required.

"We will figure it out later." During the planning phase, or in early stages of the project, when PMs come across problems and challenges regarding resource and skills shortage, it is important to alert stakeholders, but they often say that there is nothing that can be done about it now and a solution will be found later on. Unfortunately, it is unlikely that there will be an easy solution to these problems later in the project; furthermore, by then the project is probably going to struggle to meet even its least challenging commitments.

"This is not my problem to worry about." There are many things in a project that are out of the PM's control, such as vendors and other external deliverables, dependencies on other projects, and cross-project risks. When PMs voice their concerns about these matters, the response is often "it is not your problem to worry about," which is a mistake. There is a difference between not having control over certain things and failing to address them. PMs cannot micromanage other projects or try to solve their issues, but they do need to communicate with external stake-holders to learn about situations that may affect their own projects downstream.

This involves building relationships and a collaborative environment that enables a mechanism to address these challenges in a timely manner. Hiding behind the silo-driven thinking of "this is not my problem" will lead to significant problems later.

"Do it just this time. It's an exception." This statement represents special requests that stakeholders make, with the most common ones being requests to do something differently than it should be performed or to include additional scope or features that were originally left out of the requirements without using the change control process. These requests may be accompanied by "I will view it as a personal favor," or "we go way back." It reiterates the importance for PMs to understand the project success criteria, manage the trade-offs between them, and let no external (unrelated) factors interfere with success considerations.

"But I sent you an e-mail." In the early 1990s, e-mail was viewed as the best thing since sliced bread. Since then, many e-mails have been sent and received, and e-mail has become a problem in itself, creating many misunderstandings. E-mail and other forms of written, informal communication may be convenient but cannot replace the basic need for people to talk to each other. It is not enough to send an e-mail and hope that the recipient receives, reads, understands, and responds to it. There are too many potential failure points in any type of communication, and e-mail fails to provide safeguards for most of these. In fact, it introduces potential failures and misunderstandings in the form of tone, style, structure, and at times, intent. To foster effective communication, it is important to introduce a set of best practices for e-mail conduct so that e-mail becomes a value-producing tool, as opposed to one that is misused and falls short of delivering its potential value.

"Just add some resources and do it faster." Not all project delays can be fixed by adding resources. Even when resources are available to perform the work, which is unlikely, it does not follow that they will add value. When sitting on a delayed flight, no one proposes that the airline call in an additional copilot in order to fly faster and arrive on time. The reality is similar for projects: there are activities that, even if the organization adds resources toward performing them, may not yield any gains to the project, despite adding costs. Due to the law of diminishing returns, adding resources may backfire and slow the process down or lead to more defects. The PM needs to determine whether the situation can benefit from adding resources or other trade-offs need to take place in order to meet project objectives.

NOT ENOUGH OF . . .

Similar to the "reality in quotes," there are some statements that are not said enough in projects and organizations. There are some exceptions to this rule, but not hearing these statements enough serves as an indication that something is not working the way it should. For any one of these examples, PMs need to ask ourselves: When was the last time we said one of these sentences to one of our colleagues? When was the last time we were on the receiving end of one of these comments? Here are some examples of things that should be said more often, in the hopes that they will become part of the culture in more organizations. Each example is followed by some background, and the book will address ways to help make these expressions more commonly used.

"How I can help you?" We are all overworked, have significant resource constraints, and are in a constant reactive mode to issues, problems, and crises that take place in our projects. It is challenging and complicated enough to handle our own workload, let alone offer help to someone else. However, our skills, knowledge, experiences, and access to resources may be relevant for someone else in the organization and can be used to their benefit. Building a culture of helping others will make us much stronger as a collaborative team and in turn, will encourage other team members to reciprocate. It is not about creating a utopia or a fantasy world, but about showing genuine care about each other, sharing success across the organization, and realizing that: sometimes I may be doing the helping, and other times I will need to leverage someone else's capabilities to my benefit.

"Thank you. I appreciate your effort." (Or: **"Good job."**) We are often quick to complain or tell someone that they did not do what we expected, but what about a good word? I once made a comment in a project meeting to one of the resources, showing appreciation for his effort, only for that person to approach me afterward to tell me that it was the nicest thing anyone had ever told him in that company over his 10 years there. There is no need to single out people, to compliment the same people over and over again, or to compliment someone for no reason, but a good word does not cost anything and goes a long way in building confidence, strong relationships, a sense of pride, collaboration, and a positive atmosphere.

"What can I do to help us work better together?" Many of us do not really have meaningful conversations with our colleagues at work. We talk to each other and see each other in meetings, but the conversations are not meaningful. We often address issues, deal with problems, report status, or ask technical questions, but usually this is where it ends. There are no meaningful conversations about how to work better together or how to change the way things are now. I once had a new manager that, when she got to her new position, said one of her first orders of business was to cancel the regularly scheduled one-on-one meetings with her team members. Her reasoning was that she did not have time for it, and it was no surprise that it weakened our team and our ability to perform. This was because our manager no longer had the insight necessary to identify underlying issues and to understand, firsthand, what team members were going through.

She essentially eliminated her best way to know what was going on with her team, and by using the excuse of a lack of time, she slowly relinquished her control, along with her ability to know about and proactively deal with situations, challenges, and other team interactions. Informal one-on-one meetings with colleagues and team members are priceless—they establish good working relationships, open the lines of communication, and even spark friendships. They allow us to address issues informally and collaboratively and to improve our ability to work together and understand each other. An attempt to reach out and try to help or look for areas of improvement will most likely trigger a reciprocal reaction and create a positive dynamic with our colleagues.

"We need to do some team building." This is not something we fail to say to each other; it is rather an observation that we do not have enough team building in our environments. Whether it is a time or a budget constraint that inhibits team building activities, in many organizations, employees find it hard to recall the last time the team went out together for lunch. It does not have to be fancy or paid for by the company; it is enough just to go out, as a team, to celebrate a milestone or alleviate some tension. During any type of team building activity, there is an opportunity to learn something about our colleagues, which may help us to build better relationships with them. With a friendlier atmosphere among our team, it is more likely that individuals will seek win-win resolutions to situations and try to work with each other, rather than against one another. This is not about turning our workplace into a country club and going for a team lunch every day but about striking a balance and creating the conditions for success.

"Let me see if I understand you correctly." Paraphrasing is a tried-and-true way to help communicate effectively. We often do not fully understand each other, and, by paraphrasing, we improve our chances of understanding each other by the end of the conversation. It takes more time, but it is time well invested, as it saves us from the likelihood that one of us misunderstands the other. Some people that I know (including myself when I was young) do not see the need to repeat what was just said. Yet, with experience, we come to realize that it is an effective way to show the person we are conversing with what we understood and to make sure that was the intent.

"I understand where you are coming from." Because we are quite self-absorbed in our own tasks and projects, we often do not take the time to see where other people are coming from, what their intentions are when they ask for something, or what exactly, they need. At times, we may find ourselves arguing with someone over something, even though they agree with us. Failing to listen to each other and to understand each other's needs makes our communication inefficient and ineffective.

"Do you have what you need to do it?" Asking someone to do something and looking the other way, hoping they can do it, is not the right way to show support or to achieve results. Even though I am not the technical subject matter expert, my job as the PM is to ensure that my team has the right resources and conditions to perform the work I ask them to do. Some may describe it as "throwing someone under the bus" by telling them: "I told you what I need; go figure it out." I view it more as part of Deming's 85-15 rule,[1] which states that it is the job of management (and in this case, the PM) to make sure that the team has what it takes—context, training, conditions, and goals—to perform the work.

There are many other adages that are missing in action and/or not used enough, if at all, in our environments. However, I feel that the selection presented here expresses the main problems we face in our projects and organizations.

INSTANT GRATIFICATION

We live in an era of instant gratification. People want to see results right now, the customer wants to realize project benefits yesterday, and many have not heard of "paying your dues." This reality forces us to undermine the importance of planning and to cave under the pressure of delivering results. Almost every PM I know has had to face a situation in which a sponsor or a senior manager asked them to "do something" or "produce results" rather than plan. This leads to a situation wherein we do not plan sufficiently and end up taking on projects, not only without proper understanding of what we are entering into, but also without a roadmap of how to handle them, how to realize the intended benefits, or how to define those benefits altogether. Surveys, studies, and other research are all available, which give us much information, but with mixed signals about the state of project management.

THE SHORT HISTORY OF PROJECT MANAGEMENT

Looking at the modern history of projects, there are a few important milestones to note, as illustrated in Figure 1.1.

Are we doing any better today than we did in the past? Arguably, yes. Our projects deliver faster, better results and achieve more with less, even though our standards are now higher, perhaps higher than what we can deliver. On the other hand, are we doing any better? We produce less than what we commit to, and it almost always involves bugs and defects; we pass more of the onus onto the customer ("let's pass it to warranty"); and our realities are plagued with service calls,

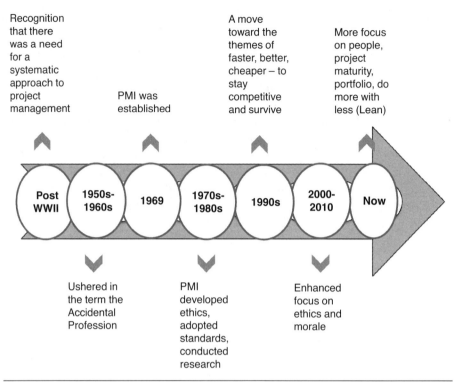

Figure 1.1 Project history milestones

strained relationships, and recalls. One would think that, with about half a million Project Management Professionals (PMPs) worldwide,[2] we should be able to deliver better project results.

So, what is the problem? Project management can be traced back thousands of years. Long before we decorated our business cards with letters that represent designations, people led and managed projects: the Giza Pyramid, the Colosseum, and the Taj Mahal were all planned and delivered and are still standing (for the most part). There have also been some projects throughout history that did not necessarily deliver on their intended success. For example, Table 1.1 compares highlights between the Empire State Building and the Leaning Tower of Pisa.

SIGN OF THE TIMES

One might think that, with all the progress we have made in project management over the years—especially in the past two decades—along with the methodologies and approaches we have in place, we should achieve much better results in our

Table 1.1 Tale of two projects

	Empire State Building	The Leaning Tower of Pisa
Start date	During the Great Depression (1930)	Year 1173
Scope	102 stories (at the time, the tallest building in the world)	8 Floors, 207 Columns
Timelines	14 months start to finish	Year 2001. 828 years
Costs	$14M (with a 50:50 ratio of labor to materials)	Unknown (probably slightly more than intended)
Effort	7 million hours of labor with 3,400 workers on site at the peak of construction	Final modifications made in 2001

projects than we actually do. Unfortunately however, this is not quite the case. Our current performance might be better than it used to be, but it somehow does not deliver on the promises we make and for the most part, falls short of expectations. It may be an expectations management issue, a somewhat consistent state of under-performance, or a combination of the two.

The *Chaos Report* from the Standish Group[3] refers to three definitions of project outcomes: (1) Successful—the project was completed on time, on budget, and according to specifications (features and functionality); (2) Challenged—the project was completed and operational but was over-budget, late, or did not meet all of the original specifications (features and functionality); and (3) Failed—the project was cancelled before completion or never implemented. These options offer the full range of possible results; however, on their own, they can be easily taken out of context. For example, there might be quite a wide range of project outcomes that fall under "challenged," and some failures might be "painted" in the brighter color of "challenged." This is common when there is no clear understanding of, or agreement on the definition of, success.

In other cases, the project circumstances may be distorted when labeled with one of these three definitions. I have worked on projects that, although over budget, were considered successful. On others, we delivered late, but it was the right thing to do. Most commonly, I have been on projects that delivered less than the full intended functionality, but they were still a success. It is easy to come up with labels, but this needs to be done within the context of the project and measured against the real reasons for which it was undertaken. Applying these success/failure definitions may also lead to a project derailment, where stakeholders may prefer to "qualify" to the success criteria rather than ensure that the project benefits and value are delivered at the end.

Since part of my career involves professional development and training, deferring to success criteria reminds me of classes with an exam at the end. Quite often, students ask me what is going to be on the exam, and my answer to them is that they should not focus on the exam, but rather on learning something and having takeaways that will add value to their roles and jobs. Clearly, it is important to pass the exam, but the course's success is about the value participants obtain from it; only one of its components is the exam, but the main one is the learning. My goal is to ensure that students remain focused on what matters and not merely on the exam. The same applies to projects: I hope to have the project labeled as a success, but it is more important for me to have the organization/customer benefit from its results. These considerations are about philosophy, style, expectations management, and focusing on what really matters—delivering value and benefits.

MORE WITH LESS

Virtually every organization tries to do more with less. Or rather, continues doing what they're doing, but with fewer people and less money, hoping to maintain an acceptable level of quality and the same service level. It may be successful—for a while and to a certain extent—but at some point, customers will start to notice and the results will start to show. Imagine that you are sitting on an airplane and there is an ad playing on your TV screen where the builder of the aircraft boasts about how they manage to manufacture it for less cost by awarding all their contracts to the lowest bidder. Would you feel safe about your impending trip? Would it make you feel better about choosing this airline? The answer is pretty clear, yet the majority of organizations out there put cost savings at the top of their priority list and look for every possible way to constantly reduce costs.

The compression of products' lifecycles, an ever growing need for faster results, and the reality of having to do more with less, lead us to look for shortcuts in the way we manage projects. The "usual suspects" to suffer from these shortcuts are the initiation stage, planning processes, and testing. There are attempts to cut costs in all of the other parts of the food chain as well, but these three areas are often the first ones to suffer cuts. The misconception is that these cuts will not affect the bottom line because these are not cuts to the product or functionality that we can't get by without.

Since we cannot reduce the scope of the project without authorization, we lessen the effort, time, and capacity allocated to these three areas in an attempt to cut our losses, so we can dedicate whatever capacity we are left with toward producing the project deliverables. The main reasons for these shortcuts are: (1) the need to show results due to stakeholder pressure and a false sense of complacency; and (2) thinking we will be able to tie up all sorts of loose ends later in the project. This is obviously a misconception that keeps haunting us and proving us wrong again and again. The range of shortcuts taken falls between a superficial, meaningless effort that is done mostly for the sake of doing it, to failing to perform some of those "critical to success" activities, such as planning and testing.

Let's take a closer look at these three areas that are most often cut from a project, and what they involve:

1. **Initiation**: the work that needs to be performed throughout initiation includes those foundational things that define what the project is about and sets the tone for the entire project. It involves putting together the project charter, performing stakeholder analysis, carrying out a project readiness assessment, and leading a kickoff meeting. Chapter 2 has a detailed discussion of these topics.

2. **Planning**: it is safe to say there is a fine line between not enough planning and overdoing it; however, in most cases we err on the insufficient side of this range. Effective planning does not necessarily need to involve a cumbersome plan, but it does need to cover everything relevant to our project. Many organizations know how to plan and prove it with effective planning for their large projects, but unfortunately they leave the smaller projects with vague plans that resort to luck and heroism. A good plan needs to clearly state the project scope and include realistic timelines, resource plans, and budgets for all the work. It should also include plans for the remaining knowledge areas—including meaningful risk, quality, and communication plans—as well as a procurement plan, if needed. All of these plans must be integrated based on the project objectives and success criteria.

3. **Testing**: we all know how important testing is, yet it is one area that consistently does not get the amount of time and focus it requires, or even the time initially committed. The sequence of activities in technology projects has the development effort preceding the testing, and—since the former quite often takes longer than planned—any extra time needed will subsequently come out of the testing effort. This extra time leads to delays in the start of testing, but—since the project deadline will not get extended—the blame will typically fall on the testers. There are other contributing factors to the prevailing attitudes toward testing:

    a. The misconception that a combination of good developers and a serious development effort may reduce the need for testing.

    b. The incorporation of hope into our plan—hoping we can get by without actually testing the system in full.

    c. The belief that some types of testing, mainly user acceptance testing and scalability and performance testing, may not be necessary. These are often the first to go, but—just as they were part of the test plan for a reason—removing them will have a negative impact.

    d. Sometimes we also need to remind stakeholders that testing does not really start at the end of the development effort: test planning and the writing of test cases need to take place early in the development effort and at times, need to be part of the design. Therefore, even if we allow sufficient time for testing, waiting to begin this process until development is complete will most likely lead to time and quality issues.

These three areas are mentioned here, not because they are more important than others, but because they tend to be squeezed more than other parts of the project. It almost seems that due to their less tangible nature, team members and stakeholders tend to think it is possible to not perform them sufficiently, or at all, and still get by.

GIVE ME A SCHEDULE

A few veteran project practitioners argue that it used to be easier to find a PM who could produce a realistic schedule than it is now. This claim does not imply that PMs cannot produce schedules: building a schedule is fairly basic, and a PM should be able to perform it easily with the abundance of tools and techniques that are out there. Yet many PMs are not capable of building an effective or realistic schedule. A few possible explanations for the PM's limited ability to build a decent schedule and our diminished aptitude to deliver other project artifacts and plans will be addressed here: focus, overreliance on tools, the "two layers" concept, insight, communication, poor risk management, and team performance.

Focus

As PMs, we are often spread too thin. The old adage, "Jack of all trades, master of none," is applicable in cases where PMs are focused on managing so many transactional aspects of their projects (e.g., schedule updates and deliverables) that they fail to see the big picture and to handle the transformational aspects—such as quality, risk, communication, and organizational objectives. An elaborate discussion of this matter takes place in Chapter 7, "Manage Those Things that Make a Difference," where I demonstrate that our effort should not only be focused on producing project deliverables but also, if not mainly, on managing those things in the project that make a difference, so we can successfully complete our deliverables.

Many PMs do not have sufficient understanding of what organizational objectives the project is intended to achieve, which results in a failure to focus on activities that can achieve those objectives, which further results in an overall impaired ability to pick our battles. While it is not necessarily the PM's role to identify the areas that help in picking the right battles, Chapter 7 will provide insight into how to look for this information and what questions to ask in order to manage the project effectively.

Overreliance on Tools

With the need to do more with less (and faster), we resort to tools, templates, and other "silver bullet" solutions that present a solution, but often not the one we need. Tools are only as good as our ability to utilize them. No tool is good for all conditions, and when choosing one, we need to carefully check how it aligns with our goals and which aspects of the tool can help us deliver better results. I often see situations where there is an overreliance on tools with the expectation that they will provide us with answers to questions we don't even know we need to ask.

The "Two Layers" Concept

In our projects, most of what we do will have two layers: the content and the context (the "what" and the "how"). We try to build a schedule by resorting to any kind of help available. However, because this help is not tailored to our needs and does not take our circumstances into consideration, it fails to deliver the intended benefits. In addition, when we don't know what the objectives are, or what the nature of the trade-offs (with all the other constraints) are, any schedule we manage to put together, even if it indicates that we can meet the deadline, is most likely out of touch with reality—it will fail upon contact with reality. When I was a kid, my older brothers told me that no matter what I had to say, it was always going to be better to say it nicely. The same applies to our projects: it is not only what we do but also how we do it that matters.

Insight

Most PMs put little to no thought into their projects about organizational culture, politics, and the true impact of certain actions upon the project trade-offs. The result is little to no insight about the reality in which we operate, which leads us to drive the project "blindfolded." Chapter 4 provides an introduction to organizational politics and offers several ideas for better understanding them. It is complemented by Chapter 5, which deals with stakeholder analysis, understanding how to handle and treat stakeholders, and what to expect from them. Without performing proper stakeholder analysis, or with no stakeholder analysis at all, we do not have a clear picture of who calls the shots in our projects and what their decisions are driven by.

Communication

In most projects, there is a communication plan that includes an illustration of the information that is going to be communicated, including its frequency, mode, and other details. The communication plan should be an extension of the stakeholder analysis and as such, deal with which aspects each stakeholder needs to know, to what extent, and the appropriate style in which they should be delivered. Along with these items, the communication plan should serve as the repository for setting behavioral expectations, setting up ground rules, and providing guidelines for conduct in and around the project. Chapter 11 lists those items and provides a roadmap to building a meaningful communication plan that not only allows the PM to proactively manage the project's communication but also to leverage effective communication to better manage risk and overall project success.

Poor Risk Management

Insufficient, untimely, ineffective, or unrealistic—one of these descriptors can often depict the way risk is managed in the majority of projects. The result often leads to "management by emergencies," where our reduced capacity allows us to attend only to project emergencies and to do so almost exclusively in a reactive mode. Proper risk management analysis, incorporated with a strong communication plan as outlined in Chapter 8, helps us to gain a clear view of the challenges we are facing and to address them sooner and more effectively than we would otherwise. A more composed approach, driven by a plan, will also reduce reactions to project events that are driven by panic, which may lead to further mishandling and errors.

Team Performance

We can review team performance according to three aspects: capacity, capability, and culture. Doing so allows us to properly assess the areas in which the team might need development or additional focus.

- Team capacity deals with the ability to achieve a set amount of productivity within a defined unit of time. While it is not easy to increase a team's capacity in this day and age, the process is straightforward—adding resources or hiring new people will increase a team's capacity.
- Team capability is about what our team knows about our subject matter. It can often be broken into business or functional categories; and similar to capacity, it is possible to enhance our knowledge by providing our team with business or domain training and development opportunities.
- Team and organizational culture is not always easy to capture or define. It is a powerful undercurrent in the organization and as such, is extremely difficult to manage and to change. It can be viewed as a team's or an organization's shared values, beliefs, symbols, and behaviors. Understanding culture is roughly equivalent to providing the PM with a map that shows the lay of the land, which can help him/her navigate the organizational pillars and speed bumps. Before we try to change a culture, it is important to note that one culture is rarely better than another, and we first need to understand an organization's or team's culture and how it can help support

the organizational and business objectives. Changing an organization's culture is one of the most difficult leadership challenges, as it is a complex combination of all the organization's goals, values, processes, roles, attitudes, communications practices, and assumptions.

THE STRUCTURE OF OUR BRAIN AND PROJECT MANAGEMENT

There is one more thing that is deeply ingrained in the way we run our organizations and projects: the structure of our brains. One of the secrets to success in anything we do is to perform it in a way that is in line with our natural tendencies so it does not contradict the way we are "wired" to think. This relates to the way our brains are structured into the right and the left hemispheres. The right hemisphere of the brain is associated with our analytical, people, and political acumen; the left side is associated with techniques, methodologies, and systematic thinking.

When considering the two, we can see that the majority of project management training and professional development has been focused on aspects associated with the left side of the brain, involving discipline and knowledge. People try to apply proven concepts from other projects into ours; we look for templates, concepts, and processes to drive our delivery of benefits; and we focus on introducing more tools and techniques into our projects. These kinds of improvements are easier to teach, simpler to measure, more tangible to manage, and more transferrable than those associated with the right hemisphere.

The areas associated with the right side of the brain are more "artistic" and skill-driven. As such, they are harder to teach and much more difficult to comprehend and quantify. If you are "right-brained," it is not about teaching leadership, but

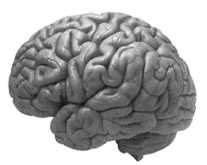

Project Management: focus on the right
side of the brain

Image 1.1   The human brain

rather about how to apply the most appropriate leadership style to the situation that is comprised of your personality and project and organizational circumstances. The tool to utilize does not matter as much as managing your stakeholders (also known as people) and their expectations. It is not about handling the technical skills of your team, but rather about how to manage the team dynamic, the individual needs of its members, and how to extract more from their limited time and available skills. When my projects failed to deliver on their promises, I used to look for excuses and came up with my team members' lack of technical expertise as a possible explanation. It was not a blame game, but an attempt to look for the fault somewhere else. It was convenient to point at lack of technical skills as a possible reason. I essentially pointed at the left side of the brain and tried to find some comfort in believing that, had we had the right or sufficient technical skills, it would have been better. I later realized that it was not the technical skills that were the problem, but my inability to extract those relevant skills and capacities from the people on my team.

Another consideration related to the structure of our brain is the way we think. This is not a biology or science class, but after several years of leading teams, I have learned that most people tend to think in a linear way: we tend to view actions and their associated reactions as not only related but also correlated. That is, we expect that an action will almost always trigger a reaction that is similar in size, magnitude, and impact. Unfortunately, our realities (and especially our project realities) are not so simple, and the gap between the way we think and the way things take place may serve as an explanation as to why—despite all the skills, tools, and techniques that we possess—our projects often do not yield the desired outcomes.

For example, when I ask my development team why they are working on something that is not in the plan, they often tell me that it will only take them an hour to finish it before they go back to doing what they were supposed to be doing. For them, it is only one hour; but even if that turns out to be the case, it may spell the difference between being on time and delivering late. Due to the heavy interdependency among project activities, along with the constant resource constraints we are under, every activity in the project can be compared with taking a commuter train: for the developer, a one-hour delay may only be one hour, but for the PM, with the constant need to manage conflicting priorities, an hour delay may translate to a day or more in project time overruns. When taking the train, I may only be 2 minutes late to the station, but since the train has left, it will not translate into a linear delay that is equal in size but into a much more significant one. If the train comes only once every hour, my arrival two minutes late to the station may lead to arriving an hour late to work.

We can therefore view chaos theory as applicable to project reality: an action may have a reaction that is in proportion to the action, or it may lead to a much greater, smaller, or nonexistent reaction. Some call it the "butterfly effect," where a butterfly may spread its wings on one side of the world, and this action may trigger a tropical cyclone on the other side at some later point. More often than not, a simple action or lack of action in the project may lead to much more devastating results downstream. The ability to anticipate and properly measure the impact of anything we do in our projects is one of the things that distinguishes good PMs from average ones.

CULTURE OF ALLIGATORS

When you look around at your colleagues in your organization—whether within or outside of the team (team members, leads, functional managers, other PMs)—there are a few things you may want to ask yourself: Are these team members allies? Are they trustworthy? Do they work with you or against you? These questions are all related to each other, and they are not about the knowledge or technical skills of those colleagues and resources. In many organizations, it appears that the answers to these questions are not quite what you would hope for. Each of your colleagues manages his or her "territory" with little or no regard for the organizational and business objectives or for anyone else's needs. It is likely that these colleagues not only do not share with you the same set of priorities but also have priorities that directly conflict with yours. It may be that you both need the same resources at the same time or that you are aiming for opposite outcomes for certain situations and deliverables.

As for other projects in the organization, the situation is quite similar: every project careens toward its destination with little consideration for other efforts that are taking place in the organization at the same time. We can argue that it is our reward system that forces each PM to focus only on one project because, if you do not focus on your own project priorities, nobody else will. With that said, however, many PMs find themselves promoting their own project agendas—even though, by doing so, they may compromise the performance of a different project. As we have limited capacities in our organization, it is normal to need to juggle priorities. Unfortunately, there is often no clear guidance (or any guidance whatsoever) from senior management concerning the right thing to do and which project is more important to focus on for aligning with organizational priorities.

You can also find this behavior among resource and functional managers. Most of us are single-mindedly focused on our own specific objectives and have no clear priority setting or directives on the organizational level. These narrow and some-what self-centered views translate into turf wars, lack of collaboration, lost trust, and conflicting priorities. In turn, they lead to wasted time on infighting, arguing, and resource reallocation, rather than to a constructive, unified, and focused effort that serves the organization as a whole over each individual's agenda. It is quite apparent that many, if not most, requests of an individual for help or for additional resources from a colleague are faced with some form of rejection, often accompanied with an excuse and an explanation for why this person is too busy and could not possibly help. We need to face the reality that most team members remain self-absorbed and driven by individual, personal, and project objectives. With little consideration for other's needs and with the self-centered view that many team members have, most communications among team members to request resources will start with a descriptor or an adjective, as shown in Figure 1.2.

Over time, we get better at adding a descriptor that is more imminent, severe, urgent, or alarming than the previous one in order to get our needs met. As a result, we become oblivious to our colleagues' requests and calls for help, and we shift our focus to the description and intensity of what we need instead of on its merits. In an atmosphere where we only take care of our own interests and treat our colleagues' needs as nuisances, our teams gradually become dysfunctional. We are not efficient in our efforts as a team, which will inevitably lead to inferior results.

A suitable name for this natural progression is a *culture of alligators*. Why alligators? We treat each other similarly to the way alligators treat each other. Anyone

Figure 1.2   Examples of adjectives and descriptions of emergencies (alphabetically)

who has ever watched one of those nature shows on TV can recall the way alligators interact: when they find something to eat, they fight over it with each other, pushing and shoving, grabbing and pillaging. I have never seen an alligator that stops for a second, looks at their fellow alligators, and says: "You seem to be in much greater need. Here is some food." Naturally, they just take care of their own needs, and most of us and most of our colleagues act in a very similar fashion: we are self-focused, only taking care of our own needs and showing disregard for those of our colleagues, even if their needs are legitimately more urgent than ours.

This behavior occurs for a variety of reasons, some of which are not up to us, such as unclear organizational priorities and reward systems that encourage us to self-focus. Nevertheless, it produces the same results. Trying to make excuses—it is not up to us and there is nothing we can do about it—will not change our project realities and will not bring us closer to a more collaborative environment. We therefore cannot dismiss it or discount its impact, but rather should look for ways to improve and fix it.

Where can we start? Look for ideas on how to change the way we interact with our immediate environment and let it grow from there. It is less a change in culture than a grassroots change in attitudes. We should all take a look at our own conduct and try to get more out of the relationships we form at work. We should look for ways to improve collaboration within our team and with our colleagues and for ideas on how to create an environment that not only produces a win-win resolution to challenging situations but also fosters win-win thinking among team members. This will ultimately lead to building trust and stronger relationships, and working together more efficiently toward our goals—instead of working against each other. Here are a few examples of simple things we can do to kick-start the effort to improve the culture of alligators and help our interactions, communications, and relationships with our colleagues and team members:

1. Take the ego out of our meetings and conversations. It is not about who prevails, but about how to generate buy-in for doing the right thing for the project. When we are wrong, we need to learn to admit we are wrong; help others save face when they are wrong; and build a case for our position by providing evidence and information that supports it. In addition, we should not take it personally if our position is not accepted, as it is not a battle against other stakeholders but a joint effort.

2. Learn how to reach out to team members and stakeholders and tailor our message to them based on their style, drivers, and values. Chapters 3 and 4, concerning stakeholder management and politics, deal with this in more detail.

3. Attitude: I have learned that attitudes take projects down more dramatically than schedule problems or defects. Negative attitudes that develop

among team members tend to spread like wildfire and infect individuals who, up until that point, were not distracted by political games. Although difficult to manage, we need to take the extra step to manage relationships, reach out informally, and develop rapport with team members and stakeholders. Having an informal conversation over a cup of coffee, giving others an opportunity to confide in us, and showing genuine care for team members' concerns is key for success in these matters. When we see those negative attitudes begin to develop, we need to focus on addressing them quickly, effectively, and privately: not in front of other team members, not during a large meeting, and not in ways that will divert the team's attention and focus away from the work it needs to do. Work one-on-one with the person involved and let them feel that you are there to help—not to discipline and discount their concerns.

This chapter has provided an overview of many problems we face in our project environments, in order to jumpstart a discussion on how to start the process of changing them. It contains a review of the state of project management and the reality that, with nearly half a million PMPs worldwide, it is not easy to find a "good" PM. Moving forward, each chapter of this book deals with a different aspect of our projects and outlines meaningful steps to take to better achieve our goals and improve our project management practices and environments.

Every significant change in the right direction needs to start with something small, and just as moving a large mountain begins with moving one rock, this book breaks down ideas, insights, and checklists into meaningful and easy-to-follow concepts. The ideas and proposed solutions in the book are aligned with current methodologies, and their value comes from rearticulating concepts by putting them in the context of our project challenges. The ideas are driven by out-of-the-box thinking that will help you identify the situation you are facing as what it really is and optimize your ability to handle it successfully.

REFERENCES

1. Mary Walton, *The Deming Management Method* (New York: Perigee Books, 1988).
2. Project Management Institute (2013).
3. J. I. Eveleens and C. Verhoef, "Quantifying IT Forecast Quality," *Science of Computer Programming*, vol. 74, no. 11+12, 2009, 934–988.

2

Project Complexity and Readiness Assessment

> **"All of the Success Criteria and Constraints Are Equally Important."**
>
> This is related to "I need an answer now." While organizations make commitments that are at times ambitious, project managers (PMs) need to inform senior stakeholders about what information is needed in order to deliver the value they are looking for. The next step is to check which success criteria may be more flexible so a plan can be put together to deliver success.

People plan, prepare, and conduct informal readiness assessments for most things that we do. Sometimes we use a checklist to make sure we take everything we need when going somewhere, although usually we just have this list in our heads. Before we leave home in the morning to head to work, we conduct an informal, undocumented, readiness assessment. It involves doing all the things we need to do prior to leaving home (e.g., shower, brushing teeth), and before heading out, we make sure that we are dressed appropriately for the occasion, that we have our computer and other work-related materials, and that we have all the things that we need, such as car keys, wallet, "European carry all," purse, or umbrella. Although it is not documented as a formal process, we know what we need to do and in which order, and we conduct it like a best practice. If we fail to check whether we have what it takes to get out the front door, we may end up going to work without our computer bag, with no car keys, or even in our pajamas instead of work clothes.

Although many people recognize the importance of being ready to handle whatever we need to do, it is rather astonishing that organizations consistently fail to invest enough in measuring their level of readiness for upcoming projects. Related to this notion is one of the leading concepts in quality management: DTRTRTFT (Do The Right Thing Right The First Time).[1] In other words, it is imperative to make sure that we understand how prepared we are for the project and that we make the effort to deliver success in our first attempt. Without any measurement of our readiness, it is unlikely that we can prepare sufficiently for what we are facing, and the results will, unfortunately, fall below expectations.

This chapter discusses ways to measure your project readiness and its complexity. It also introduces criteria and measurements that can help you determine the impact of the assessment's results and, in turn, come up with recommendations or next steps. It also provides suggestions of other activities that you should conduct early in the project—ideas about how to prepare for and conduct an effective project kickoff meeting and a framework for building the foundations for such a meeting. There is always the challenge of finding time and capacity for these activities, along with (somewhat legitimate) doubts about their cost-benefit ratio.

At the end of an effective readiness assessment process, the PM should have the ability to articulate the organization's readiness for the project and, in turn, to manage or change the expectations and risks associated with the undertaking. By the end of this chapter, readers should be able to measure the effort required to produce a readiness assessment and consider the criteria related to whether the project is worth the organization's time and effort. Similar to all the other concepts introduced in this book, the ones in this chapter are straightforward, easy to implement, intuitive, and yield easy-to-realize benefits. Another feature that makes them practical and easy to implement is that they introduce a new way of managing projects that is based on existing and proven concepts, methodologies, and best practices. Let's first familiarize ourselves to the two concepts just introduced—project readiness assessment and complexity assessment—and then expand on them.

INTRODUCTION TO THE READINESS ASSESSMENT

The readiness assessment measures how prepared you and your organization are for the upcoming project. There are many ways to measure readiness, and the level of intensity and thoroughness should depend upon multiple factors, such as organizational risk attitude, project complexity, and the specific situation you are facing. A "proper" readiness assessment may include evaluations of: the organizational culture, processes, and procedures; leadership styles; resource management; overall complexity; and historical performance. The readiness assessment can help you identify project and organizational needs and serve as a foundation to planning. The readiness assessment is not about planning—it is about evaluating how prepared the organization and the team are for the project.

If the assessment ends up indicating that the organization is not prepared for the project, it does not mean that it has to be called off, or that the PM should refuse to work on it; rather, it should serve as a warning sign that it is time to either reconsider whether the project is viable or consider taking extra measures to ensure that the organization is better equipped to handle it. These extra measures should take place during the initiation and planning of the project if a decision is made to move forward with it. Many organizations enter into projects without being fully ready for them or without knowing how prepared they are for the journey. Sometimes it may be more dangerous to have no indication about the readiness level than to realize that the organization is not fully prepared.

Readiness deals with a variety of matters, where the leading ones are related to: resources (i.e., availability, capacity, skills, timing, and fit), project dependencies, domain experience, approvals, budgets, and schedules. It can be viewed as a type of gap analysis between where the organization currently is and its capacity for the project. Failing to effectively address these gaps and proceeding with the project will result in elevated levels of complexity and risk. In some cases, the team identifies areas of the project that indicate a lack of readiness, and in others, there is simply a lack of information about some aspects of the project. Either way, these are both warning signs to the organization that this project requires special attention.

Why Readiness Assessment?

There is a guideline that keeps reminding me of the importance of effective project planning, and although not proven scientifically, I have verified it in practice: for every unit of time I spend in (quality, meaningful) planning, I end up saving three units of time down the road. Even it if it is not always the case, it averages out this way for every project. The project readiness assessment is an important precursor to planning and provides an indication of what to expect, which makes the planning easier, more efficient, and more effective. The goal of the readiness assessment is to help the organization become aware of, and then try to avoid, obstacles that may prevent or delay the delivery of the project's value and benefits. By identifying potential hurdles, your organization can address potential dangers proactively before they materialize and become issues or problems.

The readiness assessment not only gives an indication of whether the team is ready to start the project but also, by doing it early—before problems begin to emerge—reduces costs. Any issue, problem, risk, or hurdle the team manages to anticipate, get ready for, or avoid before it actually materializes saves a significant amount of money during and after the project. It also introduces another benefit related to team building: Engaging our team during the assessment period builds relationships and provides a reliable indicator of the team's readiness for the project. It also sends a message to both the team and the customer that the organization is taking its projects seriously. That alone puts the organization and the team in a better position than it would have been in otherwise.

The downside is that like many other good ideas, it is hard to implement—not because of the cost or complexity associated with it but because of the difficulty in "selling" this idea to senior management. The readiness assessment does add to the cost and time at the front end of the project, but this is time and money that is essentially guaranteed to be "returned" later in the project in the form of savings and efficiencies. This book's approach to a readiness assessment and the list of benefits it articulates will serve both as a framework and as a list of justification points for selling the idea to your senior management. The merits test—proven results, improvements, and success—are the best selling points for any idea. As these readiness assessment ideas prove to be contributors to success, they may encourage organizations to change project planning and preplanning efforts to accommodate them. Part of this step toward success is project performance and delivery that is free of surprises and most PMs will attest that project surprises are high on their list of least favorite things.

A Word or Two About Integration

One of the many differences between project management methodologies and project realities lies within the integration stage. There are few specific guidelines on how to perform a meaningful integration of all the aspects that need to be managed in a project. Chapter 13, "Project Integration," provides a detailed approach to integration and the activities associated with it; however, part of integration is to realize that it happens all the time and everywhere. It means that anything that needs to be done will *always* end up impacting at least one other part of the project—most likely, more than one. This may not come as news to you, as it is quite the same in life: every action that people take has some sort of impact, direct or indirect, on multiple other things. For example, when a central bank raises interest rates, it sends shockwaves throughout the economy—some are direct (higher costs of borrowing, slowdown in investments) and others are less so (currency fluctuations). This is not to mention the unpredictable impact it might have on real estate, foreign flow of capital, discretionary spending, unemployment rate, and overall economic growth.

Projects are similar in nature: any action causes some sort of an impact or reaction somewhere else in the project or the organization; however, no one can be sure of the nature of the impact—whether it is linear or nonlinear, positive or negative, clear or vague. The more information the team manages to gather and understand up-front, anticipating as many of the potential hurdles that the project will encounter as possible, the better off it will be. Another part of integration that people tend to forget is that every action eventually has some sort of impact on quality (the readiness assessment is the first step to achieve quality). Moreover, the attitude an organization has toward the readiness assessment is an early indication of its attitude toward quality.

WHAT THE READINESS ASSESSMENT IS ABOUT

The readiness assessment consists of measuring at one or more of the following levels: organizational, program, project, and team. It checks whether you are prepared to perform the work, how open you are to changing the way you do things to accommodate the new needs, and your overall implementation capability. On a high level, it includes the proposed readiness assessment areas, as demonstrated in Figure 2.1.

The assessment will help you to focus on things you or your organization might need to prepare for and to overcome any potential obstacles that may impede your project. Parts of the team readiness assessment may overlap with the stakeholder analysis; this is an example of integration and should not be viewed as a duplication of effort, but rather as an input to the stakeholder analysis that will be performed once the project gets the "go ahead." The readiness assessment precedes the stakeholder analysis as it is performed even before the project is a go. If done at the right time, the readiness assessment's results may demonstrate that the entire project is unfeasible.

Figure 2.1 Readiness assessment areas

For the most part, readiness assessments yield results that range between fully ready and completely not ready, but rarely will deem a project as one of these two extremes. If an assessment produces results that show that the organization is fully ready for the project, this may truly be the case, or there is the possibility that the assessment was not performed properly. In the end, an assessment that indicates that an organization is completely not ready for a project may point at a more fundamental problem in the organization by considering the project in the first place. Generally, it is expected that the assessment will reveal gaps and articulate areas that can help your organization put together stronger teams and focus on the relevant areas of planning that it needs.

Know If You Are Ready

There are a few questions you can ask yourself before starting the assessment, to get a better idea about where you stand in relation to your project readiness:

- Is there a project readiness measurement process in your organization?
- Has it been an issue in previous projects?
- Did lack of readiness cause project complexity or mire project performance?
- Is there a formal process in your organization for a readiness assessment?

Even if the answers are not the ones you are hoping for, it does not necessarily indicate looming trouble; it simply reinforces the need for meaningful readiness planning and serves as a reminder of what might happen, or rather what has happened, when readiness assessment was not done properly. It can also serve as an indication of how well you are positioned for such an assessment and how easy it might be to conduct one.

ASSESSMENT CONSIDERATIONS

In essence, the assessment tries to determine how aligned the main stakeholders, the organization, and the customers are with each other about the goals, objectives, approach, and capabilities of the project. Before devising a list of questions that help measure the readiness level, there are a few things to take into consideration, as illustrated in Figure 2.2.

The questions should be treated as discussion points, for which PMs need to engage in conversations and look for answers, rather than walk around and ask stakeholders direct questions that could be taken out of context. Each question has the potential to turn into a risk if the answer is not positive in terms of the project context, or when there is not enough information. The answers to these questions

The list of questions serves as a repository.

- Not all questions are applicable for all situations and organizations.
- It is not realistic or cost effective to attempt to answer them all.

Identify half a dozen applicable questions.

- The more answers found, the clearer the picture about project readiness.
- Failing to find answers may indicate greater project risk.

Having no information may be riskier than knowing that you are not prepared or that conditions are not favorable.

- People are generally optimistic by nature and there are two things that tend to take place when information is missing:
  - People do not look for additional information to gain more knowledge about the matter.
  - They are inclined to believe that it will be ok and that they will have the power and means to deal with the situation if and when something happens.

Figure 2.2 Assessment considerations

may help in performing a stakeholder analysis. PMs can build their own proprietary measurement tool by performing a few simple steps, as demonstrated in Figure 2.3.

The Assessment Questions

With the considerations from Figure 2.3 in mind, let's delve into the questions. Keep in mind that some of these questions may not be relevant to your environment, and you may identify other questions that are not in this list. The goal is to have a set of questions that will ultimately give an indication of whether you are prepared to move ahead with the project. A simple scale of 0–5, as illustrated in Table 2.1, should be sufficient (0 indicates missing information and a need to make assumptions). The list of questions has been organized into logical categories and is presented in Figure 2.4.

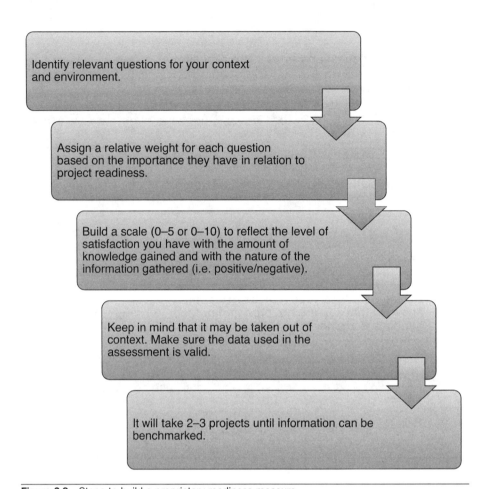

Figure 2.3 Steps to build a proprietary readiness measure

Table 2.1 Preparedness scale

0	1	2	3	4	5
No information. Make an assumption.	Very Low	Low	Medium	High	Very High

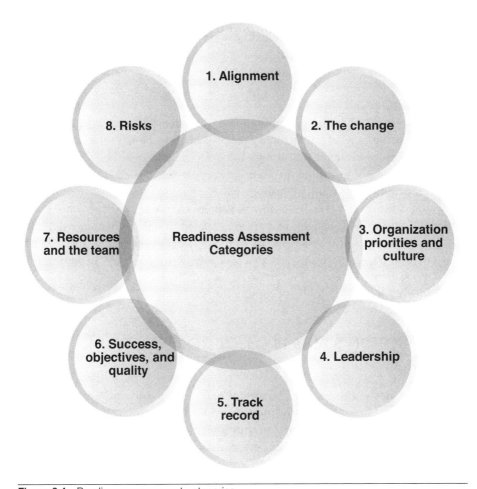

Figure 2.4 Readiness assessment categories

ASSESSMENT RESULTS: HOW DO YOU KNOW WHEN YOU ARE READY?

The results of your assessment may not be conclusive or specific, and they may not give a clear signal for where things appear to be heading. However, they can give you better insight and additional knowledge about your project's environment and possibly about the overall chances of successfully completing it. More specifically, your assessment may produce value from the following points of view:

- Help your organization identify changes that need to be made to invest in its project, including: reassigning responsibilities, shifting staff schedules, and changing the cost structure.

- Ensure that the project coincides with organizational strategies and goals. Beyond the potential waste of efforts and resources for pursuing misaligned goals, it may confuse employees and may further impair the chance for success if the project is not aligned with the organization's overall strategies.
- Indicate whether the organization has allocated adequate budget, staff, and technology infrastructure to the project and whether other resources are in place to support it through to implementation.
- Provide input to the organizational priorities and if needed, lead to conversations about resource reallocation.
- Indicate where we are and how well prepared we are for the project. It may also provide insights and answers related to stakeholder analysis and preliminary risk assessment. In turn, the assessment results serve as a natural transition to the next area we cover here—the project complexity assessment—since the less prepared we are, the more complexity we can identify in relation to the upcoming project.

INTRODUCTION TO THE PROJECT COMPLEXITY ASSESSMENT

This section deals with another important measure for your project, which also serves as a subset to readiness—the project complexity assessment. In a world where virtually all organizations engage in running multiple projects simultaneously, resource sharing, and at times, dispersed resources, project dependencies, and outsourcing, every project is essentially complex. Because PMs should treat every project with the appropriate level of focus and intensity, we should still try to learn more about how complex each project is (relative to others), how to define what complexity is, and how to measure it. Obtaining a realistic reading of project complexity will help assess our readiness level and, in turn, allow us to plan properly.

While trying to categorize and measure complexity, there are a few common types to consider: technical, organizational, environmental, people, and overall complexity. The ability PMs have to detect complexity within these generic categories and to prepare for it will have a significant impact downstream on the degree of project success we can deliver. The breakdown of complexity into categories helps channel our focus toward where complexity may come from, and the categories can serve as a checklist to remind us which areas may produce complexity. Generally, not every category that is illustrated in Figure 2.5 will produce complexity for every project.

PMs need to look into all of these areas, and—based on the result of the complexity measure each one produces (details and the how-to's will be discussed in greater depth later in the chapter)—we should check whether it impacts project

Technical

- Involves anything related to technology, innovation, system interactions, compatibility, scalability, and design

Organizational

- Tangibles: resource management, best practices, policies and procedures, cross-project dependencies, cross-project risk impact, and logistical aspects such as co-location

Environmental

- Culture and politics in the organization, markets and competition, regulators, suppliers, external political environment, economy, social aspects

People

- Teams, group dynamics, values, personalities, conflicts, and styles

General Uncertainty

- Project size, constraints, internal dependencies, and overall level of uncertainty

Figure 2.5 Complexity categories

readiness and update the project risk section accordingly. Arguably, this list of categories may not have significant impact on all projects—some projects are more straightforward, with little complexity, and other projects are just small enough that even if there are some areas that produce complexity, it is easily contained and managed. However, my experience shows that in many organizations, the large, potentially complex projects get the right amount of attention and understanding of their complexity. The problem is usually with smaller projects that generally do not get the right amount of focus and attention, including a failure to conduct a complexity assessment. These often end up causing the most problems and grief for organizations.

Project complexity tends to grow in direct proportion to the size of the project, with a high level of complexity in any specific category, and—in cases where no category is labeled as complex—it may be the sheer number of areas of uncertainty that make it complex. A project complexity assessment measures the combination of any given project's complexity categories, their magnitude, and the number of interactions between them. All of this should then be factored into the readiness assessment to gauge the organization's and the team's capability to deal with the project. PMs should not be deterred from taking on high complexity projects, but having a realistic view of what we are facing in advance will help in the planning process.

Project Complexity Assessment

One of the challenges with the word *complexity* is that it is of a relative nature. It is similar to hot, cold, pretty, big, or small, which are all relative descriptors. When team members say something is complex, one thing is certain: it is complex for them. In this case, you cannot question the legitimacy of what they say, but you may have a different view about it. I personally do not like cilantro; so, when my friend tells me that he likes cilantro, I can question his taste in food, but I cannot tell him he is wrong. With this consideration in mind, let's try to build a definition of what might qualify something as complex, and go with that definition. This will lead to consistency and prevent all sorts of subjective judgement calls that may mislead us.

WHAT IS COMPLEXITY?

Complexity is a difficult concept to define. According to Webster's dictionary,[2] Complexity is:

1. (Apparent) the degree to which a system or component has a design or implementation that is difficult to understand and verify;
2. (Inherent) the degree of complication of a system or system component, determined by such factors as the number and intricacy of interfaces, the number and intricacy of conditional branches, the degree of nesting, and the types of data structures.

With a better idea about what complexity is, it is important to note that it may still be difficult to identify and articulate a complexity level. It is possible to have a complex project—even if there is no single area of complexity that stands out besides a combination of factors that together indicate complexity. In a similar manner, the leader of the Tour de France, who wears the yellow jersey, may not have produced the best time on any single day but has the combined best time. The complexity assessment, coupled with the readiness assessment, will serve as a gateway into risk management—every item that is deemed complex will need our attention later, when we look at project risks.

Project complexity is typically described in general terms but is often not fully understood by everyone involved. The word "complex" comes from Latin (*complexus*), which means "entwined or twisted together." It is also described as an aggregate of parts. As opposed to "complex," we use the word "simple" in the context of dealing with only one part, as opposed to multiple parts acting together. Everything we do can be measured as having some level of complexity—low, medium, or high—and therefore all projects will have some degree of complexity. The complexity assessment is something that needs to take place early in the project and needs to be maintained throughout the project, based on the progress made, and then needs to be reviewed at the end to make sure it is in line with reality. This provides a layer of validation and continuity to the assessment and makes it more sustainable for reference by future projects.

For more effective results, the complexity analysis should involve, at least in part, selected project team members completing a questionnaire, individually, in order to quantify the level of complexity drivers. If there is capacity for such an exercise, the results should be compiled, analyzed, and elaborated upon in a workshop, to allow further discussion, clarification, and issue resolution. The goal is to achieve a consensus or an understanding among team members and, if required, stakeholders of the level of complexity and the main challenges and weaknesses the project is going to encounter. For more context and validation, it may need to be complemented by a stakeholder analysis for a prioritization scheme of what to address first.

How to Measure Complexity

First, let's define what types of project complexity we should be on the lookout for, and then find ways to measure them. They can be broken down into two main categories—technical and organizational/management complexity—and into subcategories associated with each of them:

1. Technical complexity is about the technical aspects of what we need to do and deals with the degree of difficulty we might face in building our product and the business scope of what we do. It can be broken down into aspects related to the product and those related to the project work, as demonstrated in Figure 2.6.

2. Organizational/Management complexity (or nontechnical) is about the business aspects of the project, the team, the relationships of the project with other projects and organizational functions, and the project organization. Under this category, there are several subcategories:

- Product related: scope, design, technology, processes, integration, scalability, and methodology
- Project work related: schedule and cost, schedule detail level and data sources, and financial arrangements for funding the project

Technical

Figure 2.6 Complexity assessment subcategory: Technical

   a. Environmental complexity refers to intangible aspects of the environment in which the project takes place, such as political and cultural impacts, agendas, communication efficiencies, and the overall business climate inside and outside the organization. It is difficult to measure, and there is a need for access to knowledge about how things really work in the project's environment, including the list in Figure 2.7.
   b. Team and people complexity is about team dynamics, styles, values, and the abilities of resources to work well together. It addresses conflicts, conditions for conflicts, and personalities.
   c. Overall level of uncertainty combines aspects of complexity from other categories and subcategories and includes considerations of whether we have done it before, how estimates are done, and other non-tangibles that may be related to a combination of complexity from other categories.

There are cases where no category produces a high level of uncertainty complexity on its own, but the combination of all categories together generates a higher level of overall uncertainty complexity. It is similar to when someone has a cold that is moderate in severity but lasts longer than usual: it may not be the most severe cold or the longest one, but the combination of the two aspects makes it feel like a severe cold.

It is now time to look at the attributes of a project and try to measure which one may introduce complexity into the project and under which category it should be classified. It is important to categorize the complexities into types so we can focus

Environmental

- Design of the management structure
- Risk management
- Project partnerships, dependencies, and organizational interface
- Decision making and approval processes
- Logistical issues related to co-location and interdependencies

Figure 2.7   Complexity assessment subcategories: Environmental

our efforts on addressing areas that are more complex and try to handle them proactively in order to reduce any future complexities they may produce. Each type of complexity may be fed by any one or more of the project attributes. Let's review the project attributes and the questions we need to ask for each, and then match them to the complexity types. For each attribute question, you can create a measure (0–5 or 0–10) to reflect the total rating score of the attribute. The scale should reflect the conditions in your project and their relative importance to and potential influence upon it. Make sure the scale is consistent, so that 1 represents simplicity, smaller scale, or smaller size, and higher numbers represent greater complexity.

PROJECT ATTRIBUTES

The main attributes of a project should include the project knowledge areas,[3] along with a couple of additional items to complement them. The scope, time, cost, and quality attributes fall under the technical complexity type, and all of the other attributes listed in Figure 2.8 belong under the management/organizational type. The attributes are then listed in the complexity attribute table, whose headings are listed in Table 2.2.

Once again, not all of the assessment questions may be relevant to your project, but you should view them as belonging to a repository of questions to consider. Take those that are relevant to your circumstances and utilize them to measure your project complexity.

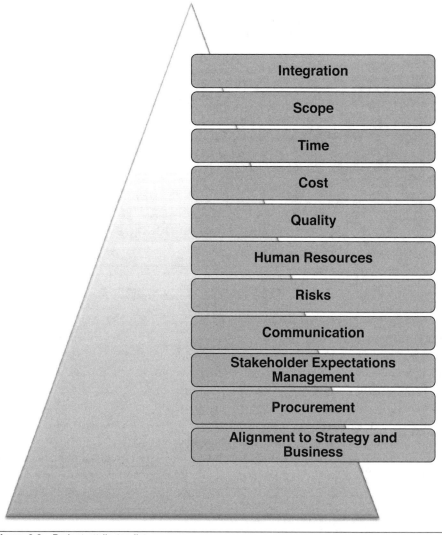

Figure 2.8 Project attributes list

Table 2.2 Complexity attributes table headings

Project Attribute	Attribute Related Questions	Relative Weight (0 = unknown, 1 = Low, 5 = High)	Score per Question (1 = Low, 5 = High)	Complexity Type

The Questions

When information is not known about a complexity assessment question, the most viable option would be to resort to making assumptions. However, it is important to note that more assumptions imply higher potential complexity. The table should include scores for each question and an overall score for every category. Identifying areas with high complexity will help focus the team's and the organization's efforts toward the more complex categories. Many of the areas of complexity can be addressed through the risk management process.

THOUGHTS ON COMPLEXITY

Many of the areas of complexity can be addressed through the risk management process; however, realizing the degree of complexity early on in the project may help direct the PM's focus toward those areas that are most important during project implementation. With a higher level of complexity in your project, you will need to define the appropriate approach to take and in turn, think about risks—in the event that one of the areas of complexity materializes into an event that threatens project success. Risk management will help you handle the problems that may occur. The complexity assessment deals with how hard it is going to be to implement the project and serves as a precursor to risk management. There is one additional thing to remember about the project complexity level: Even if there is a high degree of complexity, it does not mean that the project requires a complex solution.

Understanding the level of complexity will inherently direct you toward an appropriate solution. On a side note, readiness and complexity assessments are useless without follow up, communication, and action. When an area of complexity is discovered, the onus is on the PM to let the appropriate stakeholders know about it—if it is not communicated to the project stakeholders, no action will take place to address the complexity. Furthermore, even if PMs alert the stakeholders, they should make sure to clearly articulate the impact of not addressing these complexities in a way that resonates with each stakeholder. Otherwise, stakeholders will not take any action, and the complexities will turn into risks and trouble downstream. Chapters 3 and 4 deal with organizational politics and stakeholder analysis, respectively, and provide valuable information on how to approach and manage relationships with colleagues and project stakeholders.

KICKOFF MEETING

There is one more thing that complements the readiness assessment and complexity level, essentially completing them—the kickoff meeting. There is no question about the importance and the value of conducting an effective kickoff meeting. In fact, most projects begin with a kickoff meeting, which essentially sets the tone for the rest of the project. Unfortunately, many kickoff meetings fall short of sending the project off on the right foot and do not live up to their potential. It may be that this failure is do to the PM lacking leadership skills or simply failing to understand the true purpose of such a meeting. As this is often the first time that stakeholders meet each other and the PM, it is important to keep all the clichés about first impressions and the importance of setting the tone properly in the forefront of your mind.

The PM needs to conduct a kickoff meeting that is effective and efficient—effective, to ensure that it achieves its intended goals, and efficient, so it is done with less effort, interruption, and distraction, focusing only on whatever value-adding aspects it provides. Planning starts with setting up the goals that the meeting needs to accomplish and the techniques to employ to meet these goals, including such details as the seating arrangement, style, agenda, and a list of topics, actions, and behaviors to avoid.

Ideally, the kickoff meeting should serve as an "opening ceremony" for the project, injecting it with excitement and energy to inspire the team to jumpstart the process of generating ideas for a solution. However, the reality is usually far different: kickoff meetings often do not have a sufficient level of focus and fail to achieve the goals for which they are intended—to set the project expectations, send a clear leadership message, and identify areas that require special attention.

Many kickoff meetings are uninspiring and do not provide a comfortable sense of direction and leadership. Lacking a clear message may well serve as a message about the state of affairs in the project—that there is no leadership, direction, or drive behind it. With all the logistics and preparation time that go into kickoff meetings, they often turn out to be an expensive repetition of already-known project information and add little or no value. The kickoff meeting should serve as an analysis and strategy session, wherein the PM generates confidence in the direction, leadership, and approach for the project, and stakeholders spend time interacting with each other and establishing working relations for the project.

Pre-Kickoff

There are a few key ingredients for a successful kickoff meeting, including preparation work, putting together a good plan, and outlining the meeting's goals and expectations. One aspect of preparation, which may have the most potential impact, is to conduct a pre-kickoff, or project-definition series of meetings. If you are assigned to the project at this early stage, you should reach out to high profile stakeholders for a series of one-on-one conversations that in turn, may result in several potential benefits, as listed in Figure 2.9.

While it makes sense to reach out to as many high profile stakeholders as possible, keep in mind that with limited time and resources, you will need to strike a

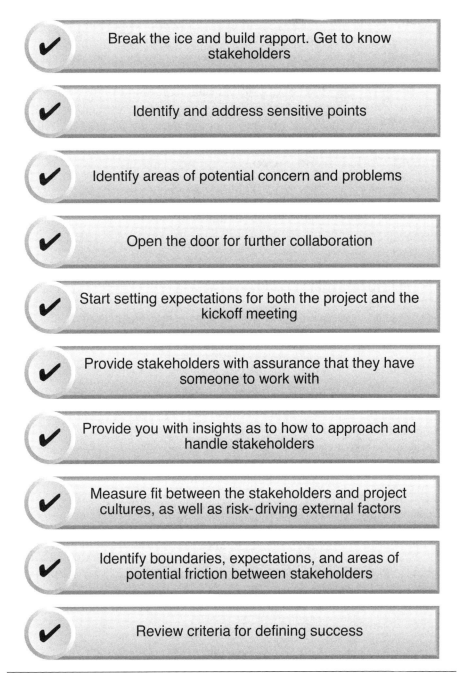

Figure 2.9   Pre-Kickoff meeting benefits

balance that provides you with access to roughly a handful of stakeholders, to whom you can provide value while obtaining the information you need. When trying to shorten the list of stakeholders that you interview, try to reach out strategically to stakeholders who are directly responsible for what you are producing (e.g., heads of departments) or to stakeholders with greater abilities to benefit or harm your project. In an attempt to get the required information from key high-profile stakeholders, PMs should identify the ten most relevant questions for their environment.

Plan and Conduct the Kickoff

The official kickoff meeting of the project is an opportunity to get creative and incorporate various activities into it, in an attempt to address specific problems or issues, understand stakeholders' needs and behaviors, set up ground rules, and make introductions.

KICKOFF SUMMARY

Since the kickoff meeting is the first real event of the project, one would think that it should be handled with the appropriate level of attention and focus. Therefore, it is surprising to see so many projects launch without one. There is a long list of reasons for this, but for the most part, they should be viewed as excuses:

- Virtual or global projects where stakeholders are not co-located;
- So much work has already been put into negotiations, feasibility, early planning, requirements, and statements of work, that the kickoff meeting appears to be nothing more than a ceremonial aspect that adds no value;
- Some projects are on hold or are so late to start that there is no time allocated for preparation and planning. Stakeholders want to see things getting done;
- Scheduling conflicts—stakeholders are busy and it is hard to coordinate a meeting.

Since the benefits of conducting a well-planned kickoff meeting outweigh the circumstances and the excuses, even if it produces only one benefit for the project, it will still be worthwhile. Figure 2.10 contains a list of potential benefits that a kickoff meeting can yield.

READINESS AND COMPLEXITY FINAL THOUGHTS

This chapter has dealt with four elements that occur early on in the project; ideally, they occur prior to, or very early, in the initiation process. A project readiness

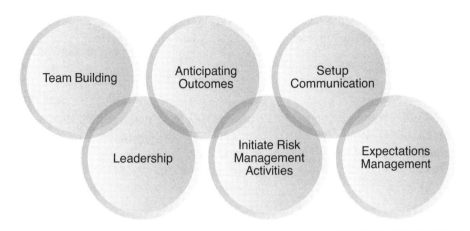

Figure 2.10   Potential benefits moving forward—kickoff meeting

assessment provides the organization with an indication of whether it is ready to take on the project and has what it takes to bring it to a successful outcome. The complexity assessment is related to readiness and indicates areas of potential complexity (and subsequent risk) that may arise throughout the project, whether the complexity is due to lack of readiness or to anything that may pose challenges to the project teams.

The advantage of determining the readiness and complexity levels early on is that it will be easier and less costly to address them than if we stumble upon them later, unprepared. Even if the findings of these two assessments show that we are not quite ready, or that the project is going to be complex, they do not call for an outright cancellation of the project but rather warrant more attention to the identified areas. Once the project is a go, it is worth investing in trying to establish relationships with key stakeholders early on to help identify and address issues and challenges and to help build good rapport with them. This is the "pre-kickoff," or project definition stage. Finally, the kickoff meeting provides an opportunity to set the tone of the entire project and demonstrate leadership.

Many projects proceed without one or more of these activities in place and still make it to successful destinations. However, they end up doing it with significantly more effort, cost, time, and aggravation than they otherwise would—if they had made the up-front effort to perform these four activities. Other projects that end up falling short of delivering success can usually look back at the onset of the project to find the reason: no effort, or insufficient effort, was invested up front to assess readiness and complexity or to prepare for and conduct a meaningful kickoff meeting. With that said, it is clear that these activities are not simple to perform, and they are time-consuming and costly. However, like many other planning activities, a serious look at their cost-benefit analysis will show that these up-front investments significantly benefit the project and the organization moving forward.

References

1. Philip B. Crosby, *Quality is Still Free* (New York, NY: McGraw-Hill, 1996).
2. "Complexity," from Merriam-Webster's online dictionary, at http://www .merriam-webster.com/dictionary/complexity.
3. Project Management Institute, *A Guide to the Project Management Body of Knowledge (PMBOK® Guide—Fifth Edition)* Newtown Square, PA, 60–61, 2013.

3

Culture and Politics: The Organization's Pillars and Speed Bumps

> **"That's the Way We Have Always Done it Here."**
>
> This is one of the most innovation- and improvement-inhibiting statements out there. Processes and best practices may be key success factors, but they need to be balanced against the need for continuous improvement. Challenging existing processes with alternatives that appear legitimate and better should not be suppressed by excuses, such as "this is how it is done around here." This argument is likely an attempt to hide behind existing practices and to shirk responsibility. Ironically, it is most prevalent in organizations that are in the direst need for improvement.

Organizational politics: no one likes it, and no one wants to be part of it. However, everyone must engage in it to some degree; unfortunately, most people do not do it well. Organizational politics is all around us and here to stay. No one can wave a magic wand and make it disappear, although it is possible to learn how to cope with it. This chapter deals with how to handle organizational politics, play it the way it should be played, benefit from it, and at the same time manage not to overdo it. The information in this chapter is complemented by Chapters 4 and 11, which deal with stakeholder analysis and management and with project communication, respectively.

Although virtually everyone is engaged in organizational politics, sometimes without even realizing it, it starts bothering people only when they are on the losing end of a political transaction or when they feel manipulated by other team members. One of the main difficulties with organizational politics is that the "political rules" are not written anywhere, and often they are not transparent or even apparent.

An attempt to change organizational culture or politics, or to "fight" them, will most likely end in frustration, disappointment, out of control conflict, or even losing a job. To make things more complicated, culture and politics are different from one organization to another, within the same organization, and sometimes even within the same department. It is hard to detect politics, yet it is something that may have a significant, and at times severe impact on essentially everything that goes on in the organization.

To illustrate the presence of organizational politics that people often do not even realize, I have posed the following question on several occasions to job candidates I have interviewed, particularly when they adamantly insist that they do not engage in office politics: Imagine that you intend to ask your manager for a long vacation during the busy time of year and, for various reasons, you have procrastinated doing so to the point where it can no longer wait. You finally decide to approach your manager this morning, but as she gets out of a meeting, she appears visibly distraught and stressed. Would you ask her about the vacation now? Most candidates answered that they probably would not, and that was when they realized this was organizational politics—even if they did not initially recognize it.

Some people may be "straight shooters"—transparent, up-front, candid, or politically correct—while others are hard to read, but everything people do, say, and react to, the way they do it, and sometimes those things that are not said or done become part of the organizational culture of politics. One of the first things to keep in mind when trying to get a better handle on politics is that everything people do has two layers: the layer of "what," which is the content and substance, and the layer of "how," which is the style, timing, context, and form. The "how," at times, may be more important and impactful than the "what."

This chapter also provides a look at some of the influencing factors on politics, such as: conflict management and resolution, typical sources of conflict, team formation, egos, personal needs, and personal styles. Together, they all make up the organizational pillars and speed bumps: likening politics to driving in the dark and still managing to navigate our course without stumbling on obstacles that are along the way.

WHAT IS POLITICS?

One of the first things to do in an attempt to figure something out is to define what it is, and there are as many definitions of what organizational politics is as there are people in the organization. An example of a possible definition would be: team members who do not work hard and yet manage to hold onto their position or even get promoted due to political undercurrents in the organization. Other examples include the following:

- Employees who act like "boy scouts" when a senior stakeholder is in the room and turn into "loose cannons" when senior managers are not in sight;
- Team members who only do things to gain attention and appreciation from other stakeholders;
- People who act irrationally only to obtain advantages over others.

Quite often, politically-driven behaviors lead to a negative stance at the workplace and to negative attitudes that are developed by other team members and stakeholders that, in turn, may create a vicious cycle that is hard to break. To be clear, this chapter is not intended to encourage behaving in a political manner or being driven by politics; rather, it is meant to give some insight into how to better handle those who do conduct themselves politically and how to deal effectively with the situations that ensue.

Soft Rewards

Beyond salaries, benefits, job titles, achievements, fulfillment, and growth that people look for as part of working for an organization, there are several non-tangible rewards. The organization does not provide them as part of the benefits package, and they are not documented anywhere, so they are difficult to measure, and each person's combination of these "soft rewards" adds up to a different set of personal priorities.

One way to pursue these intangible gains is to engage in politics (though not in the negative context). However, many people are not sure what these benefits and rewards are, and without knowing what they're aiming for, they cannot come up with a strategy to achieve them. This is one of the things that makes organizational politics so elusive and complex: many people do not focus their efforts on the things that will help them achieve soft rewards, and others do not even know that these rewards exist. Figure 3.1 provides details about these elusive and coveted soft rewards.

Measure of Personal Power

In the right combination, soft rewards represent many of the aspects of personal power. They are contextual, related to the specific situation people are in and to the organization and the area they are trying to influence. Ranking personal power can help individuals articulate their own sources of power and become more goal-oriented in channeling their efforts toward building personal power. With the

> **Soft Rewards**
>
> - **Friendships (for social, career, or personal gains)**
> - **Recognition and perceived expertise**
> - **Opportunity (for growth, personal gain)**
> - **Seniority and status (learn how it is measured; how those with status got it)**
> - **Sense of confidence (show knowledge without appearing arrogant)**
> - **Information (about work and about other people may be confidential or off-the-record)**

Figure 3.1 Soft rewards

information about soft rewards in place, there are various ways to measure the components of personal power, and individuals can rank themselves and quantify their level of power by asking a series of questions, as demonstrated in Table 3.1. For each question, make sure to address the areas where there is a gap between the way you feel and the perception your colleagues have about you. Answers to these questions must be candid, so that they serve as an indication of your current level of personal power, as well as provide a foundation to improve your overall sense of power in the organization to a level that suits your needs.

Table 3.1 Personal power question categories

Category
Friendships
Interpersonal skills
Confidence
Status
Information

For each of these categories there are a couple of questions to be asked and the result should be tallied to measure one's personal power.

UNDERSTANDING POLITICS

People see organizational politics in either a positive or a negative light. As a positive, it is about the process of gaining support for actions or positions, having political wisdom, and being prudent, practical, and diplomatic. Those who practice "positive politics" are viewed as smart, savvy, and go-getters. The negative context refers to devious and deceitful behaviors to gain power and earn status—at its worst, it can be downright dishonest. For the most part, those who practice this kind of politics tend to put their own goals ahead of the organization's objectives.

Values

Organizational values are where politics and culture meet. Values are not necessarily documented anywhere, but it is quite easy to see them in action. No two organizations are the same, and even within the same organization, there will be differences in values from one department to another. Politics is partially about understanding the organizational culture, or understanding the values the organization holds. It is also about how closely people share the same values with the organization, and their ability to fit into it.

Influence

One of the common reasons for engaging in politics is an attempt to gain organizational influence. Influence is an attribute associated with leadership, and according to Dictionary.com,[1] it can be defined as "the capacity or power of persons or things to be a compelling force on or produce effects on the actions, behaviors, opinions, etc., of others." Most people want to be more influential because it gives them more power and places them in a better position to seize opportunities and get things done their way. There are different ways to gain influence from one organization to another, and each method has different organizational implications. Overall, politics and influence are both means for individuals to get more access to people, information, and resources, and—whether in an organization or outside of the corporate world—cultures value similar things:

- Wealth (resources, money);
- Knowledge (experience, professional, history, domain);
- Skills (interpersonal, business, innovation);
- Leadership.

There are a few things to aim for when trying to build political power in an organization, ranging from building and understanding our personal power base to staying focused and building respect and trust. They may be easier said than done, but the following list outlines the specific activities to do (including what not to do) to achieve political power:

1. Build and understand your power base. You should first become aware of the values that prevail in your organization and understand their meaning and your existing and desired interaction with them. You should then ensure that you understand the area, industry, and business in which the organization operates and develop or focus on your expertise (which could be any subject matter, functional area, or overall communication and leadership) through identification of your core competencies and what makes you special in this area.

2. Think like a leader (but not too much). There is a story about Robespierre, the famous agitator of the French Revolution, which tells of how he leapt up from his chair as soon as he noticed a mob assembling outside and is reputed to have said: "I must see which way the crowd is headed, for I am their leader." Thinking like a leader is (among other things) about putting yourself in other people's shoes and trying to understand where they are coming from. It is also about being the "bigger person" by trying to find a win-win resolution to issues in a way that addresses both sides of a conflict and the organization as a whole. Conflicts and disagreements need to be addressed with the appropriate rigor, and any proposed options must not be in isolation—they need to consider the needs and priorities of the whole organization. In the process, keep the organization's culture and values in mind and check how many of these you possess so that you can apply a style and aim in a direction that are aligned with them. If you no longer represent the organizational values and those of the team you are trying to lead, you will lose the ability to influence them, and your personal power will decline.

3. Build trust. It is a well-known fact that trust is difficult to build, hard to maintain, and even harder to regain once lost. It is the foundation of virtually any progress and achievement down the road, and we must conduct ourselves in a calculated and focused manner that delivers consistent insight, expertise, treatment of others, and responses to situations. More specifically, trust depends on a set of actions and behaviors, presented in Figure 3.2. It is common to see people engaging in behaviors that eat away at the trust they are trying to build. It is not only about failing to deliver on these trust-building behaviors, but also about trying to avoid any of the behaviors listed in Figure 3.3.

4. Know your team. There are a few actions we need to take to get to know our teams, with the ultimate goals of: performance, team cohesion, and the ability to demonstrate leadership and exercise personal power. The building blocks for achieving these are listed in Figure 3.4.

Figure 3.2   Ingredients of trust

Figure 3.3   Trust destroyers

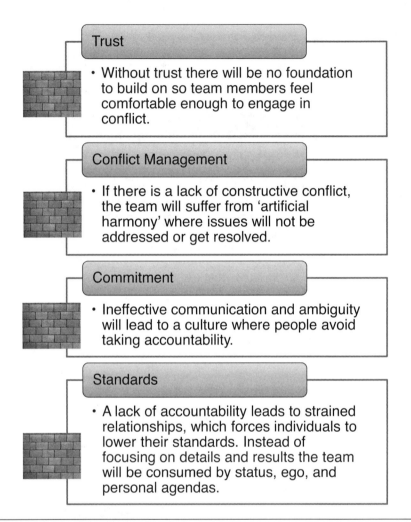

Trust

- Without trust there will be no foundation to build on so team members feel comfortable enough to engage in conflict.

Conflict Management

- If there is a lack of constructive conflict, the team will suffer from 'artificial harmony' where issues will not be addressed or get resolved.

Commitment

- Ineffective communication and ambiguity will lead to a culture where people avoid taking accountability.

Standards

- A lack of accountability leads to strained relationships, which forces individuals to lower their standards. Instead of focusing on details and results the team will be consumed by status, ego, and personal agendas.

Figure 3.4 Team building blocks

5. Stay focused. The work of a leader, of one hoping to become a leader, and of one trying to build and maintain trust (the entire population should qualify under one of these conditions) never ends. We should constantly be on guard, check our actions, and try to improve how we conduct ourselves and do our work. In a way, this relates to the process of continuous improvement and to the need to both excel at the technical domain (the what) and at the process (the how).

6. Pick your battles. This can be viewed as a subset of staying focused, since it is about channeling our efforts toward the things that matter for our

causes. There is no need to prove we are right all the time, and when appropriate, it is important to be humble and admit mistakes.

BLOOD IS THICKER THAN WATER

In some organizations, there are people who appear to hold positions and jobs they are not qualified for and therefore, do not have what it takes to handle the challenges they present. It often triggers thoughts of: "How did this person get the job?" The answer lies within organizational politics: oftentimes, some of these less-than-suitable employees are friends with, or related to, powerful people in the organization. It is safe to say that, when push comes to shove—when there is uncertainty, and when it comes down to making tough decisions—it is all about relationships, friendships, and who is connected to whom, much more than it is about skills, facts, logic, or actions.

In times of need, people help those they trust, with whom they are friends, and quite often, who have helped them in the past. This fact reiterates the importance of managing relationships and keeping in mind how easy it is to make enemies and how critical it is to remain on the "good side" of as many stakeholders as possible. These relationships, friendships, and alliances can spell the difference between success and failure and may break a deadlock when there is a tie.

LET'S TALK ABOUT POLITICS: THE INTERSTATE STORY

Many years ago, when I performed some project work for my brother's company, while returning together from a client site, we encountered what turned out to be one of the most important lessons anyone could ever learn about organizational politics. It was such a potent experience that I view it as one of the defining moments in my career. We were driving on an interstate highway in the United States and found ourselves following a driver of a black Cadillac who had a radar detector. He drove very pragmatically: he slowed down when needed and accelerated as the road conditions allowed. In project management speak, his scope for the day was to drive from point A to point B safely and get there on time, dealing with any impediments along the way (e.g., slower traffic in sections of construction with a lane reduction from two to one lane in each direction).

At some point, the driver of the Cadillac decided to add one more item to his day's scope, which was to become an educator for other drivers (the equivalent of a change request). Just as we approached a section of the highway that was under construction, as the pylons started to close in from the left, he decided to pass an eighteen-wheeler, as illustrated in Figure 3.5, which in turn, triggered the following chain of events:

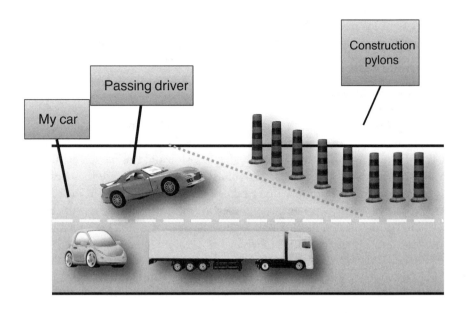

This is how it all started, leading to the accident.

Figure 3.5 Before the accident

1. My brother, who is more risk averse than I am, said, "He shouldn't do it," to which my response was, "Let's see what happens."
2. The truck driver did something dangerous and uncalled for: he veered to the left in an attempt to block the Cadillac from passing.
3. The Cadillac driver was determined to pass and kept going.
4. I screamed, "Abort, abort!"
5. Then the unimaginable happened (see Figure 3.6). Huge clouds of smoke and dust covered everything and traffic came to a dead stop.

When the dust and smoke finally settled, both vehicles were stopped on the side of the road, and despite severe damage to the front of the Cadillac, we noticed that the driver was okay and already on the phone, notifying someone that the change request did not go well.

When we drove away from the scene, my brother and I engaged in a conversation about this collision, which was completely preventable. Although there were no physical injuries, it could have had a much more severe outcome. My brother, who is several years older than I am, wanted to check whether I learned something

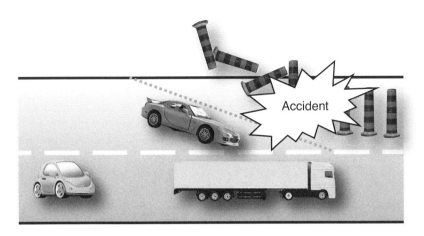

The moment of the accident. It was preventable and not a matter of which
one of the drivers was to blame.

Figure 3.6   After the accident

from that event and asked what I would have done if I were the Cadillac driver. I
was certainly not going to "play chicken" with the truck, but then my brother asked
what I would have done if I had finally passed the truck. I replied that, at a safe
distance, I would have probably gestured to the truck driver that I didn't appreciate him veering into my path and trying to block me. My brother, who knows me
very well and probably saw that one coming, asked why, and my surprising answer
was: "For me, inner peace." It sounds as ridiculous as it really was; I would have
paid a derogatory gesture to the truck driver, just to make myself feel better and
make a point.

That was many years ago, and my driving style has changed considerably since
then, in part thanks to the conversation with my brother that followed. That conversation also helped me relate this experience to the corporate world and to my
day-to-day conduct in projects. We talked about my need to make a point to the
truck driver and established that it was not necessary and would have added no
value whatsoever to my life in any way. We then tried to map this onto an equivalent
office situation and came up with one that fit the bill: In a project meeting, one of
the team members, who is known for his antics, said something that was worthy
of a nasty reply on my part, which would have triggered a good laugh and fifteen
minutes of fame for me. It makes no difference whether we work together directly,
who is more senior, who is smarter or more successful—there is one question we
need to ask ourselves before we react: Is it going to add value to the cause?

EMOTIONAL RESILIENCE

It is hard to take emotions out of what we do. Emotions are usually the result of caring, and most people care about what they do. Moreover, emotions dictate the course of action in conflict situations, especially if the stakes are high. We want to be successful; we invest time, money, and energy into doing something and we become emotionally involved. Yet without removing the care, concern, and attention that come along with emotions, it is important not to let emotions interfere with decision making, relationship building, or work. When a team member says something that provokes a witty comment, the power of not saying anything should prevail. Even if there is a strong urge to react with a comeback, it can be done one-on-one after the meeting. Making unconstructive comments will derail the discussion, may deter others from associating themselves with you, and will possibly hurt the person your comments are directed at. While many people tend to forget their commitments, they do hold a grudge, and according to "Murphy's Law," they will get even at the worst possible time.

It has been called "Verbal Judo,"[2] which uses martial arts concepts for managing communications and in this context, means: "if you are going to say something just for the purpose of making yourself feel better, do not say it." While easier said than done, there are some techniques that can be applied in an effort to overcome that urge: one of them is the good, old fashioned, "count to 10" technique. When someone says something that infuriates you, or when that invites an inflammatory statement from you, take the time to count to 10, and if it is still relevant and applicable after 10 long seconds, you can say it then. At the very least, it will inhibit you from saying something that you will regret later. Keep in mind that almost anything can be undone, except for reversing time and taking back what has just been said.

Another tactic to apply is also related to martial arts:[3] when in a conflict situation, and the other side goes on the attack (especially if personal), it is important to resist the urge to retaliate and counterattack. Instead, there should be an attempt to either cool off and consider not responding altogether or to take their motion and use it to your benefit by turning the same argument around on the other side so it serves your point in an attempt to solve the problem. For that, you need to have emotional resilience, know the subject matter, understand the situation, realize the stakes involved, and make the point in an assertive, professional, and effective manner—without getting personal or antagonizing others.

WIN-WIN

It is only possible to achieve a win-win resolution by separating the emotion from the situation and judging things by their merits—not by who said what or by attempting to make a point. It is not about who is right or wrong, but about the style and the way we feel about each other and the situation. To help the point come across as effectively and distraction-free as possible, try to apply the following:

- Remain professional;
- Focus on the problem;
- Stay objective;
- Maintain a goal of achieving a win-win resolution.

The pursuit of a win-win resolution will bring the other side to a state of mind of potential agreement and will help you build a reputation as a composed individual, who remains focused on the greater picture—solving problems and ensuring everyone's needs are met. Taking the discussion of emotions a step further can show that it is not mandatory for people to genuinely like each other or be best friends in order to build productive and collaborative relations. In fact, alliances have formed among people who had conflicting priorities, did not see things eye-to-eye, and were not on friendly terms. Working together toward solving each other's problems was achieved through the ability to take emotions out of the equation and see past personal differences, identify areas of mutual gain, and complement each other's needs.

A focus on a win-win approach is fundamental, not only in building strong relationships and managing projects effectively but also in negotiations. It is an approach that can be applied to any conflict situation by shifting the focus of the discussion away from a collision course of opposing positions. These positions represent what each side wants, and sometimes they have little to do with the real needs. Focusing on uncovering each side's interests, as demonstrated in Figure 3.7,

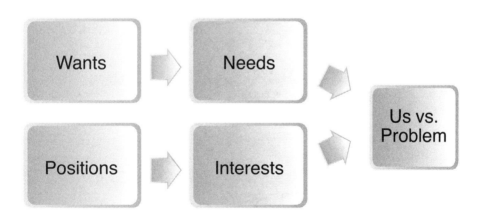

For a win-win resolution, shift the conversation from what each side wants to what they need and try to position both parties in the conflict on the same side, dealing together with the problem, rather than one against the other.

Figure 3.7   Move from wants to needs

addresses underlying needs and is likely to produce a win-win resolution when these needs are met.

In addition, try to further shift the conversation away from viewing each other as the problem, to focusing on how to solve the problem together by approaching it as "us against the problem." When people view each other as the problem, there is very little progress made toward a resolution, and it usually leads to both sides entrenching themselves deeper in their original positions. Once again, less emotion and more focus on the merits of the situation are keys to success.

COFFEE AND VALUE

One of the most challenging tasks in projects is managing meetings. Too long, too many items to address, unproductive, ineffective, confusing, and depressing are some descriptors that can be used to depict unsuccessful meetings. There is a lot to say about meetings in most project environments, as badly managed ones may serve as an indicator that something in the project is not right. While Chapter 11 extensively examines communication, including how to manage successful meetings, the discussion here is about how to deal with stakeholders outside of large meetings.

Meetings may get emotionally charged because they involve multiple team members and stakeholders, representing multiple points of view, and all with ego.

Coffee. Important to find time for one-on-one conversations
in order to build relationships.

Image 3.1   Coffee can go a long way

I try to establish norms in my projects, which, on the one hand reduce the number of participants in meetings (without compromising the meeting's value), and on the other hand, encourage people to communicate information in a timely manner and preferably through one-on-one methods, rather than through official meetings. One-on-one communication removes walls, fosters honesty and openness, and reduces the number of unwelcome surprises, which are far too common in meetings. It is not an alternative to meetings, but rather an opportunity to catch up on some details, address issues, clarify misunderstandings, and get different points of view about project events. As most one-on-ones are informal, every project manager (PM) should encourage and facilitate a norm of informal meetings on a regular basis, reaching out to as many stakeholders as possible, while maintaining control over official project communication.

With tight and busy schedules, it is hard to find time for these meetings, which is why a cup of coffee can help: it is easy to lure people into a one-on-one meeting with a cup of coffee. They usually find time for it, and the coffee will go far beyond the impact of the caffeine—establishing rapport and forming a comfortable environment where information flows and relationships are built. These routine, informal meetings over coffee prove themselves effective in establishing rapport with stakeholders and team members and, likewise, open an informal channel of communication, wherein high quality and insightful information is exchanged about people, processes, issues, and the overall project. It also contributes to building long-term relationships that sometimes lead to alliances, understanding each other's needs, and greater collaboration.

TEAM BUILDING

In most organizations, team building activities have been reduced to a minimum. There are many reasons for this—namely, lack of time, budget and time restrictions, and organizational priorities. Such activities are critical for building relationships and rapport among team members and between team members and the PM. There are a number of options for the type of team building activity that can be employed, which should be established in the communication plan. However, more important than the nature of the activities or the costs associated with them is ensuring that team building activities actually take place. Time and budget constraints force most team building activities into local chain restaurants and are limited to celebrating major team or departmental milestones—and those team lunches often get canceled. Yet with the lack of other activities, these gatherings are something for the team to look forward to, and the value they produce far outweighs the time and costs they consume. They create team harmony and conformity, and team members are often appreciative of the gesture, but above all, team activities get team members to interact outside of the office. During these events, people sometimes end up sitting next to colleagues that they normally have little or no interaction with, which often triggers conversations that would not otherwise take place in the office about unrelated topics (e.g. families, hobbies, and personal life), potentially allowing new friendships to form.

Back to Friendships

Friendships formed at work are not merely about building personal power and should not be driven by political agendas: friendships should be about establishing a more pleasant workplace and finding common areas of interest with colleagues. There are organizations in which there are few friendships among employees, to the extent that some people say they "do not want to associate with colleagues past 5:00 p.m." It must be quite depressing for those who think like that as they come to work every day and spend most of their day with people they do not like. It is possible that people place more importance on their families and other commitments outside the office, and therefore it should not be taken out of context: the goal is not to have friendships at work, but it may be a means to improve performance and a sense of belonging. These goals can be achieved without friendships, but they are better advanced when friendly relations are present.

Workplaces with few or no friendships may also indicate that there is something in the leadership of the organization that simply does not work because there is no tradition of teamwork and conformity to the culture and the organization. Performance and project results may suffer as it is unlikely for a group of people who do not like each other or get along to produce results that meet or exceed expectations on an ongoing and consistent basis.

There is another significant benefit when team members are on friendly terms: when there is a problem or conflict of interest, friends are likely to work things out together and seek a win-win resolution that looks after the underlying interests of all sides involved. When we do not get along with each other, it is unlikely that we will work together toward a resolution; furthermore, we may even extend the conflict to purposely work against each other's efforts.

IS THERE AN "I" IN TEAM?

All that talk about team building, cohesion, collaboration, and friendships at work may sound like chatter about a utopia or fantasy world, where everything is ideal. Though project management is first and foremost about managing people, and while not all of these ideas may work for every environment, these are the proven keys to project success when applied properly. While a major undertaking, this effort needs to start somewhere. Similar to an attempt to move a mountain, there is one rock that needs to be moved first. This philosophy illustrates the need for a new way of managing projects that starts with paying attention to those things that matter: the team and the individuals who make up the team.

There is an important distinction between teams and groups: teams are a group of people who work together for a mutual cause that is more important than any of the personal needs of its members. A group, however, is a collection of people who happen to do something together—but for their own benefit, rather than for the group's success. When referring to teams, there is a cliché that there is no "I" in team. It is driven by the notion that a team is not about the individuals within it, but about a common, higher cause.

The cliché also plays on the spelling of the word "team," which contains no "I."[4] However, in an interesting twist, some are saying that there is an "I" in team. To demonstrate this, we need to use a specific font that makes up a lowercase "i" within the A (see Figure 3.8). In fact, teams are composed of many "I"s, and—although their needs do not come before the team's needs—special attention needs to be given to their needs in order to enhance team performance. Individuals in that collection of people that make up the team have needs, feelings, attributes, and characteristics that make them who they are and determine their level of contribution to the team's effort.

A DIFFERENT VIEW OF LEADERSHIP

PMs inundate themselves with techniques, tools, methodologies, and disciplines in an attempt to know what to do and how to do it better. At times, PMs may even have the expectation that the tools perform some of the thinking for them. Other real life examples include, cars parking themselves and applying breaks when they see fit and mobile phones that are full of applications (apps) that remind people what they should do and what they should remember—some apps even tell people their moods. While tools and methodologies are good for routine ongoing activities, they may not be appropriate for leading people. Some tools may be difficult to utilize

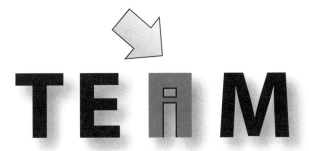

Every team is made of individuals who have needs and characteristics that must be taken into account in order to optimize the team's performance.

Figure 3.8   There is an "I" in team

properly, but one thing is clear: there is an overreliance on tools in the hopes that they can replace basic things that people should do: think, lead, assume, inquire, question, consider, empathize, and feel. This overreliance on tools and techniques often leads to disappointment, as they do not deliver on their promises.

I once heard a speaker at an event[5] comparing the tools and techniques we use to the algorithms used by many online service providers. They take user demographics and factor in anything they learn in the process—search topics, location, preferences, and other tendencies—to build a profile about each user and make related options available—options that are as close as possible to the user's preferences. Search engines do it to propose related topics; online book stores do it to suggest books we might be interested in; and e-mail providers post banners with advertisements (ads) related to the user's preferences. I recall that I was initially impressed (and then somewhat worried) when my webmail provider posted banner ads for diapers on my page right around the time my wife and I had our first daughter. Since then, the line has gotten progressively more blurry between things that can be improved through an algorithm and those that cannot be so managed. Leadership, communication, stakeholder relationship management, proper resource allocation, realistic estimates, and proactive risk management cannot be managed by a tool.

Buffet vs. Branson

Tools and algorithms will not solve problems on their own. The way to solve problems is to match the leadership to the specific situation and to the needs of the people involved. No two leadership styles are the same, and no two will be applicable to different situations or to different PMs. When thinking about leadership styles, it is not quite about "picking" one, as we do not really have much choice—leadership style is a function of personality, so the choice is usually between no more than two styles. We cannot apply someone else's style or personality to ourselves, nor look at someone and say: "I would like to adopt this person's leadership approach." An effective way to illustrate this is to imagine Warren Buffet trying to lead in the same way as Richard Branson. It would not be appropriate and may even look ridiculous—not to mention how uncomfortable Buffet would feel trying to act in a manner that is completely out of character for him. We sometimes come across leaders from whom we would like to learn leadership or whose charisma we would like to have, but none of us can mimic another's style and persona.

LEADERSHIP STYLES

There is no formula for leadership, and there is no algorithm for managing and engaging people. However, an algorithm-like system can be applied to create a list of leadership styles that acts like a multiple choice questionnaire, from which we can choose one or two preferred styles. The word "preferred" is not about the style that we like better or the one we want to adopt but about the style we tend to use, gravitate toward, or default to. Of the leadership styles in Figure 3.9, each of us can identify one or two that apply best.

Every person can find one or two styles to use that feel more comfortable than the others on this list. We need to realize that we cannot be everything to everyone and that we have to make choices as to what we can offer and which stakeholders and directions to focus on based upon our personalities, our styles, and the situations we are dealing with.

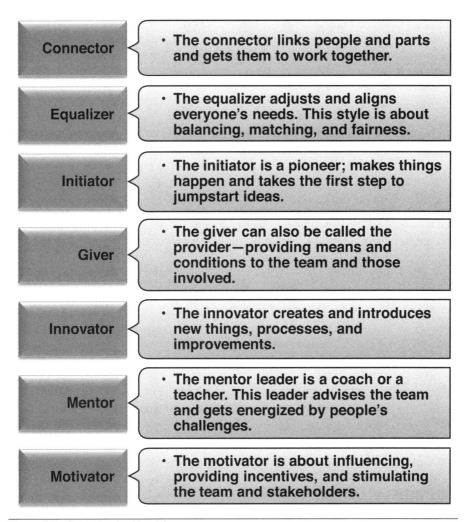

Connector
- The connector links people and parts and gets them to work together.

Equalizer
- The equalizer adjusts and aligns everyone's needs. This style is about balancing, matching, and fairness.

Initiator
- The initiator is a pioneer; makes things happen and takes the first step to jumpstart ideas.

Giver
- The giver can also be called the provider—providing means and conditions to the team and those involved.

Innovator
- The innovator creates and introduces new things, processes, and improvements.

Mentor
- The mentor leader is a coach or a teacher. This leader advises the team and gets energized by people's challenges.

Motivator
- The motivator is about influencing, providing incentives, and stimulating the team and stakeholders.

Figure 3.9   Seven leadership styles

Keep in Mind

The way we conduct ourselves and the level of integrity we project will determine how others view us in the organization and, in turn, will have an impact on our credibility and ability to lead. There is another underlying concept to keep in mind: "the buck stops here." The leader is ultimately accountable for the results and outcomes of the project. The leader is not necessarily accountable for every individual action, but rather for the project's bottom line. Pointing fingers, blaming others, and coming up with excuses are practices that some people adopt, but this is not a fair, sustainable, or credible way to lead. It is easy to say that others are to blame, but—if we want respect from others—we need to earn it first, which is not done by shirking responsibility. The buck stops at the top, and anything else is an excuse.

CONFLICT

There are some things about conflict that most people can agree on:

- Most people do not like conflict;
- No one wants to be involved in it;
- Most people seem to be engaged in conflict on a regular basis;
- Most people view conflict negatively and do not see the benefits that can be realized from conflict that is handled properly.

What is conflict? It is a clash or fight as a result of a problem, disagreement, or competition for resources—conflict occurs when people do not think the same way about something, or when they want the same thing at the same time, but there is not enough of it. People view conflict negatively, partially because of the somewhat unpleasant process associated with it, and as a result, we fail to see the potential benefits it may lead to. The type and style of a conflict will be shaped by the combination of three aspects:

1. Human nature, which is universal.
2. The culture, which is specific to an organization or a group and can be learned.
3. The personality of those involved, which is specific to individuals. While personalities cannot be changed, attitudes and behaviors can help adjust personalities.

TEAM DEVELOPMENT

The context of the conflict can be viewed through Tuckman's[6] model for stages of group development, as illustrated in Figure 3.10. Virtually all teams go through

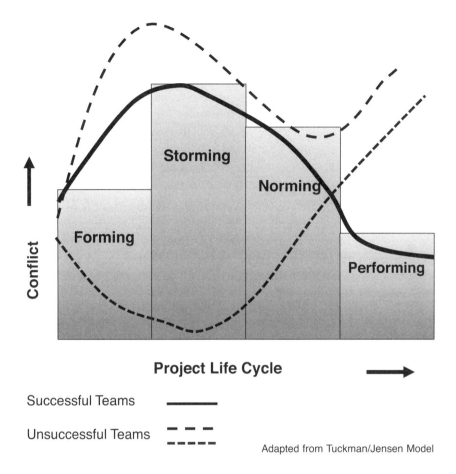

Project Life Cycle ➡

Successful Teams ⎯⎯⎯

Unsuccessful Teams ⎯ ⎯ ⎯
⎯⎯⎯⎯⎯

Adapted from Tuckman/Jensen Model

Teams that go through a proper storming stage (solid line) are likely to be more successful than teams that either avoid conflict or get consumed by too many conflicts (both types of dotted lines).

Figure 3.10   Stages of team building

team building stages, in which the conflict level rises before settling and moving toward higher performance levels.

This is one of the most familiar team development models, which includes the following stages:

- Forming:[7] Groups initially concern themselves with orientation—accomplished primarily through testing—which serves to identify the boundaries of both interpersonal and task behaviors. Forming includes the establishment of dependency relationships with leaders, other group members, or preexisting standards. It may be said that orientation, testing, and dependence constitute the group process of forming.

- Storming: This is characterized by conflict and polarization around interpersonal issues that serve as resistance to group influence and task requirements.
- Norming: This is when resistance is overcome, in-group feeling and cohesiveness develop, new standards evolve, and new roles are adopted. Intimate, personal opinions are expressed.
- Performing: Finally, interpersonal structure becomes the tool of task activities. Roles become flexible and functional, and group energy is channeled into the task. Structural issues have been resolved, and structure can now become supportive of task performance.

Special attention should be given to the storming stage, since it is important for shaping the team and is a critical contributor to the team's performance. Obviously, teams are formed in order to produce results. Therefore, it is safe to say that the storming stage is not about the reason for the team formation; yet the way teams handle it will have a significant impact on subsequent performance. There are three approaches to the storming stage:

1. Many teams just avoid it. Team members do everything in their power to circumvent any potential conflict and suppress disagreements. It appears that their main goal is to avoid conflict at whatever cost and with no consideration of future implications it might have on the team's performance. While it is not a scientific observation, teams that avoid the storming stage, or simply skip it without handling their differences, issues, and disagreements, tend to end up performing to a lesser degree of success than teams who storm effectively. Avoiding conflict tends to yield benefits only in the short term; without conflict, teams do not set their goals and expectations and do not "clear the air" to move forward. As a result, these teams find themselves consumed by conflict and have difficulty focusing on what matters (the project work), becoming distracted by misunderstandings and misaligned expectations.

2. There are teams that go through a good and healthy storming stage. It is not that they sit down and decide, "Let's have some storming and conflict now." Rather, they generally embrace the storming stage, recognize that conflict needs to take place, and handle it in a way that helps clear the air and remove obstacles to the team's future performance.

3. Other teams get stuck in the storming stage. With the right combination of personalities, teams may find themselves caught up in the storming stage and not able to get themselves out of it toward norming and performing. It is usually a result of one or more of the team members enjoying the thrill of conflict and engaging in what appears to be a perpetual conflict, just for the sake of having a conflict, to the degree that it

consumes the team and drains its energies. These teams usually end up underperforming.

The storming stage is a natural occurrence that most teams will undergo, and teams should allow it to take its course. Mishandling this stage, whether consciously or subconsciously, is likely to result in team-building challenges and performance issues moving forward.

Disagreements, discussions, and even arguments (not personal, but about merits) among stakeholders are often sources of creativity and innovation and are generally good for the project. When stakeholders challenge each other, it usually leads to a variety of ideas and approaches, rather than an artificial harmony. When we do not engage each other, or when team members and stakeholders have no opinion, it is usually a bad sign for the project—and possibly an indication that a more significant and less contained conflict is to come. When we are involved, it is a sign that the matter is important enough for us to care and that we have enough knowledge to form an opinion.

When stakeholders are involved and caring, it usually leads to collaboration and often to improvement and innovation. With a variety of opinions and an environment that encourages discussion and sharing, stakeholders are not afraid to express their opinions, which usually leads to collaboration and consensus. (Consensus is an agreement among a critical mass of the stakeholders, but not necessarily a unanimous decision.) While it costs more time and effort to collaborate and reach a consensus, it is a good investment for the team and the organization; whereas the alternatives are not likely to bring the conflict to a resolution.

Keep in Mind

There are a few things to be aware of when engaging in conflict so that it actually yields benefit. When facing conflict situations, we should ask ourselves what the alternative would be, so we do not end up with more damage and unresolved issues in the long run. After a conflict takes place, we need to ask ourselves whether the team is now better off as a result of the conflict. If team members or stakeholders engage in a conflict and, at the end, we cannot identify any associated benefits, the following question should be asked: "Why go through a conflict if it does not improve our position as a result?" If the issue is not resolved, or the team is not more cohesive after the conflict, then it was not worth it—especially because there is a high probability that the same problem will resurface in the near future.

SOURCES OF CONFLICT

There are clear guidelines for conflict resolution techniques (to be discussed in this chapter), yet there is no single remedy for all problems. Before trying to resolve a conflict, it would be helpful to determine where it stems from. Figure 3.11 lists a few typical sources that tend to lead to conflict if not handled effectively and in a timely manner.

- Organizational and project priorities: unclear or poorly communicated priorities lead to gaps between views of what needs to be done, and different interpretations of priorities are usually influenced by personal motives and agendas.
- Unclear expectations: one of the most important roles of the PM is to manage expectations, which can be broken down into three aspects, as listed in Figure 3.12.
- Communication: the Project Management Institute says that PMs spend most of their time communicating, 80–90%, which means that they

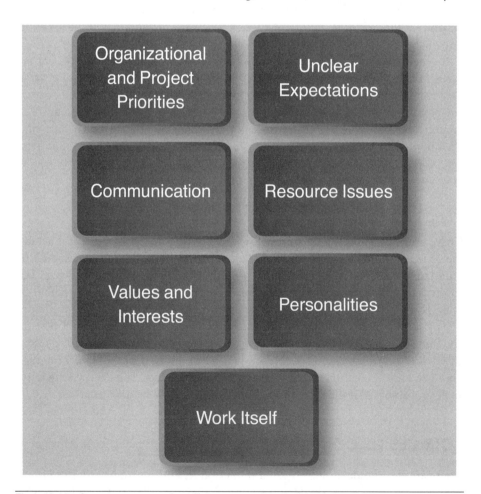

Figure 3.11 Common sources of conflict

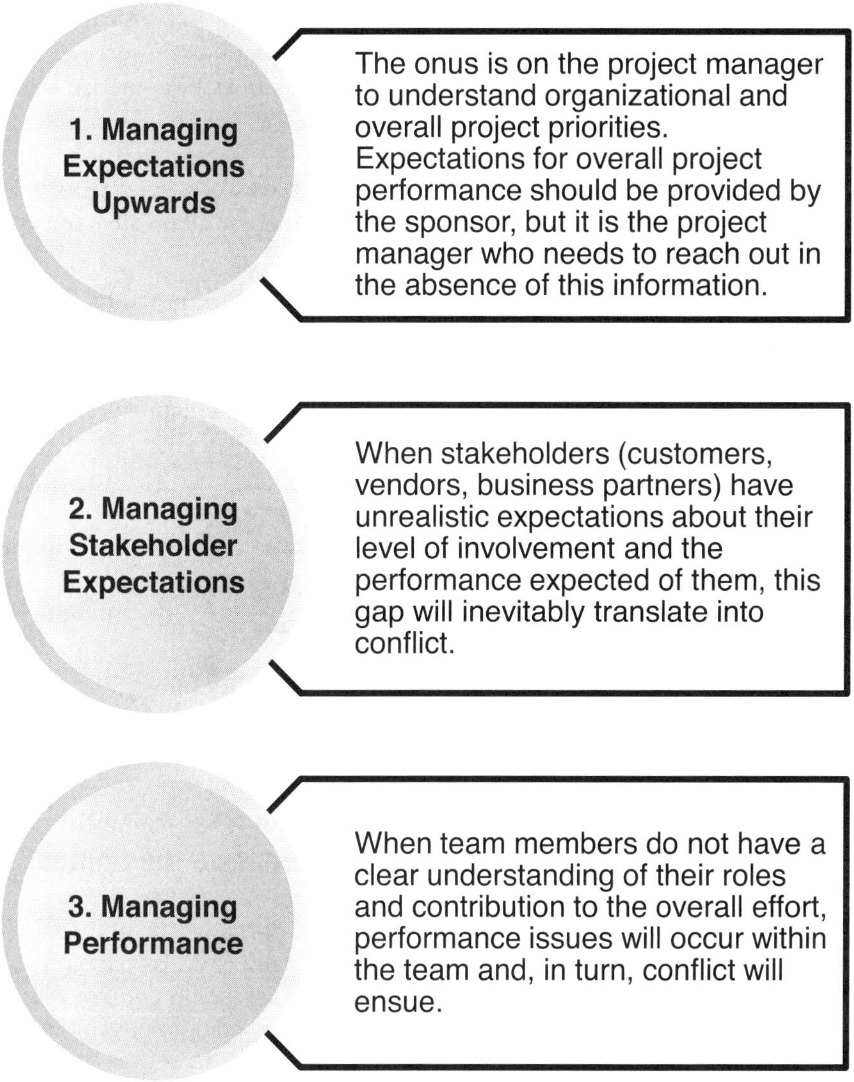

1. Managing Expectations Upwards

The onus is on the project manager to understand organizational and overall project priorities. Expectations for overall project performance should be provided by the sponsor, but it is the project manager who needs to reach out in the absence of this information.

2. Managing Stakeholder Expectations

When stakeholders (customers, vendors, business partners) have unrealistic expectations about their level of involvement and the performance expected of them, this gap will inevitably translate into conflict.

3. Managing Performance

When team members do not have a clear understanding of their roles and contribution to the overall effort, performance issues will occur within the team and, in turn, conflict will ensue.

Figure 3.12 Three aspects of managing expectations

essentially function as communications hubs. It requires them to own the communication function within their project in order to avoid misunderstandings, mismanaged expectations, performance issues, and frustration.

- Resource issues: virtually every project has to contend with resource concerns—whether it is a shortage of resources; timeliness, or duration of resource allocation; "stealing" of resources in the middle of tasks; or a mismatch between the team's skill level and the task.

- Values and interests: people do not share the same set of values and interests—which includes priorities, goals, definitions of success, and happiness—since we have different backgrounds and viewpoints. At some point, things may not turn out the way others feel they should, and it is a short road to conflict from there.
- Work itself: different views and approaches to the tasks at hand, work volume, task size, data interpretations, and processes are all possible sources of conflict.
- Personalities: the contribution of personalities to conflict can be broken down into two components, as appear in Figure 3.13.

It is up to the PM to conduct research about the stakeholders and team members (that is, perform a stakeholder analysis) and identify the different personality types

As a source of conflict

Project teams are made up of people with different personalities which can be a source of conflict, especially if team members do not accept each other's points of view and approaches to work and problem solving.

As a factor with impact on the conflict style

The personalities of those involved (e.g., passionate vs. easy-going people) will have a major impact on the style and the course the conflict will take. Effective conflict management will help prevent every little disagreement from developing into full-blown conflict that will eventually consume the team.

Figure 3.13 Personalities' impacts on conflict

in the project and how they could potentially interact. Even if (as in most cases) the project managers have no control over which resources work on their project, they need to try to quickly recognize the challenge and create the conditions for the team and the stakeholders to work together effectively. When life doles out lemons, we need to make lemonade. This is no different for the project: even if stakeholders and team members are not likely to get along, the main goal should not be to suppress the conflict, but to manage it properly, following the steps in Figure 3.14.

The PM's ability to manage conflict effectively is a strong indicator of leadership and credibility and a significant factor that impacts personal power in the organization and, therefore, the individual's political clout. People constantly examine how effective PMs are at managing conflict and establish an opinion about their ability to lead and bring the project to success. The word "effective" refers to avoiding unnecessary conflict, engaging in necessary conflict, managing the conflict that takes place—not suppressing conflict just to avoid it—and resolving it in such a way that the issue does not resurface shortly thereafter. Every action PMs take, even if

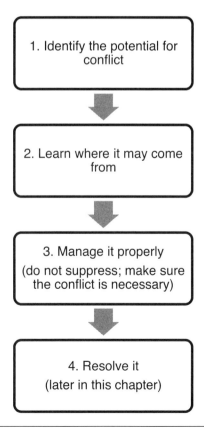

Figure 3.14   Steps to manage conflict properly

unintentional or part of a larger crisis, is being evaluated—consciously and subconsciously—by all stakeholders involved. Based on these actions, other stakeholders form opinions and perceptions about the PM's personal power and leadership capabilities.

A Deeper Dive Into the Causes

Beyond the causes of conflict already mentioned (and without crossing the line into psychology), there are conditions that most people go through at different points in time that are likely to lead to conflict. These situations, listed in Figure 3.15, happen regularly in projects, and the reactions they trigger often lead to conflict.

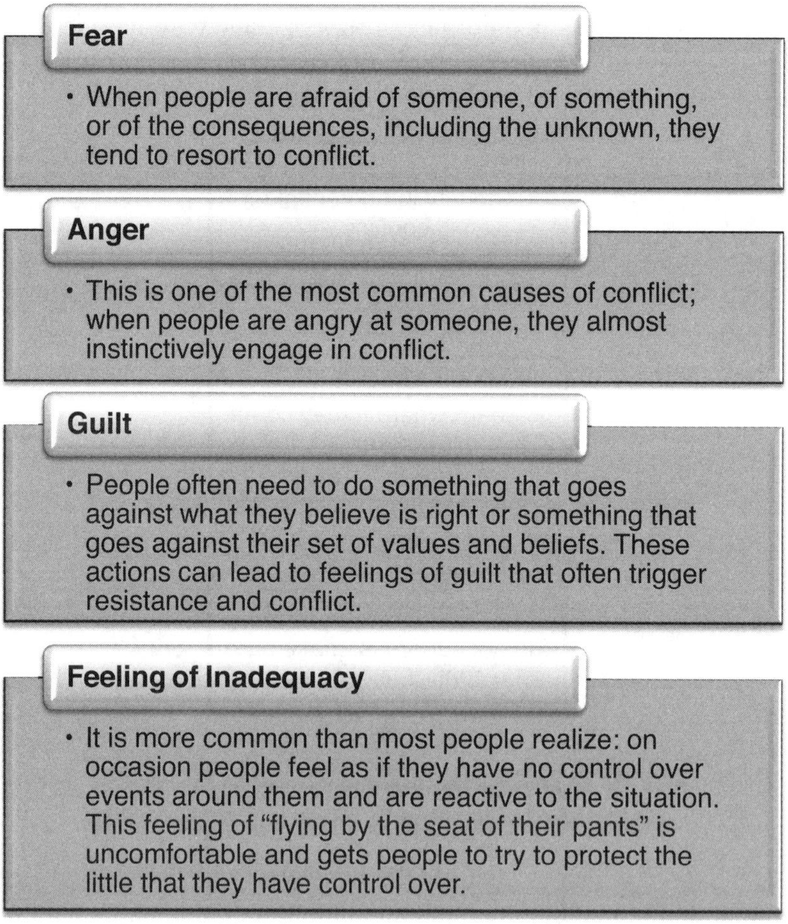

Fear
- When people are afraid of someone, of something, or of the consequences, including the unknown, they tend to resort to conflict.

Anger
- This is one of the most common causes of conflict; when people are angry at someone, they almost instinctively engage in conflict.

Guilt
- People often need to do something that goes against what they believe is right or something that goes against their set of values and beliefs. These actions can lead to feelings of guilt that often trigger resistance and conflict.

Feeling of Inadequacy
- It is more common than most people realize: on occasion people feel as if they have no control over events around them and are reactive to the situation. This feeling of "flying by the seat of their pants" is uncomfortable and gets people to try to protect the little that they have control over.

Figure 3.15 Causes of conflict—a deeper view

This is yet another reason to pay more attention to the stakeholder analysis and gain a good understanding of the people involved, where they come from, their values and expectations, and whether there is anything about them that may predispose the team or the project to unnecessary conflict: It is the PM's job to set and establish clear expectations, ground rules, guidelines, and boundaries, so that everyone on the project knows what to expect and is on the same page. Chapter 11, on communication, elaborates how to set up a meaningful communication plan, which will set clear boundaries and expectations, so the PM has a better ability to control the team's and stakeholders' behaviors, thereby reducing distractions. In most projects, communication is nowhere near ideal, and PMs almost never obtain all the information they need to effectively manage communication. The chapter also indicates when information is missing, or when there are challenges surrounding the quality of the information. Either way, it can help PMs figure out when there is a need to dig a little deeper and take more serious measures to manage stakeholders and team members. In turn, it may also lead to realizing that the project has more complexity and risk than previously thought.

CONFLICT—THE GOOD, THE BAD, AND THE UGLY

Despite the modern view of conflict as a good thing for an organization, most people still try to identify sources of conflict and work on these areas in order to reduce conflict. If conflict is so good, then why avoid it? Let's break conflict down into three types, and then articulate what should be done about each:

- **The good.** Good conflict takes place for reasons related to the merits and objectives of the project and is recognized and managed well. For conflict to be managed well means that it is dealt with effectively. It is about taking the circumstances into consideration and trying to get the most out of the situation, including trying to find a win-win resolution, which addresses as many needs of the opposing sides as possible. In the end, if the conflict is handled effectively, the problem that led to the conflict is no longer an issue, and the team is good to move forward with its work—and is better off than it was before.
- **The bad.** Bad conflicts are the ones that do not take place. It is almost instinctual that most people do not like conflict and try to make things better the "good way"—that is, without actually confronting the other person or the issue. Unfortunately, this approach is not a real attempt to make things better, but rather a *hope* that things will (somehow) get better. It is a form of being "passive aggressive," as the issue at stake is not really addressed. It maintains some level of (artificial) harmony, and although it may work for a while, it is usually not sufficient. It is human nature to try

to keep the peace, and for that reason, people refrain from complaining, arguing, addressing the issues at stake, or standing up for their beliefs—just for the sake of avoiding conflict. It may be appropriate in certain situations; it may serve as a blueprint for disaster in others.

- **The ugly.** Standing up to beliefs, arguments, and disagreements and addressing unpleasant issues does not have to get out of hand, turn ugly, or become personal. Most of us associate conflict with its potentially ugly side, not realizing that issues need to be addressed and that it can be done in a civilized way. That is, talk about the issues, work together toward a resolution, seek a win-win resolution, understand where the other side is coming from, and collaborate. In short, conflict should not become an all-out fight and should not be viewed as such. Even when there are disagreements, it does not mean that the two sides need to hate and disrespect each other or that they should sabotage each other's efforts. In fact, disagreements and differences in opinions are the foundations of innovation and creativity—perhaps the term creative tension comes from this. The shape and style of the conflict will be factors of the personalities involved, the stakes, and the organizational culture. No one wants to engage in perpetual conflict, but there is a fine line between the effort to avoid conflict altogether and the point of too much of a good thing.

Overall, there is nothing wrong with disliking conflict; however, PMs should focus their efforts on the following:

1. Identify sources of conflict so they can manage the conditions that predispose teams to conflict and as a result, reduce "unnecessary" conflict, which is conflict that is a distraction and does not add value to the team and the project. The goal is to manage the conditions that lead to conflicts in an effort to reduce the undesired types of conflict.

2. For those issues that are directly related to the work at stake, PMs need to establish a system to handle the conflict and manage it effectively. This includes establishing a mechanism to deal with it and escalation and decision-making processes to ensure buy-in and transparency. Depending upon the circumstances, there may be situations that require different types of handling, but collaborating and problem solving is the most sustainable way to address issues overall.

3. Properly managing conflicting situations will prevent them from escalating and turning personal. Some people still believe that if they ignore a problem, it will just go away on its own—as if looking the other way will simply make it go away. Ironically, many conflicts that are left unaddressed end up escalating to become ugly, out-of-control conflicts.

CONFLICT RESOLUTION TECHNIQUES

There are essentially five approaches to resolve conflict, and some are perceived to be more effective than others. However, just as no two conflicts are the same, no two conflicts require the same treatment. The following list,[9] also illustrated in Figure 3.16, offers a quick overview of the approaches to resolving conflict and establishes how effective each is:

1. Avoiding/Withdrawing: PMs who avoid or withdraw from conflict exercise low assertiveness and do not seek cooperation, which is an approach that does not take care of the needs of either of the sides involved in the conflict. This approach repeatedly delays the conflict in the hopes that

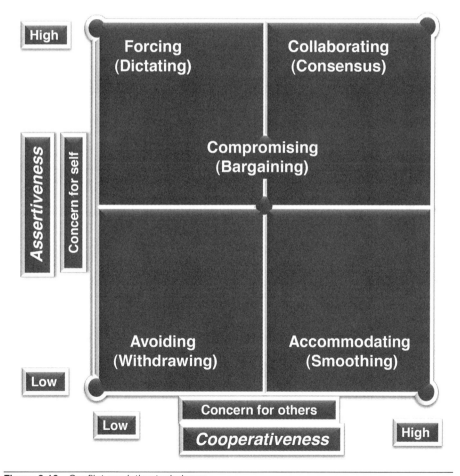

Figure 3.16   Conflict resolution techniques

it will not return, which does not make the problem go away but does maintain harmony—even if artificial.

2. Accommodating/Smoothing: PMs who accommodate opposing views or smooth over a conflict exercise low assertiveness but do seek cooperation. PMs try to accommodate others but without taking their own needs into consideration. It is similar to saying: "we are one big happy family and sometimes we fight." However, giving in may give the wrong message to some, who might take advantage of the show of kindness.

3. Forcing/Competing: PMs who force a competitive "winner" in a conflict exercise high assertiveness, which directs the sides toward a solution but by focusing on finding *a* winner, rather than on finding a win-win resolution. Seeking a winner, rather than cooperation, may be applicable for certain situations, but it does not make the underlying problem go away and often leaves one of the parties injured, which may lead to resentment, residue, and future conflict.

4. Compromising: People love to say, "Let's compromise." It is driven by good intentions but often does not yield the desired result, as it is more about bargaining. It applies a mix of assertiveness and cooperativeness, and its goal is to find a middle ground. However, there is a significant "but:" people often feel that they give more than what they get, even if it is seemingly equal. Furthermore, it deals with the sides' positions, rather than their interests, hence it does not address the underlying needs or the real problem. If a buyer wants to pay $100 for something, and the seller wants $200 for it, settling on $150 may sound like a good solution, but it is probably not. It is possible that the buyer does not have more than $100 or that the seller's cost to produce the product was $180, in which case, $150 will not address anyone's real needs. In some situations, it may also give the wrong message: if one side knows that the other is drawn to a middle-of-the-way solution, they may come up with unreasonable opening points in order to force the other side closer to what they really want. If the sides are genuine in their effort to solve the problem, it can yield an effective and long-lasting solution, but it often leads to disappointment.

5. Collaborating: PMs who use a collaborative approach effectively work toward solving the problem. It applies assertiveness and cooperativeness and is about finding a win-win resolution. The sides in the conflict actually work together (not against each other) by:
   a. Trying to understand where the other person comes from;
   b. Shifting the conversation from positions to interests;
   c. Working on giving something that the other side values in return for something that they value;
   d. Trying to make the problem go away.

In collaborative conflict resolution, the goal is to move on and have a new reality that is free of the problem threatening the team. The good news is that it is perceived to be the best and most effective conflict resolution approach. The bad news is that it is resource and time hungry and requires emotional resilience, investments (time and resources) by all sides involved, as well as genuine care about the organization, the situation, and the other side—enough to justify the effort to solve the problem. Another piece of bad news is that most projects are short of resources and time as it is; PMs are spread too thin and have no capacity to spend in trying to reach the ultimate resolution. If done properly, this technique will leave the team with a clean slate to go back and focus on the main reason for which they are there: to produce the project deliverables and benefits, without being consumed by a conflict that distracts them from the task at hand.

Which is the best approach? Clearly, there is no one approach that would serve as a silver bullet for every situation. At times, due to deadlines or other urgencies, the right thing to do is to withdraw or accommodate. Compromise, even though it does not really solve the problem, may be the best solution available after conducting a cost-benefit analysis of the effort required against the benefit it may yield. Even forcing may be an appropriate solution under circumstances of tight deadlines or other pressing priorities. However, if the goal is to make the problem go away, there is a need to invest in the solution and somehow find a way to collaborate.

While some PMs treat conflict as a problem and sometimes try to avoid handling the situation altogether; more experienced PMs view conflict as a good thing: the team members have opinions and knowledge of the subject matter, and they care enough to engage in a conflict. It is not about PMs rubbing their palms together with glee, saying, "finally there is a conflict to resolve;" rather, it is about taking the opportunity to help the team work together and help them solve the problem. It empowers them and allows the project manager to demonstrate effective leadership—not by telling the team members what to do (i.e., forcing) or giving them the solution, but by getting them to reach a resolution together and equipping them to handle future problems on their own.

Ask Yourself

If you take the time to examine these five approaches to managing conflict, you can probably identify two that you tend to gravitate toward. Then think about how effective you are at resolving the conflicts you face (your own or others). The measure for effectiveness can be ascertained by asking:

1. Did you fix the problem?
2. Did you manage to make the problem go away without it coming back?

If your answers are not "yes" to both questions, your preferred tendencies for conflict resolution may not be effective. The implications go beyond the immediate problem that is not resolved: your conflict resolution effort is a reflection of your leadership, the perception the team and other stakeholders have of you, the team's morale, and how much personal power you have in the organization. Unfortunately, most of us naturally gravitate to "Avoiding" or "Accommodating" as at least one of our two preferred approaches, and we seem to answer "no" to at least one, if not both questions about the resolution's success, indicating that the problem we dealt with was not resolved. It is never too late to work on changing your approach to handing conflict.

Another piece of advice for PMs is to avoid being one of the sides in an all-out, loud, or unnecessary conflict. This is often a sign that the conflict is being mis-handled, and inevitably both sides will be associated with the problem, regardless of who is right. When PMs find themselves involved in a conflict, it should be in the capacity of a mediator, "conflict resolution facilitator," or leader (though with-out being tempted to force a resolution). The downstream negative impact of being associated with a mishandled conflict is the PM's objectivity and credibility, which will likely be called into question. And, with that, the PM's ability to exert influence on and effectively manage future conflicts, even projects, will be compromised. All that will result is reduced personal power and political clout. A common question that often comes up in relation to the advice of not taking sides is: "What if someone is being forced to take sides?" The answer is that it takes two to tango, and it should be within each individual's power not to be part of the problem and try to be the bigger person by handling the conflict effectively. In such cases, all of the downsides will be reversed into positives.

ESCALATION

Escalation comes when two sides cannot reach an agreement and seek resolution from a higher authority. Naturally, when a disagreement reaches a certain point, someone may threaten to escalate. However, it is not always so simple:

1. If the other side does not end up escalating, the threat will hurt their credibility.
2. Even if they escalate, the higher authority may not side with them.
3. It gives the higher authority the impression that the two sides cannot deal with their own relationships. A common reaction may be "do not come to me with these issues—this is the reason I hired you, so you figure it out."

Escalation usually makes both sides look bad, as they are usually part of a dysfunc-tional face-off putting one side against the other, which involves finger-pointing and an inability to work together. However, there is better a way to handle a deadlock: if the sides cannot work out a solution, you can propose escalation as an option to educate the other side about the consequences of escalation (but not as a threat). Even if there is eventually a need to escalate, both sides should approach the higher authority together and position themselves against the problem, rather than viewing each other as the problem. In such a case, the higher authority will recognize the collaboration, and someone who was likely going to become an enemy turns into a partner for potential future collaboration.

Astute PMs try to reduce the number of enemies they have in the organization, keeping in mind that when facing a disagreement with team members and stakeholders, they should not make the opposition into an enemy. Some people instinctively take disagreements personally and view the other person as the enemy. It is not constructive to let emotions take over and to judge others, as it leads to more negative politics—such as distracting the team away from focusing on the actual work at hand and distorting future decisions, which will be made based on who comes up with ideas rather than on evaluating the merits of those ideas. When there is a disagreement, it should be viewed as an opportunity, insofar as one side knows something the other does not. Either way, if both sides make the effort to work together and find out where the other is coming from, it is likely that they will end up finding a new ally for future decisions.

MISCONCEPTIONS ABOUT CONFLICT

There are a few misconceptions, or myths, about conflict that are important to mention so we can handle conflict optimally and embrace it with all the potential benefits it can lead to. They are:

1. Conflict is bad and always damages relationships;
2. Conflict needs to be reduced or avoided;
3. Ignoring the problem will make the conflict go away;
4. Conflict indicates personality issues and psychological problems;
5. Harmony is always good and conflict is always bad;
6. Conflict is an indication that people do not care.

MAY COME IN HANDY

There are a few more things that can help reduce "negative" politics in project environments: they are not easy to implement, and any attempt is likely to trigger resistance, but they are a necessity too important to skip. It is easy to hide behind the excuses that politics is too substantial and out of one's control, but to make a positive difference, PMs need to start somewhere, and there is no better time than the present to start working on the following:

Big picture—Focus on the big picture and encourage teammates to do the same. Many people get bogged down by small things that distract them from seeing the overall picture. It will also help refocus people on the end goal, helping them realize that things take time and that it is not about pursuing temporary fixes, but rather about doing the right thing and keeping the objectives in mind.

Roles and Responsibilities—Define and communicate roles and responsibilities early and clearly. Any gap in this area will end up backfiring later.

Expectations—Articulate and communicate goals, objectives, and success criteria so progress can be measured and results evaluated. Along with clear roles and responsibilities, it will ensure focus and accountability. It will also help deploy resources more efficiently.

Feedback and Support—Mentoring, coaching, and performance reporting are important for telling people how they're doing, for communicating areas for improvement, and for team building exercises in which members help each other, provide feedback, and collaborate on ways to work better together.

Collaboration—Encourage collaboration and reward those who do it.

Leadership—Ensure clear boundaries are set and demonstrate leadership clearly during the project, while remembering that power may come from knowing what not to say and when not to enforce things. Leadership involves empowerment, coaching, mediating, and fostering team growth through trust, relationship building, and teamwork.

Rules—Make sure you abide by organizational rules, policies, and procedures and work within them to achieve your goals. Even if you have great ideas and want to do the right thing, breaking the rules will get you into trouble. There is no excuse for not following the rules, and it never pays off to do so. There is a difference between breaking rules and bending rules, and by understanding the stakes involved, you should be able to take calculated risks that will help you get closer to achieving your project goals.

Alignment—Make decisions and recommendations based on evidence, logic, and facts as much as possible, ensuring that they are aligned with the project and the organizational goals.

Openness—Disclose the truth early and build a supportive environment that encourages truth—and never shoot the messenger. Lead by example by remaining constructive in giving feedback, encouraging clarifications when things are not clear, sharing information, and trying to reduce stress and anxiety among the team.

Dialogue—Establish open dialogue with your team that allows people to express themselves openly, exchange ideas, and work together on improving working relations and productivity.

Positive Feedback—Be sure to give positive feedback when it is warranted. We do not do it enough, as we are often consumed by finger pointing, blaming others, and taking things for granted. Do not single people out, do not dismiss what they have to say, and distribute authority equally.

Substance—Be sure to focus on the substance and merits of what you do, rather than on the ceremonial aspects, status, and red tape.

Transparency—Be sure to conduct yourself with transparency, objectivity, and visible fairness. Provide feedback and encourage learning without smothering the team. This is obviously not easy; most of us are often consumed by deliverables and other project work and overlook these important things, and find ourselves with no capacity to take care of them. Chapter 7, "Manage Those Things that Make a Difference" provides more insights as to how to channel focus, energy, and limited capacity into value-adding activities, which enable effective management of the project and clearer focus on those things within the organization that matter.

Recognition—Politics in the organization is here to stay, so you should learn how to play the game in order to promote your project's best interests while trying to improve your environment and its ground rules. Learning to work within the existing political system will help the organization and everyone involved adapt, change, and achieve goals.

FINAL POLITICAL THOUGHTS

One of the best kept secrets about project management is that it is about managing people. There are different schools of thought about the need for technical knowledge, subject matter expertise, and market experience; but at the end of the day, project management is about the PM's ability to manage the people in and around the project. A large chunk of this difficult task is to navigate the people, personalities, culture, and politics of the organization. There is no on-the-job training for this, and while some stakeholders befriend the newly appointed PM and give advice that may or may not be true or useful, it is up to the PM to learn (fairly quickly) where the speed bumps and the pillars of the organization are.

Speed bumps and pillars are the unmovable things that make up an organization's culture and politics, and the PM must recognize their existence and positions. For example, the son of the owner of a company may be a pillar in the organization since he is not going anywhere: he may either be effective or a walking disaster, but any hope to move him, or to remove him from the organization, is simply unrealistic. The quicker the PM learns about these organizational characteristics, the quicker he/she will become effective on the job and actually add value. If the PM ends up stumbling on one of these characteristics inadvertently, this may still be tolerable as part of the early "honeymoon phase" of the project, but soon enough, this will be seen as overstepping boundaries—with a political cost.

Knowing organizational politics is not rocket science, and the only difficult thing about it is the time and energy it consumes. There are some people who really know their way around the organization—they know who to go to for what, and they always have the scoop on what is happening in the organization. They are politically savvy, which is usually a result of paying constant attention to the people around them, in addition to their subject matter expertise. With such knowledge of the organization, culture, people, and overall politics, they know how to navigate their way to their destination. The good news is that each of us has the skills to do it properly; the bad news is that most of us do not have the time to do it or the awareness of its importance. This chapter has provided insights on how to deal with organizational politics, and now it is time to work on it, starting with a stakeholder analysis that will give the PM an idea of who is involved in the project and how to handle them. The information in the next chapter, which deals with managing project quality, will build on the knowledge in this chapter and will further help you deal with organizational politics.

References

1. Based on http://dictionary.reference.com/browse/leadership?s=t.
2. Inspired by the book, *Verbal Judo: The Gentle Art of Persuasion*, by George J. Thompson and Jerry B. Jenkins (New York: Harper Collins, 2004).
3. Adapted from http://flamesonfifthavenue.com/archives/310.
4. Inspired by the book, *There Is an I in Team: What Elite Athletes and Coaches Really Know About High Performance*, by Mark de Rond, (Boston: Harvard Business Press Books, 2012).
5. Ideas in these section are loosely based on ideas presented by Marcus Buckingham, the keynote speaker at the Project Management Institute's (PMI) Global Congress of 2012 in North America, Vancouver, October 2012.
6. Bruce W. Tuckman, "Developmental sequence in small groups," in *Psychological Bulletin*, 63, (1965), 384–399. The article was reprinted in *Group Facilitation: A Research and Applications Journal*, Number 3 (Spring 2001).
7. M. K. Smith, (2005) "Bruce W. Tuckman—forming, storming, norming, and performing in groups," from the encyclopedia of informal education, at www.infed.org/thinkers/tuckman.html.
8. *A Guide to the Project Management Body of Knowledge* (*PMBOK® Guide—Fifth Edition*), 287 (Sylva: Project Management Institute, 2013).

9. Five approaches to conflict resolution model adapted from "Conflict and Conflict Management," by Kenneth Thomas, in *The Handbook of Industrial and Organizational Psychology*, edited by Marvin Dunnette (Chicago: Rand McNally, 1976).

4

Understanding Stakeholders and What They Want

> **"What is the Meaning of Stakeholders' Impact?"**
>
> Stakeholder analysis involves placing the stakeholders on a grid in order to rank them, better understand their needs, and learn their potential responses to various challenging situations. The ultimate goal of stakeholder analysis is to understand anything about the stakeholders that can help the project manager (PM) manage the stakeholders' expectations and deliver success. It includes understanding stakeholders' needs, their ability to influence the project, their level of involvement, and how much they care about the project and its results. From the analysis, a stakeholders' management strategy should be formed as part of the communication plan. The terms to use on the power/influence-interest/impact grid should be intuitive to those participating in the process and those who need to interpret its results. The Y axis should be for influence, to measure stakeholders' ability to influence the project and its results, and the X axis should measure how impacted the stakeholders would be by the project. It can be called interest, or stake, so the PM understands how much stakeholders care about the project outcome.

The only way we can understand stakeholders' needs early enough in the game is to perform a stakeholder analysis. There is growing recognition of its importance, yet most PMs do not conduct stakeholder analysis at all; and most of those who do something like a stakeholder analysis do not do it sufficiently and fall short of getting the intended results. Failing to perform stakeholder analysis has a negative impact on the project success downstream, due to an increased risk of spending time on items potentially unimportant to the key stakeholders. Project failures can often be traced to a missing or poor stakeholder analysis, and while there is never sufficient time to conduct one, there really is no way around it. Stakeholder analysis and management is a growing area within project management, and it is becoming recognized as a critical contributing factor to project success. Although not necessarily formal, somewhat intangible, and not a project deliverable, the stakeholder analysis is a "background" effort that serves as a building block of the project.

Before performing a stakeholder analysis, it is important to ensure that there is a clear understanding of what (or who) a stakeholder is. According to the Project Management Institute's (PMI) *Project Management Body of Knowledge (PMBOK® Guide)— Fifth Edition*, "Project stakeholders are individuals, groups or organizations who may affect, be affected by, or perceive themselves to be affected by the decision activity or outcome of a project.[1] PMI has enhanced its focus on this important aspect of project success, stakeholder management, and analysis. This chapter deals with what it takes to gather the right and sufficient amount of information about the project stakeholders to both effectively manage and meet their expectations and ensure they provide and receive the agreed-upon value from the project. The discussion is closely based on the Stakeholder Management chapter of the *PMBOK® Guide—Fifth Edition* and is enhanced with practical and proven ideas and concepts that will make the process second nature for most PMs. If conducted properly, the stakeholder management process can also become an introduction to organizational politics, to ensure a better understanding of what people want and channel the project efforts appropriately.

The process of identifying, analyzing, and managing stakeholders is not a one-time thing at the start of the project. It is an ongoing process that needs to take place at various points throughout the project. Defining the process and its goals and objectives can help set up a target of how to measure whether a necessary and satisfying set of information has been obtained:

1. Identify the project stakeholders: It is nearly impossible to manage the expectations of people the PM does not know exist or what their involvement in the project is. Though seemingly obvious, many PMs continue to manage their projects without noticing or taking into consideration some of the stakeholders. This almost guarantees misunderstandings and project problems, no matter what the stakeholders' disposition toward the project is. Looking the other way will not solve the problem, since the stakeholder you do not know about is the one who may take your project down.

2. Stakeholder analysis: Learn what the stakeholders want, need, expect, what stake they have, and how much influence they have on the project and its results.

3. The next step is to identify stakeholders' potential reactions to various project situations and based on the results, develop a plan to engage them and manage their expectations. Managing stakeholders' expectations is

the key to project success, and containing their reactions to unfavorable situations will help keep the project from getting out of hand. It also includes grouping the stakeholders according to their needs, planning for the specific handling of each group or of an individual stakeholder, and subsequently designing a communications plan.

STAKEHOLDER IDENTIFICATION

Identifying stakeholders involves creating a list of all involved in the project and determining whether they are: (1) actively or passively involved, (2) positively or negatively impacted, and (3) in support of the project. Beyond identifying and recognizing the stakeholders, PMs need to further investigate and elaborate on each stakeholder—including, but not limited to, positions, interests, needs, risk tolerance, ability to influence the project, as well as drivers and motivators they might have. Table 4.1 provides examples of stakeholders, broken into two main categories: internal and external.

Make Assumptions When You Have To

Now armed with a list of identified stakeholders, the PM almost has what it takes to perform the stakeholder analysis—except that this is where the gap begins between what the methodology proposes and the project reality. Early in the project

Table 4.1 Examples of stakeholders by internal and external categories

Internal	External
• Project sponsor • Organizational and functional groups (e.g., finance, accounting, marketing, IT) • Functional and resource managers • Subject matter experts • Consultants • Senior management • Steering committees • PMOs • Team members • Other project managers • Boards of directors	• The customer (may be internal, the same as the sponsor, or a different person/organization who pays for the project) • End users • Sellers • Business partners • Subject matter experts • Consultants • Vendors • Suppliers • Governments • Regulators • The public • Special interest groups • Competition • Anyone who might have any level of involvement or interest in the project
Typical stakeholders in a project broken into two main groups: internal and external. Every project will have most of the stakeholders who are listed above with varying mixes of influence, interests, needs, personalities, dispositions, and number of representatives of each stakeholder type.	

(initiation, early planning), there is usually insufficient information available about the project itself and especially about those who are going to be involved in it. This makes it difficult to identify stakeholders, let alone gather meaningful information about their characteristics and tendencies. As a result, many PMs often proceed with their planning without doing the analysis, essentially giving up on obtaining this information.

Although it may appear time consuming and expensive to invest the extra effort to perform a meaningful stakeholder analysis, a simple cost–benefit analysis will show that this investment will pay off later in the project. The cost–benefit analysis involves reviewing previously performed projects and checking for the costs and delays associated with misunderstandings and unknown stakeholder needs. Failing to realize who is involved in the project, to what extent, and the disposition of each stakeholder is likely to spell failure later, since decisions, recommendations, and actions will take place without taking certain stakeholders' needs, reactions, and ability to influence the project into consideration.

One effective solution to the challenge of gathering the full amount of information needed is to resort to one of the PM's best friends: assumptions. When information is missing about potential stakeholders, PMs can make assumptions about the nature of stakeholder involvement and their likely positions and reactions to situations. Assumptions should not just come out of thin air or be seasoned by hope. It is important to keep in mind that any assumption needs to be documented and revisited periodically until validated or refuted. Chapter 6 of this book deals with assumptions and expands on their importance, how to handle them, and the implications of not articulating and managing them properly.

Categories

To make stakeholder analysis and management easier, PMs can categorize stakeholders into groups that identify a specific set of communication needs throughout the project. While it is clear that each individual has a unique set of styles, needs, and characteristics, it is easier to manage the stakeholders and build communication and engagement plans by forming them into groups. The stakeholder analysis will uncover specific needs and challenges associated with the individuals within the groups and will enable customizing communications with them. PMs should categorize stakeholders according to the circumstances and considerations that are specific to their environments. An example of stakeholder categorization is demonstrated in Figure 4.1.

It is important to note that not all stakeholders within a category require the same type of communication, engagement, or treatment. Categorization only serves to make it more efficient for the PM by reducing the volume of customized communication channels and engagements.

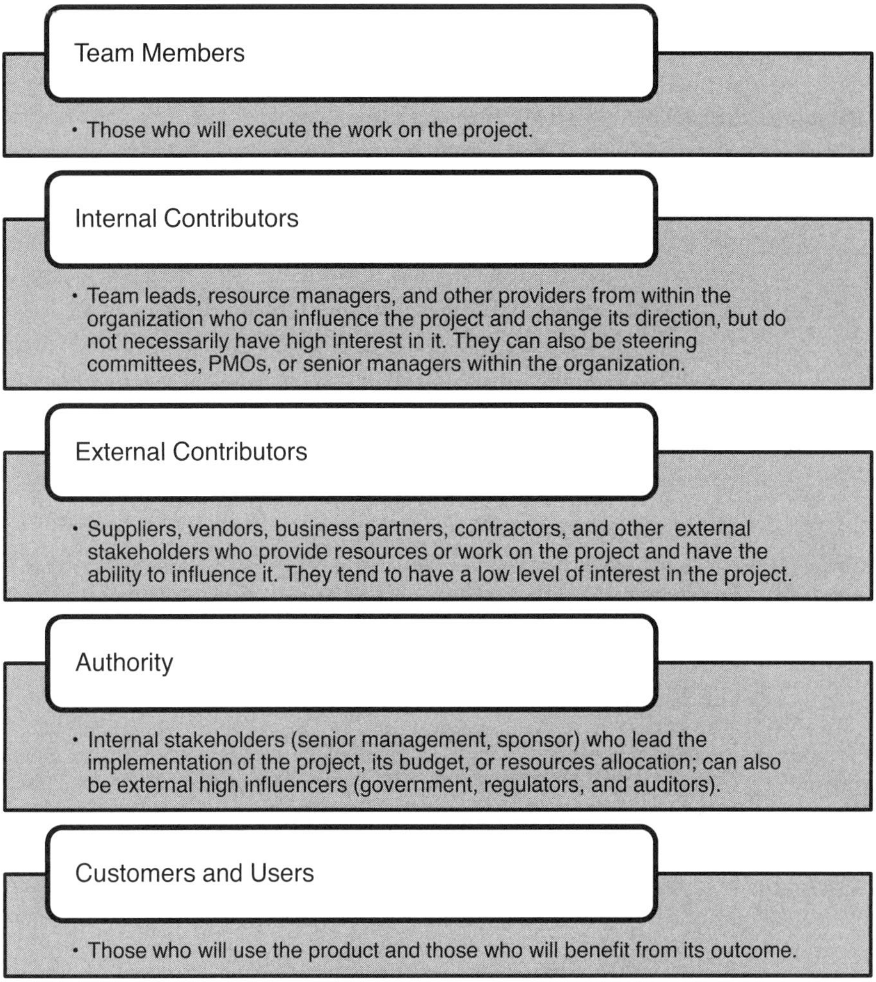

Team Members

- Those who will execute the work on the project.

Internal Contributors

- Team leads, resource managers, and other providers from within the organization who can influence the project and change its direction, but do not necessarily have high interest in it. They can also be steering committees, PMOs, or senior managers within the organization.

External Contributors

- Suppliers, vendors, business partners, contractors, and other external stakeholders who provide resources or work on the project and have the ability to influence it. They tend to have a low level of interest in the project.

Authority

- Internal stakeholders (senior management, sponsor) who lead the implementation of the project, its budget, or resources allocation; can also be external high influencers (government, regulators, and auditors).

Customers and Users

- Those who will use the product and those who will benefit from its outcome.

Every project manager must consider the types of stakeholders as applicable to the project environment to ensure effective categorization in a way that helps manage communication needs.

Figure 4.1 Stakeholder categories

STAKEHOLDER ANALYSIS BRICK AND MORTAR

The stakeholder analysis starts with traditional and commonly used tools—the result should be a clear picture of the identified stakeholders and a roadmap of how to manage them. Start by taking the list of stakeholders and placing them in the influence and interest grid.[2] The PMI names the axes "Power" and "Interest," but in some situations, the use of the word power may imply authority, and many stakeholders can influence projects, even without formal authority. The goal, illustrated in Figure 4.2, is to measure how much influence a stakeholder may be able to exert on a project and its outcomes, and how much stake and vested interest the stakeholder has in it.

The grid is broken into quadrants, which represent low and high values for each of the two measures, and is intuitive to manage:

1. **High and high**: this is where the project players and principals are and the PM should manage them closely. They rate highly in three key areas: (i) they have a strong ability to influence the project; (ii) they make key, meaningful decisions about the project (i.e., budget, resources, timelines, and priorities); and (iii) they have a high level of interest due to their heavy personal and professional investments in the project. The stakeholders in this quadrant often call the shots and define the project success criteria and its objectives—it is *their* project. There are usually no more

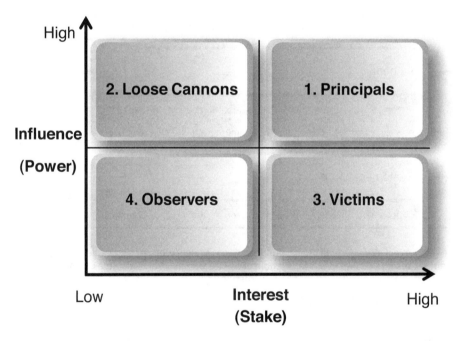

Stakeholders are placed on the grid in relation to their ability to influence the project and the level of interest they have in it. This commonly used foundational depiction requires further analysis of stakeholders' attitudes, potential reactions to events, and general position toward the project.

Figure 4.2 Stakeholder influence-interest grid

than a couple of people in this quadrant—specifically, the project sponsor and the customer. In certain situations, there may be other stakeholders as when there is more than one sponsor or there are multiple layers of accountability.

2. Logically, the next quadrant identifies stakeholders with **high influence and low interest**. The PMI says PMs should keep them satisfied,[3] but many PMs simply view them as loose cannons. These stakeholders have varying amounts of power to influence the project's course and outcome, yet they do not have a vested interest in it. They will not directly suffer the consequences of the project's failure, or they may have a direct conflict of interest or conflicting priorities with the project. This is a busy quadrant and contains most of the stakeholders involved in the project as known at this point. As the project moves forward, some stakeholders will no longer be involved in it, while others, new ones, may be introduced to the project. A list of possible stakeholders who may find their way into the second quadrant appears in Figure 4.3.

3. The third quadrant is where the victims are, and the PMI indicates that PMs should keep them informed. After attending to the needs of stakeholders in quadrants 1 and 2, PMs have a diminished capacity to address these stakeholders' needs, but attention should still be paid to what these **low influence, high interest** stakeholders have to say. Not everything they have to say actually adds value to the project, and the PM should have the ability to differentiate between their contributions. Since these stakeholders will be the ones who must deal with the consequences of the project outcome, there may be some merit in what they have to say. This quadrant is not heavily populated and is primarily made up of end users and support staff.

4. The fourth quadrant refers to the **low influence and low interest** stakeholders, or the observers. This quadrant will host any potential stakeholder who is currently not involved in the project: it may be someone who will become more influential moving forward, or other stakeholders who have a passive role but—if they do not like what they see—may get involved, sometimes in a least favorable way. Unfortunately, with all the attention being paid to managing the other stakeholders, there is little energy and time left for managing the observers. Quite often, reality plays in such a way that this quadrant produces the biggest surprises of the project, and in project management, a surprise is usually not a good thing; therefore, it is important to monitor these stakeholders, since their stakes or influence may change, as illustrated in Figure 4.4.

Another observation about the stakeholders in the fourth quadrant is related to the PM's reduced ability to pay sufficient attention to these stakeholders after trying to attend to those in the more important categories: they may become enemies.

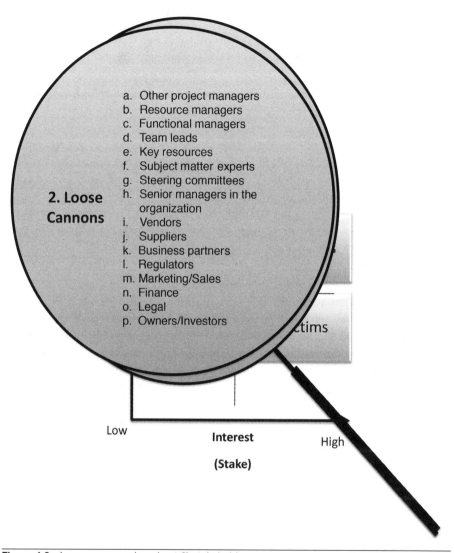

a. Other project managers
b. Resource managers
c. Functional managers
d. Team leads
e. Key resources
f. Subject matter experts
g. Steering committees
h. Senior managers in the organization
i. Vendors
j. Suppliers
k. Business partners
l. Regulators
m. Marketing/Sales
n. Finance
o. Legal
p. Owners/Investors

2. Loose Cannons

ctims

Low

Interest

High

(Stake)

Figure 4.3 Loose cannons (quadrant 2) stakeholders

However, a politically driven, yet genuine investment in a relationship with some of these stakeholders may pay off—if they turn into influential stakeholders. Many PMs fail to see a problem with making enemies, not realizing the long term negative implications it might have. At some point in their careers, PMs come to realize that even if there is no direct and immediate benefit, it is safer to maintain good relations with as many stakeholders as possible.

Many PMs who conduct stakeholder analysis utilize this influence-interest grid because it visually helps classify stakeholders and illustrates their overall

Shift (upward)
- Stakeholders who currently are not actively involved in the project may move up to quadrant 2. This is a normal progression for stakeholders. It also illustrates the importance of conducting stakeholder analysis at regular intervals throughout the project to intercept such changes when they occur.

Exert indirect influence
- Some stakeholders in this quadrant may not have much direct influence on the project, but they may be connected to an influential stakeholder. It could be friendships and relationships, or stakeholders that right now are not directly involved but they may become more influential moving forward.

Figure 4.4 Quadrant 4—observers

importance to the project. However, it is surprising to see many placing the majority of the stakeholders in the first quadrant, as principals. Only later do they realize it does not make sense for the majority of stakeholders to have both high influence and high interest in the project. It may be easy to place most stakeholders in that quadrant, but it does not provide a meaningful way to understand their importance to the project.

CONFIDENTIAL

Even before beginning the stakeholder analysis process, it is important to mention that it should be confidential. While it involves discussions and (mostly informal) information gatherings with colleagues about other team members and stakeholders, the placing of stakeholders on the influence-interest grid and the ensuing formation of opinions and action plans to engage them must be confidential. The stakeholder register should not be shared with others or posted on shared drivers—it must remain private.

Stakeholder analysis helps PMs form a realistic view of the stakeholders; it also deals with subjective relationships with stakeholders and the PM's ability to interact with them effectively. Behind the need for confidentiality is an attempt to prevent potential backlash from people who may discover that the way the PM views them does not meet their expectations and their perceived self-importance. After all, no one wants to learn that they are not high on the list of priorities or that the PM does not view them as influential and important.

In addition to confidentiality, the process is mostly informal and therefore, more difficult to plan and budget. Considering that the stakeholder analysis does not involve significant planning meetings and that the effort, intensity, and duration will vary dramatically from one project to another, there is usually no allocation of time and budget to performing it—which makes it even more challenging when trying to establish plans and expectations for the project. These challenges should not serve as an excuse for not performing a stakeholder analysis, and the extent of analysis required is typically determined during the complexity assessment, where the PM acquires an indication of the overall level of project complexity expected and the size of the project.

STAKEHOLDERS AND THE REQUIREMENTS

There are countless benefits to knowing the project stakeholders—most importantly, that it leads to engaging them and managing their expectations of and impacts on the project effectively. It can also help with the project requirements and scoping, since it is likely that the PM will need to prioritize requirements. There may be many underlying reasons for this, but the result is either the need to remove some requirements altogether or to change the order in which they are delivered. Removing features, functionalities, and their associated requirements is never an easy decision to make, especially since stakeholders get quite attached (sometimes emotionally) to their requirements. Moreover, cross-requirement dependencies and other considerations make the process much more complex than it is initially thought to be.

Most projects have some sort of prioritization scheme for the requirements: from the MoSCoW method (Must, Should, Could, Would) to functional and technical considerations, and sometimes there are proprietary methods for ranking and prioritizing requirements. Despite the strong need for prioritizing and the available tools to assist with it, surprisingly, many projects have no method or approach for requirements prioritization whatsoever—leaving it to chance and causing fierce arguments as part of the de-scoping exercises.

One challenge to requirements prioritization is that there is often no systematic way of checking which stakeholder is associated with which requirements. This can be managed by gaining knowledge about the association of stakeholders to requirements (i.e., which stakeholder requested, paid for, or needed each requirement) and applying a visual scheme, as in Figure 4.5, to map each requirement's importance to the project with the level of complexity associated with it.

Placing the requirements grid next to the stakeholder grid gives the PM an opportunity to map requirements to the stakeholders associated with them. Complexity is related to technical considerations, and importance is about whether a requirement is part of a minimum feature set and which stakeholder is associated with it. The location of each requirement on the grid should be based on the criteria that follow.

Requirements Complexity

The PM should pursue clear measurements for the criteria in order to help define the complexity of each requirement. For the most part, the technical team will be

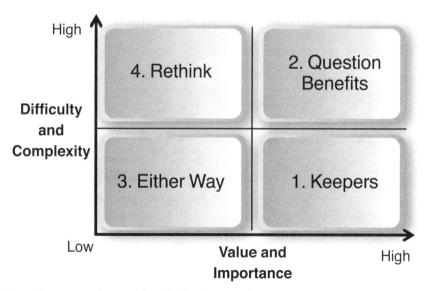

This grid maps requirements for prioritization based on their complexity and importance to the project.

Figure 4.5   The requirements grid

able to provide the majority of answers for these items, allowing the PM to come up with a difficulty ranking for the requirement at stake.

Value and Benefits

Ranking the value and benefits of requirements should consider the functionality each requirement represents, dependencies other functions have on it, value/benefits realized for the organization, and which stakeholders are associated with it. This is where the two grids can be placed next to each other, as illustrated in Figure 4.6. Map the stakeholder grid against the requirements grid by drawing arrows from the stakeholders to the requirements each is associated with.

It is not necessarily the case that every requirement introduced by a stakeholder from quadrant 4 (i.e., currently perceived to have low influence and low interest in the project) is complicated to perform and unimportant, but the example illustrates that beyond functionality, there might be a correlation between who requests a requirement and its importance to project success.

The characteristics and importance of the stakeholder behind each requirement will essentially determine the position of the requirement on the requirements grid. If a requirement is found to be critical to a set of functionalities, then it will be deemed valuable or important. Quite often, an important stakeholder (principal) champions and promotes a specific requirement, and—despite it being trivial from a technical perspective—the requirement is given high priority by virtue of being associated with that stakeholder. The opposite may also apply: stakeholders who

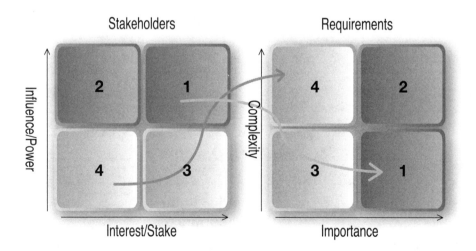

This diagram helps map the requirements to the stakeholders that are behind them.

Figure 4.6 Connecting the stakeholders to the requirements

are positioned as observers may request difficult and technically complex requirements, and the PM should recommend doing the right thing for the project: removing the requirement.

It is important to note that like the rest of the stakeholder analysis, this prioritization scheme needs to remain confidential. It may damage relationships with stakeholders if they learn that the leading reason for recommending the removal of a requirement is merely their association with it. However, the PM should protect the best interests of the project, so—when an observer stakeholder, who currently has little stake or influence, no accountability, and no financial investment, comes up with a requirement—the PM needs to be firm in protecting the project's objectives. Ironically, it is often an observer stakeholder who comes up with the most complex and expensive requirements. Determining the relative importance of stakeholders should be done in such a way that it will not compromise relationships with them or turn them into adversaries. Additional considerations on how to further learn about stakeholders' reactions and tendencies are presented later in this chapter.

TAKE IT UP A NOTCH

Many PMs feel it is sufficient to place the stakeholders in the stakeholders' influence-interest grid and to acquire some level of understanding of who means what to the project. Although this is a big step in the right direction, it leaves many important questions unanswered. There are many more things the PM needs to know about the stakeholders in order to take the analysis from its current foundational state to a multidimensional one. It involves asking a series of questions, to which the PM needs answers—but one of the challenges is that the PM should not pose these questions to the stakeholders directly but try to find answers without asking outright. The stakeholder assessment tool can help PMs through the task of looking for answers and is illustrated in Table 4.2.

It is not realistic to expect to obtain answers to all of these questions, but if the PM gets some answers, they will serve as an important foundation for the stakeholder engagement strategy. A stakeholder engagement strategy is about establishing the objectives of stakeholder engagement, indicating how to achieve stakeholders involvement at each stage of the project. It is driven by the stakeholder analysis and includes the vision for stakeholder engagement, together with details

Table 4.2 Stakeholder assessment tool

0	1	2	3	4	5
No info. Make an assumption	Very Unfavorable	Unfavorable	Medium	Favorable	Very Favorable

Use this scale to rank the information obtained for each question.

of how to and who should engage the stakeholders. In what follows, the questions for which the PM needs to seek answers as part of the stakeholder analysis are identified.

Support vs. Level of Activity

Regardless of the level of influence or interest stakeholders have in the project, there is a need to learn about their support level for the project. This includes support on three levels:

1. The project outcomes and goals;
2. The process and method;
3. The personal support stakeholders have for the PM and his or her style.

The PM needs to take into consideration whether he/she can expect support from each stakeholder, and this consideration should also include former allies, since their support is not guaranteed. Not every stakeholder who supports the project is actually active in their support. Figure 4.7 plots stakeholders in a grid of support and level of activity.

Classifying the stakeholders on this grid prepares the PM for the next step: attempting to shift stakeholders along this grid to where they need to be. It involves applying political skills—including cutting deals with stakeholders to make them

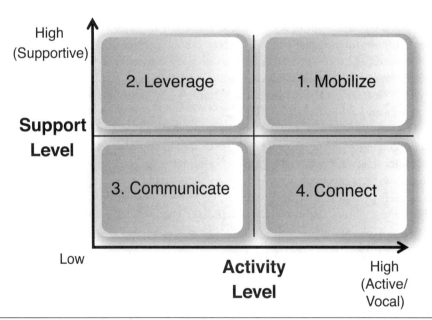

Figure 4.7 Stakeholder support vs. level of activity

more supportive of the project—and working behind the scenes to address their immediate or future needs and concerns so the PM can promote and achieve the project's goals. It is valuable to determine the following types of stakeholders:

- Promoters: active or passive (depending on the roles and involvement of the stakeholder);
- Bystanders: noisy or quiet;
- Adversaries: active or passive.

The following list contains the actions to take to engage the stakeholders, based on whether they are supporters or resisters:

1. Leverage the supporters: maximize those who are vocal supporters and help passive supporters become more vocal in their support by showing them that our needs are aligned, even tied to each other.
2. Convert bystanders: convince fence-sitters to become supporters, or at least help them focus their involvement so they promote the project, instead of potentially making distracting noise. Working with bystanders may work in your favor in the case of a tie because they can influence others to support the project.
3. Neutralize the opposition: find ways to work with adversaries to silence their resistance and convert them into supporters. This may become the foundation for collaboration and the start of productive future relationships. In situations where we encounter adversaries, there is a temptation to refuse working with those who resist our project, which is the opposite of what we should do. We should reach out to adversaries, check where they're coming from, understand their motives and drivers, and try to work with them and bring them closer. In doing so, their needs are fulfilled and their concerns are addressed until eventually the underlying causes of their resistance are defused. I have managed to create great alliances and build collaborative relationships by reaching out and working with those who were not initially supportive of my needs and priorities.

Looking for Answers

The search for answers about stakeholders involves identifying relevant questions and classifying them into categories (i.e., areas of focus), as listed in Figure 4.8.

This discovery process of stakeholders' underlying interests and success criteria occurs in conjunction with the pre-kickoff project definition meetings, wherein the PM reaches out to high profile stakeholders. It is an opportunity to engage them, which may improve the PM's ability to develop good rapport with the stakeholders. It is also an opportunity to work with the stakeholders to define: (1) their acceptance

Figure 4.8 Areas of focus for questions

criteria, which can be described as the technical aspects of their success, and (2) the approval criteria, which ensures that decision making, approvals, and sign-offs are clearly defined and assigned to specific stakeholders. Armed with information about their view of success, it will be easier to manage their expectations and address their needs as long as these do not conflict with the project objectives. In the event that there is a conflict, the options for a course of action will be based upon the nature of this conflict and the level of influence the stakeholder has—which essentially means "picking our battles," as not all differences and conflicts can be repaired.

In addition, there is a need to identify the roles and responsibilities, and it may be helpful to distinguish whether each stakeholder participates in a transactional or transformational capacity, since each type may require a different level of focus and handling (see Table 4.3). Beyond the level of influence already identified in the

Table 4.3 Transaction vs. transformational stakeholder

Transactional	Transformational
Involved in performing the work and are more on the responsive side to policies.	Decision makers, movers and shakers: more about the objectives, sign-offs, and developing policy.

stakeholder grid, it is valuable to identify the point at which stakeholders are going to be involved and to what extent.

Stakeholders' perceived attitudes toward risk is a crucial consideration in the effort to develop a stakeholder engagement strategy. Learning about their risk attitudes provides insight about what to expect from them in challenging situations, how much hand-holding they may require, and how much energy and effort the PM will need to expend to address their needs and concerns. There are generally four attitudes toward risk that stakeholders hold, as presented in Figure 4.9.

Valuable information and insights are not always shared by or with stakeholders, and there may be gaps between what stakeholders feel they need to know and their access to information. The organizational settings and conditions will have a

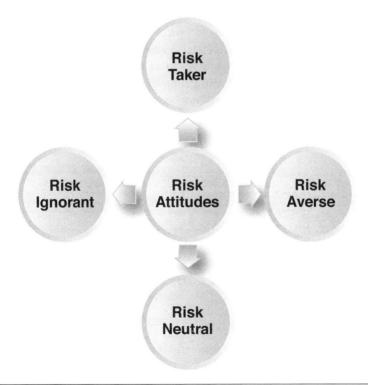

Figure 4.9 Stakeholders' risk attitudes

significant impact on how the PM can lead the project, and with conflict guaranteed to take place, there are a few insights the PM can look for in an effort to effectively handle them in a way that is helpful for the progress of the project and the dynamic of those involved.

Overall Stakeholder Importance

The placement of stakeholders into the quadrants on the influence-interest grid already prioritizes them: the PM realizes the need to collaborate with those in quadrant 1 (high interest, high influence); to work with and involve those in quadrant 2 (high influence, low interest); consult with the quadrant 3 stakeholders (low influence, high interest); and inform the bystanders (with low interest and low influence) in quadrant 4. This prioritization can be further refined and complemented by classifying stakeholders according to their ability to help the project or to harm it and how likely they are to act on these abilities. Table 4.4 illustrates the stakeholders' importance assessment, which helps determine where there might be landmines, to which the PM should pay special attention, or where allies can be found.

Manage the Stakeholders

Whatever answers PMs can get to these questions will equip them to better put together an effective stakeholder engagement plan and build a communication plan. The goals are to address the stakeholders' needs and to keep them informed at the expected and agreed upon level so they add value to the project, get the benefits they require, and remain satisfied with the progress, processes, and results. In turn, their satisfaction ensures that they will not become adversaries or derail the project.

The key to the success of stakeholder management is utilizing the information we gain by setting expectations upfront, managing the stakeholders appropriately,

Table 4.4   Stakeholder importance assessment

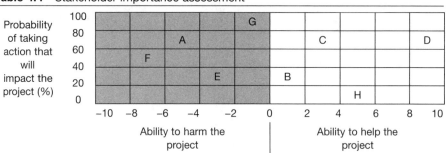

This table places stakeholders based on the chance they will take action that may impact the project, breaking the display down on a scale by the stakeholders' ability to harm the project and their ability to help the project.

and maintaining those relationships by dealing in the currencies the stakeholders understand and care about so that their needs are met on a timely basis. Following these guidelines also allows the PM to focus on what matters in the project, which is delivering its value and benefits and reducing the level of distractions in it.

Maintaining good relations with the stakeholders allows the PM to respond earlier and more effectively to challenges and performance issues, focusing on the merits and substance of the project rather than on distractions and semantics. Happy stakeholders are inclined to be more understanding of problems and performance challenges and will allow them to take place to an extent, as long as relationships and transparency are in place. Some projects can sustain performance issues for a while, and with the right approach, the PM can keep the stakeholders satisfied and less distracted in the process of bringing performance back to its intended level. When stakeholders are happy with the overall treatment they get, it gives the PM more time and leverage to fix performance issues without added distractions from the stakeholders. The opposite also applies to projects with overall good performance that is overshadowed and weighed down by strained relationships with stakeholders. Even if the team is on track to recover the performance, the distractions alone may lead to more performance issues downstream.

Stakeholder Analysis Conclusion

To make it easier to assess and compare the stakeholder analysis answers, PMs can add a tool that contains all of the questions and ranks the answers according to the nature of their information, as illustrated in Table 4.5.

Table 4.5 Stakeholder importance information summary by category

Categories of questions for each stakeholder	Level of satisfaction with information about the stakeholder					
	0	1	2	3	4	5
Underlying interests						
Roles and responsibilities						
Influence						
Risk						
Information						
Organizational impact						
Conflict and personalities						

Legend:
- Five (5): Satisfied with the information about the stakeholder.
- One (1): The question poses a challenge.
- Zero (0): Necessary information is missing; requires additional investigation and possibly making assumptions.

ATTITUDES

The common belief that it is sufficient to know who the stakeholders are is simply mistaken. PMs tend to get taken by surprise when stakeholders change their priorities, views, support, or attitudes, but it is quite common and often happens with no advance notice. When the PM knows the stakeholders in advance, the analysis is easier, since it only validates that they will act as expected; but when PMs do not know the stakeholders beforehand, there is a need for the full analysis process. Leading a project without knowing about the stakeholders is similar to driving a car blindfolded—the PM does not know how to handle the stakeholders or what to expect from them. The knowledge obtained during stakeholder analysis makes it easier to anticipate their reactions to situations, their demands, their styles, and their attitudes.

Although the use of the word "attitude" is not politically correct, attitudes exist and are so impactful that they can take projects down, even more than performance or schedule issues. By conducting effective stakeholder analysis and becoming politically savvy, the PM will build up personal power, making it easier to manage stakeholders' attitudes and reduce their potential damage to the team and the project.

Attitudes—such as negativity, envy, cynicism, and greed—are contagious. If they are not dealt with quickly and effectively, they can spread like a brush fire through the project and destroy the team's dynamic and performance. These attitudes have the ability to eat through the fabric of the team, destroy trust, and trigger unconstructive conflict that can eventually consume the team. The insights and information the PM gathers through the stakeholder analysis creates a capacity to look for attitude problems and helps provide the confidence, emotional resilience, and feeling of control to take a timely and sober look at the situation and apply the best and most appropriate solution available. The knowledge and context gained from the stakeholder analysis can serve as a toolbox, allowing the PM to identify options and anticipate whatever potential reactions stakeholders may have and the possible backlash they may lead to. Whatever the attitudes are, failing to contain them will most likely end up taking over the project team. Anything the PM can do will probably be more effective than just sitting there and watching the fire consume the project team. Waiting until the backlash is more apparent means that it is already too late to effectively address and solve the issue.

Being Proactive

The results of the stakeholder analysis should serve as a foundation for the project communication plan and stakeholder engagement plan, but even after completing the analysis, significant pieces of information may still be missing. It neither should stop the project planning process from moving forward, nor should it stop the PM from trying to obtain this valuable missing information about the stakeholders. Failure to address the needs of important stakeholders or to understand their expectations will be costly as the project moves forward.

The onus is on the PM to obtain the missing information—with no excuses. When it gets more difficult to find the information, the PM should engage other stakeholders and team members for additional insights, historical information, or formation of assumptions. The need to be proactive and reach out to stakeholders applies throughout the entire project lifecycle—not only at the outset—especially for environments that engage in adaptive lifecycles (i.e., Agile), where the stakeholders' engagement and involvement becomes more crucial for the project success and needs to be managed on an ongoing basis.

RESPONSIBILITY ASSIGNMENT MATRIX

The stakeholder analysis is not only the gateway to organizational politics, the foundation of the communication plan, and the guide to stakeholder engagement but also the first step in our attempt to match the project's tasks to its stakeholders. This matching is done through the Responsibility Assignment Matrix (RAM), as illustrated in Table 4.6, and it connects the project stakeholders with the project scope and deliverables in a practical way.

The attempt to connect stakeholders with scope and deliverables aims at these goals:

1. Ensure that each deliverable, activity, and task has a resource or stakeholder assigned to it;
2. Safeguard skill matching, so that the most suitable person is assigned to each activity and at the right capacity;
3. Get resources and stakeholders to understand the nature and level of their involvement in each activity;
4. Find gaps: completing the RAM will show us whether there is someone who can be assigned to each activity; in the event there is no one assigned to an activity, it will not get done. It sounds straightforward, but in reality, projects often go ahead without having all tasks and activities mapped out. Many times, PMs mix hope with strategy, and activities without assigned resources on the RAM are often dismissed with "we will figure it out later." Unfortunately, any gaps are usually discovered the hard way—later—at which point it is even more pressing than it was, and the team cannot perform certain activities on the project.

RACI Chart

For the most part, the RAM serves only as a generic name, and it is often called a RACI chart in practice. RACI represents the four capacities, for which resources will be assigned to the project's activities, and is short for: Responsible, Accountable, Consulted, and Informed. The use of the RACI chart is common, and the letters are

Table 4.6 RAM: RASCI chart sample

Stakeholders Project Deliverables	Ron, PM	Ari, Sponsor	Karen, IT Mgr.	Cheryl, Help Desk Lead	Barry, BA	Andy, Architect	Eva, Dir. Customer Support	Anton, Trainer
Business Requirements Document	I	I	A	S	R	C	I	
Functional Design Document	I	I	A	S	S	R	C	I
Communication and Launch Plan	R	C, I	S		S		A	I
Assess Risk	I		R		S	S	A	
Change and Control	R		A	S	S	S	I	I
Develop Training Materials	I	I	C	S	S	S	A	R
Deliver Training	I	I	C		C	C	A	R

an intuitive way to represent the stakeholders' involvement in each activity. Before proceeding with this discussion, there is another area that requires clarification: too often, PMs and team members have misconceptions about the RACI roles, and if this persists, they may fail to deliver value in creating a RACI chart, which may backfire and mislead the team during the project. Therefore, these are the true definitions of each of the RACI elements:

- Responsible: the person who is actually assigned to perform the work. Every activity must have a person to perform it because, without an "R," the activity will not get done.
- Accountable: the PM's name should not appear as the accountable party for any non-project management activity. The person accountable symbolizes where the buck stops, which will often be the functional manager or the team lead of the person performing the work. In essence, the PM cannot be accountable for any non-project management task or activity within the project (representing actual work such as writing code, testing, or building the product), since the PM is ultimately accountable for the project as a whole and does not have the capacity to be assigned to a specific task. In the event that the PM is only part time and also serves as a project resource, it will be possible for the PM to be assigned as both an "A" and an "R" for a task. There should be only one person who is accountable for a task.
- Consulted: this usually refers to subject matter experts, or other contributors, who provide inputs, knowledge, expertise, or other value to the activity but are not the ones who perform the work. There can be more than one stakeholder consulted for each activity.
- Informed: these stakeholders are more reactive in relation to the activity; they are on a need-to-know basis, and no action is required of them. For that reason, there can be multiple stakeholders labeled as informed.

It is possible to have more than one person assigned to perform the work on a certain activity, and in this case, many PMs assign multiple persons at the "R" level to an activity. Seemingly, there is no problem with this, but in practice, it is too much of a good thing. When more than one person is assigned to a task, it may lead to an ownership problem or to accountability issues at the "R" level. It is similar to sending an e-mail with a request to two or more people: each one will see the other name(s) in the e-mail and assume (or hope) that the other(s) will respond to the request. With the letter "R" over more than one name on the RACI chart, people may point fingers rather than perform the work. For these kinds of situations, the RACI chart can be enhanced into a RASCI, by adding an "S" for Support:

- Support: similar to responsible, it means that there are others who are assigned to the task. The "R" now stands for the lead, who is ultimately responsible for the task or activity, and all people labeled "S" provide support to the "R." They perform the work, but report at the task level to the "R," who serves as a central point for task accountability and reporting. This prevents the need to chase after bits and pieces of information from multiple stakeholders.

Four Steps

Although it is common to have an incomplete RAM, it is actually better than having no RAM at all. Many PMs fail to see the importance of putting together a clear and strong RAM early in the project; others simply confuse the RAM with the project schedule, not realizing it is only about assigning the resources and not about their timing and availability. If done properly, it can serve as an important milestone toward building a realistic schedule.

Another benefit it may yield is related to early detection of problems: an incomplete RAM, with tasks that have no resources assigned to them, is a risk that should be recorded. It is likely that there will be insufficient information to populate the entire matrix, particularly during the early stages of the project; in such a case, once again, the PM can resort to assumptions. The process of developing the RAM can be broken into four stages that should produce a realistic RASCI chart:

1. The first step is to take the deliverables and high level activities [from the work breakdown structure or the scoping process] and assign a high-level resource to each of them. In this way, "high level" just means defining a type of resource that should be assigned to the activity (e.g., developer, tester, designer, or engineer). This represents a generic resource that will be associated with the task in any of the RASCI capacities. This is done early on in the project, when the activities are still at a high level and there is little information about the resources and the stakeholders to be involved in the project. At the top of the matrix, resources should only be generically labeled for each of the project activities identified thus far.

2. As progress is made in planning, more information comes to light about resources and stakeholders, and it is now time to get more specific about assigning them. This is done by getting more specific about the resources involved by pointing at a specific team, a short list, or a specific skill level that is needed.

3. The third step is a result of detailed planning and should yield a set of specific resources assigned to and associated with each activity in their appropriate capacities. The top of our matrix should now include a name and a role: the name is to make sure that this person is not replaced with someone else with the same title; the role is to indicate the skills

and experience needed for the activity. This list can be viewed as a set of assumptions: every stakeholder on it is assumed to be able to perform each activity assigned. In the event that stakeholders and resources are removed or changed, the assumptions no longer stand, and a risk should be recorded. This is done not to protect the matrix but to protect the project. If the RASCI chart indicates a need for a resource, and the intended person is not available, it poses a risk for the project. Recording the risks associated with the RASCI chart and stating their associated impact is part of managing stakeholders' expectations. While maintaining good relationships with the stakeholders, the PM needs to be assertive and stand strong against the removal of resources from the project.

4. This step is about resource adjustments that will inevitably need to take place. Even if no changes occur in the project, having built the RAM early in the project means that resources may change. These changes may include availability, skill level updates, over-allocated resources, or changes in deliverables, activities, or tasks. These availability adjustments may lead to scheduling adjustments.

If populated properly, the RASCI chart can also serve as an escalation procedure guideline, as it should clearly show each stakeholder's level of involvement—including those who need to be informed about the task. This is a step toward creating a project-wide escalation procedure, where escalation becomes a "turnkey solution," which clearly specifies and communicates who needs to know what and when, and how communicating the right information to the right person at the right time can be accomplished. Communication is another potential benefit of the RAM, as it communicates the roles and responsibilities for each activity and ensures stakeholders know what is expected of them and of others.

FOCUS

Stakeholder analysis is part of a series of things the PM needs to do behind the scenes to ensure that visible success criteria (i.e., scope, time, cost, quality) are achieved. The fact that the stakeholder analysis occurs behind the scenes illustrates that although it does not produce actual product-related deliverables, it serves as support and groundwork for the project's product. At the end of the project, the customer is unlikely to ask to see the stakeholder analysis, but without one, it is difficult to deliver the success the customer is looking for.

The *PMBOK® Guide* has taken stakeholder analysis and management to a new level by making it a knowledge area, enhancing its perceived importance and putting it on equal footing with the leading aspects of the project that require the PM's attention. Every experienced PM knows that the effort put into stakeholder analysis pays off in a much stronger ability to manage them and the project as a whole. While the need for stakeholder analysis is obvious, the challenge starts with finding the time, capacity, and justification to do it properly. The compelling evidence of the benefits it yields is not likely to help PMs "sell" the need for stakeholder analysis to senior management, to convince them to mandate doing it correctly and early enough in the project. Facing this reality, PMs must make the time in their busy schedules to conduct stakeholder analysis. In summary, the stakeholder analysis can help the PM gain sufficient knowledge to detect stakeholders' needs, develop a strategy to manage their expectations, anticipate their responses to various situations, and prevent potential misunderstandings of and opposition to the project.

STAKEHOLDER ENGAGEMENT AND EXPECTATIONS MANAGEMENT

The stakeholder analysis involves gathering information about the stakeholders and making sense of this information. It is now clear that each stakeholder will have a unique combination of significance, interest, impact, longevity, and relevance in relation to the project. With that knowledge, it is time to plan for stakeholder management and engagement. While related to communication planning, it is not yet the communications plan, as the communications plan is tactical, dealing with the day-to-day aspects of the project. Rather, it is about the strategy and concepts that will shape the communications plan to make it effective, relevant, and appropriate. Effective stakeholder management supports the project by helping us understand both internal and external environments and enabling us to respond, influence, and initiate actions accordingly. It improves our ability to maintain a consistent approach and sensitivities to specific stakeholders' needs and to policies, procedures, and issues, taking both stakeholders' interests and project needs into account.

For effective stakeholder engagement, the purpose and goals of the engagement need to be determined first—which includes who needs to be engaged and how to do it—taking into consideration all of the associated risks. Figure 4.10 provides a list of considerations for engagement planning and setup. These concepts serve as a set of guidelines for how to plan the process of managing the stakeholders and from there, Chapter 11 specifies the details of a communications plan.

How to Engage

The process of conducting stakeholder engagement can be broken down into three elements:

1. Inform: there is a need to keep stakeholders informed by providing them with objective, consistent, accurate, and appropriate information.

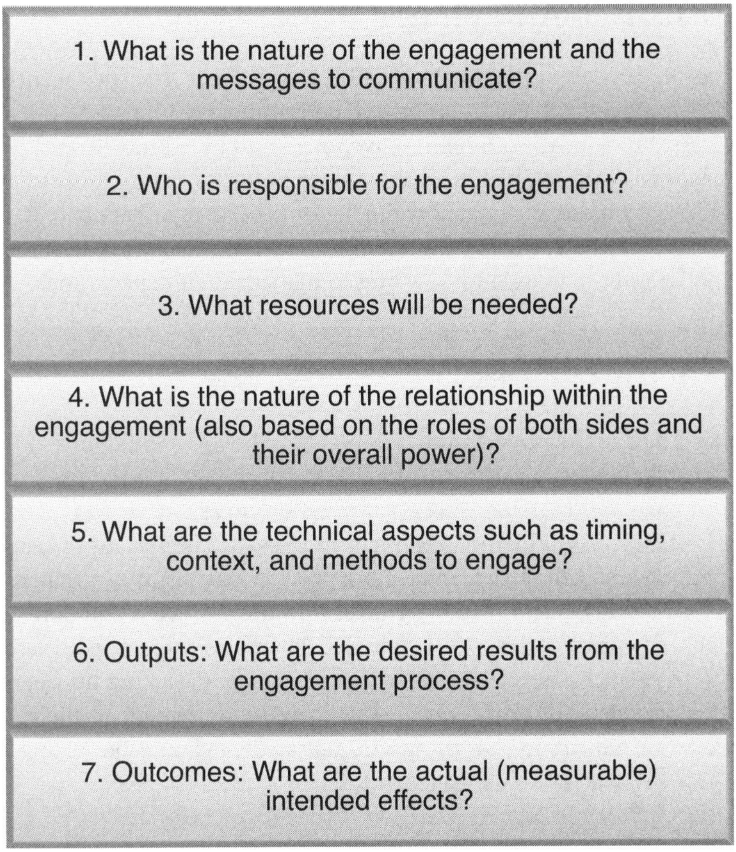

1. What is the nature of the engagement and the messages to communicate?

2. Who is responsible for the engagement?

3. What resources will be needed?

4. What is the nature of the relationship within the engagement (also based on the roles of both sides and their overall power)?

5. What are the technical aspects such as timing, context, and methods to engage?

6. Outputs: What are the desired results from the engagement process?

7. Outcomes: What are the actual (measurable) intended effects?

Figure 4.10 Considerations for engagement planning and setup

"Appropriate" refers to making sure that each stakeholder gets the necessary information—no less and especially, no more. Giving stakeholders more information than needed will lead to distractions and misunderstandings.

2. Work with them: work together with stakeholders to exchange feedback and to ensure needs and concerns are understood and taken into consideration by both sides.

3. Collaborate and energize: create working partnerships with stakeholders for decision making and process improvements. This includes providing advice to each other, considering each other's point of view, and seeking win-win solutions.

To make the relationship with the stakeholder successful, these elements need to be reciprocal, objective, responsive, open, and trusting.

STAKEHOLDER MANAGEMENT PLAN

There is no single process that works for all circumstances. The specific needs of the project, stakeholders, and the situation will determine the full nature of the engagement process, but with the guidelines given here and by asking "what," "who," and "how" questions, PMs can better organize their thoughts around how to perform a meaningful stakeholder analysis, how much rigor they need to apply to it, and what information they need to focus on in order to understand stakeholders, their needs, their potential impact areas, and how best to manage their expectations.

EVALUATE THE PROCESS

At a certain point in the project (and not too late), the PM should look at the objectives of the stakeholder engagement process to check whether the process delivers its intended goals. For that, there are a few questions to ask in an attempt to measure the success of our stakeholder management process. It is important to keep in mind that an ineffective stakeholder management process may result in strained relationships, performance issues, or—in extreme cases—outright project failure. However, even though the project may still produce deliverables as planned, there may be issues with the stakeholders that need to be addressed. Checking how effective the stakeholder management process is may uncover hidden issues in the project and may serve as an indication that things are not as they should be. Figure 4.11 lists questions for the stakeholder engagement review.

STAKEHOLDER EXPECTATIONS MANAGEMENT FINAL THOUGHTS

Stakeholder analysis and management serves as one of the most crucial underlying factors of project success. It shapes the PM's ability to know what is really going on with the project and with those involved. It acts as the foundation for other key activities, from communications planning to defining and articulating project objectives.

There are many more tools, techniques, templates, concepts, and ideas that can help us identify, analyze, engage, and manage the stakeholders. It is not about quantity, but rather quality: perform the process efficiently and effectively so it yields the desired results without an excessive burden on the team's resources. This chapter has provided insights and ideas about what to pay attention to in order to perform a stakeholder analysis that is meaningful and serves as a foundation to confidently proceed with doing the right thing and deliver success.

1. Is there a better understanding of the issues at stake?

2. Has communication been improved?

3. Are the relationships with the stakeholders developing toward long-lasting relationships based on trust?

4. Is risk being managed more effectively?

5. Is there a sense of common purpose?

6. Is there an atmosphere of collaboration?

7. Is the decision-making process aligned with project objectives and stakeholders' needs?

8. Is there a mechanism for early detection of roadblocks and problems that result in proactive handling of these issues?

Figure 4.11 Stakeholder engagement review questions

REFERENCES

1. Project Management Institute, *A Guide to the Project Management Body of Knowledge, (PMBOK® Guide—Fifth Edition)*, 394.
2. Partially based on *A Guide to the Project Management Body of Knowledge (PMBOK® Guide—Fifth Edition)*, pp. 395–397, PMI, Project Stakeholder Management Knowledge Area, stakeholder assessment grid.
3. *A Guide to the Project Management Body of Knowledge (PMBOK® Guide—Fifth Edition)*, pp. 395–397, 402–403, PMI, Stakeholder Analysis.

5

Connecting Success and Constraints

Touchless taps, soap dispensers, and hand driers have become increasingly more common and appear in growing numbers of public washrooms, airports, and workplaces. The idea behind these devices is to deliver benefits related to convenience, health, and hygiene (touch-free), as well as savings (using fewer paper towels and less water is better for the environment and cheaper for property management). They are supposed to be great, so why is it that most of us roll our eyes upwards and sigh when we think about them? Mainly because these gadgets do not quite work the way they should.

This is an example of the importance of properly defining success criteria and of considering what success looks like in the eyes of the various stakeholders. Let's take a look at why users of facilities equipped with these devices may not be completely satisfied with the results:

- The tap: water does not flow from the tap until we maneuver ourselves to create enough motion (sometimes jump up and down) so the tap senses our presence.
- Automatic soap dispenser: it is often too sensitive; while we try to get the water flowing, it keeps dispensing soap into the sink. Sometimes it is located too close to the tap, making the soap continuously hit our hands while we're trying to rinse. The excess soap builds up in the sink and can potentially damage it.
- The tap's position: often it is too short and located too far to the back, forcing our hands to rub against the back of the sink.
- Hand dryer: many do not produce enough wind and heat, prolonging the drying process, or they require us to fit our hands into a tight slot, forcing anyone with palms larger than a child's to touch the edges of the machine.

The design of many taps is primarily for easy installation and the needs of the people who actually use them are of secondary priority.

Image 5.1   The tap

The Dyson Airblade® hand dryer (on the left) and the World Dryer® Model A (right):
These models are typically very good, which comes to illustrate that
some dryers force the hands to touch their edges and others
do not blow enough air.

Image 5.2   Electric hand dryers

Figure 5.1 reviews the potential benefits of these devices and identifies which ones are realized and by whom.

What about the stakeholders' success criteria?

- The installer (representing project success): as long as the installation conforms to the requirements and is on budget and on time (with minimal interruption), it is considered a success. Quite often, operational issues and risks are not addressed by the project manager (PM). Success.
- Property management: good public relations concerning environmental benefits (less paper towels used), but no significant savings. Partial success.
- Users: the process of washing our hands after using the bathroom takes longer and is more frustrating than it should be. This extra time is marginal, but it serves as yet another non-value-adding item that contributes to productivity loss. Not a success.

DEFINING SUCCESS THROUGH CONSTRAINTS

Many PMs believe they know what they are to achieve on the project, but are unable to articulate the project success criteria when asked. There are also PMs who do not fully think through what success means. They do not take the time or get a chance to

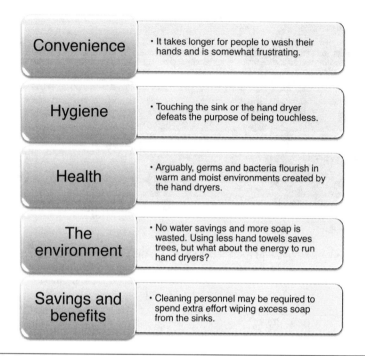

Figure 5.1 Benefits

articulate it. No one provides them with a clear list of success criteria, and at times, they are unsure whose success they're trying to deliver. This in no way implies that PMs do not perform their jobs properly. However, many PMs find themselves hard-pressed to manage projects with no opportunity to define success because of various driving forces, including: pressure to move ahead with the project, time constraints, and short-term thinking throughout the organization.

Constraints

When we are asked to define success, a common answer is: "deliver it on time and on budget." Sometimes the answer is accompanied by adjectives and descriptors, such as: "do the right thing," "make my boss happy," or "solve the problem;" but most PMs do not have a sufficient understanding of what "happy" really means. The challenge in defining success starts with the project constraints: a constraint is something that limits the project, the organization, or its team and serves as a bottleneck. It could be related to capacity, processes, speed, resources, facilities, and other operational aspects, which may impact the project team's ability to satisfy the customer's needs. Constraints are also requirements that are part of a contract, as the team needs to perform and adhere to them, and include: specifications, time-lines, budgets, performance levels, service levels, and standards.

Project success is partially defined through its constraints: scope and functionality, time, cost, and various attributes of quality—such as standards, performance level, and accuracy. These are the most quantifiable success criteria and can be fairly easily tracked and measured, if they are defined up-front and set to a baseline prior to execution. There are other success criteria that may be more challenging to track and measure, such as: customer satisfaction, rate of improvement, perceptions, value adds, future business, and relationships.

THE TRIPLE CONSTRAINT/COMPETING DEMANDS

The concept of the triple constraint in project management describes the interdependency between three main project constraints and measures of success: scope, time, and cost. The term *competing demands* enhances the triple constraint by adding resources, risks, and quality to the trade-off formula. Project success is achieved by balancing these items, which compete with each other for prioritization.

In an attempt to make the customer happy, many PMs try to exceed the customer's expectations. This is often referred to as "gold plating" and has been generally proven to not work. No stakeholder will agree to pay for unrequested extras that may not add value, may not work properly, and may eventually compromise the relationship with the customer due to mismanaged expectations. In order to define and deliver success, PMs simply need to set expectations and meet them, since an attempt to exceed expectations may be deemed too expensive and unjustified. For example, the project team may not know whether the customer is interested in paying extra for early delivery; it is the customer's decision; and if the team does not have a mandate for it, it should not be done.

It is important that the PM understands the trade-off relationship among the competing demands and ensures that stakeholders do as well. This means that not all of the constraints within the competing demands can be met as intended and concessions need to be made to ensure that the more important constraints are delivered as planned. For example, the PM needs to be able to react to schedule slippage, requests for additional functionality, and changes to resource pools or market conditions. This should be done by finding room in one area and using it to accommodate the changing needs in another based on the sponsor's and customer's mandates and priorities.

THE CONSTRAINTS FACE-OFF

Before trying to identify and articulate project success, PMs should conduct a stakeholder analysis, since they need to know whose interests they need to look after or who defines the project success and to what extent and priority. It is safe to say that most stakeholders involved in a project (internal or external) want it to succeed and do not wake up in the morning with the thought: "Today I am going to ruin someone's day." However, there are some exceptions to this rule, since there are stakeholders who have different ideas about what success is or how to achieve it.

Beyond defining whose success has to be delivered, there is also a need to figure out which aspects of success are more important than others. This can be done by asking the following questions:

- Is delivering the full scope more important than any of the following: delivering the project on budget, on time, or to specifications?
- Is delivering the project on time more important than doing it within budget or in compliance with all quality standards?
- Is delivering the project on budget more important than meeting all quality standards?

There are no easy answers to these questions, and PMs often find it challenging to determine whether one success criterion is more important than another, especially in cases where the stakeholders themselves are unable to define success criteria. Additional challenges regarding the definition of success criteria arise from changes that may take place throughout the project lifecycle. For example, when organizational priorities shift from focus on cost-savings to a need for faster time to market, the trade-offs of the project constraints may change.

The journey toward better articulating project success starts by identifying the most important constraint for the sponsor. During the project delivery, the team will channel its efforts to ensure that this constraint is delivered as intended; when there is a conflict between constraints, the one critical to success should get the right of way. In most projects, there is more than one top constraint, but PMs must not fall into the trap of deeming them all equally important, since this is almost equivalent to having no success criteria at all. Furthermore, when different high profile, influential stakeholders have different views of which constraint is more important for success, no matter what the PM does to satisfy the needs of one stakeholder, it will not satisfy the needs of others.

In an attempt to figure out priority among project constraints, different points of view must be taken into account until the PM is able to articulate and specify one or two constraints that are more important than the others. To achieve this, the PM needs to engage the high profile stakeholders for their input and conduct a face-off of the constraints against each other in a constraints face-off matrix (CFM), illustrated in Figure 5.2. While not a scientific measure of success criteria, it is an attempt to identify one or two constraints that are more important than the others to pursue.

The CFM can assist the PM in the effort to figure out which one, two, or even three constraints are more important to pursue as part of the success criteria. The

	Scope	Time	Cost	Quality
Scope	X	?	?	?
Time	X	X	?	?
Cost	X	X	X	?

Figure 5.2   Constraints face-off matrix (CFM)

analysis pits scope, time, cost, and quality against each other to determine which will prevail over all others when there are tough choices that need to be made.

This matrix needs to reflect the top stakeholders' (i.e., sponsors, customers) needs as accurately as possible. The only error that can be made is to fail to identify the actual needs of the stakeholders, or neglect to classify the focal constraints for success. Once there is an understanding of which constraints are more important, the PM can, with a high level of confidence, deliver success on the ones identified. The price for accommodating these key constraints will be paid by other constraints. For example, if the sponsor wants the project delivered on budget and on time, which is possible, the price to achieve this will likely be reducing the scope and compromising some aspects of quality (similar to the hands-free washroom).

THE BALLOON

Constraint trade-offs are often presented using a triangle to represent the competing demands, as illustrated in Figure 5.3. A triangle display has an inherent problem: the triangle will always have three sides and as a result, appears inflexible and gives the wrong impression—that pursuing more of one constraint will come at no cost to other constraints. There is, however, a better way to illustrate the way the constraints trade-offs works—with a balloon, as displayed in Figure 5.4.

The balloon is a good way to articulate to the sponsor and the customer that anything they ask for will come at a price and result in consequences that impact other success criteria. Moreover, which constraint(s) it may impact and to what extent may be difficult to anticipate.

The constraints balloon is an intuitive way to show stakeholders that when they want more of something, it will have to be paid for and offset by something else in the project, in a way similar to the law of physics that every action will have a virtually equal and opposite reaction. When you press on a balloon in one spot,

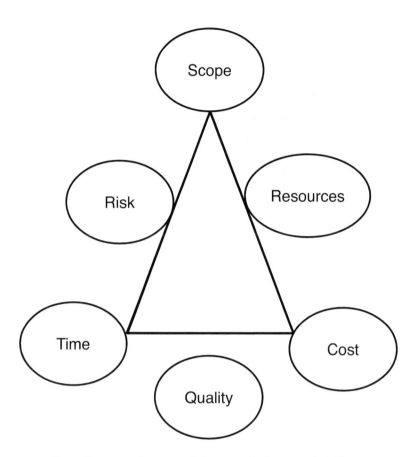

Competing demands, previously known as the triple constraint (scope, time, and cost). The triangle display is flawed since it lacks the visual ability to demonstrate the flexibility in the trade-off.

Figure 5.3 Project objectives triangle

it will bulge in a different spot: where and how much remains to be seen, but it is guaranteed to bulge. By understanding the trade-offs, the success criteria, and the stakes associated with each choice made, the PM must figure out where the impact is likely to be felt and to what extent. When pressing on one or two spots, the balloon bulges and inflates in the areas not pressed; however, when pressing too much and on too many spots, the balloon is left with no areas to give and will simply pop. This illustrates where many projects end up: by pressing on too many constraints without the ability to offset them, projects fail.

When stakeholders insist on meeting all success criteria (on time, on budget, full functionality, and to all specifications), it is equivalent to pressing on the balloon from all sides, and it will inevitably blow up. The balloon example can help

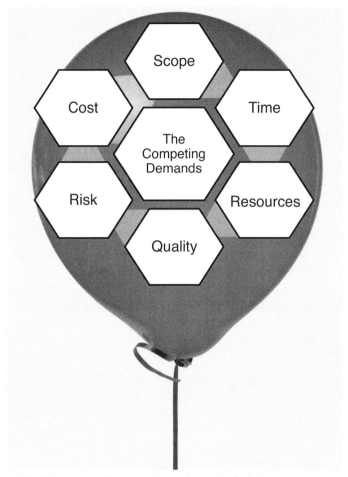

The Balloon: a good way to articulate the trade-off relations among the constraints.

Figure 5.4   The Balloon

stakeholders grasp the value of the trade-off and see that an attempt to deliver on one constraint's success may not be worth the resulting trade-off. The balloon example can also help demonstrate that the impact is usually not confined to only one aspect and often ends up being greater and more extensive than originally anticipated.

For example, if at some point during the week the project team realizes it cannot meet a looming Friday deadline, there are a few possible options to take, and each presents a set of potential consequences. The options are listed in Figure 5.5.

Possible options:

1. Work longer hours with the existing resources

2. Add resources

3. Reduce testing duration or compromise other quality aspects

4. Contact the customer and discuss a scope reduction

5. Propose a phased approach

6. Ask the customer for an extension

7. Call off the project

Figure 5.5 Possible options

Even if there is a decision to make a genuine effort to deliver on time by adding resources, reducing functionality, paying overtime, and reducing testing, there is still no guarantee that the team will meet the original deadline. In such a case—where success criteria are compromised and trade-offs are made as part of a failed attempt to meet the schedule—the team and the stakeholders should verify which constraints are more important to meet and whether the actions taken are aligned with the project objectives.

So, What Can Happen With the Trade-Offs?

While PMs recognize that the project constraints are governed by the laws of physics, senior stakeholders tend to have difficulty grasping this and as a result, often expect PMs to get things done without trade-offs. To simplify the link to the laws of physics, PMs should explain to stakeholders that there is a set of three considerations in place, regardless of the project environment or the desires of those involved:

1. The competing constraints will always balance each other: trying to get more from one will require something else to give.
2. An attempt to balance the constraints may not always be successful (as illustrated in the example of the looming Friday deadline).

3. Any imbalance among the constraints, and any failure to balance them according to the project's objectives, will have an impact on quality, benefits, and the perceived value of the product for the customer. Quality will be discussed in Chapter 9 and is demonstrated in Figure 5.6.

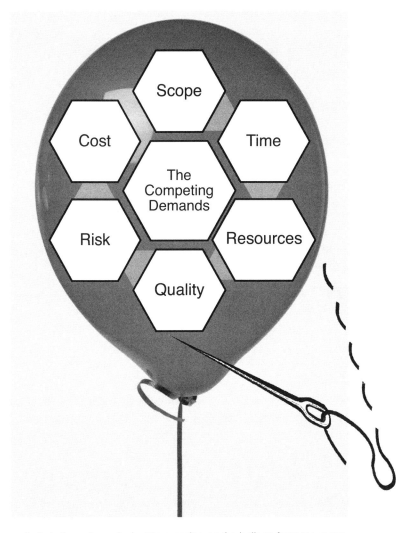

An imbalance is equivalent to pressing on the balloon from too many sides. As a result it will blow up and it virtually guarantees a negative impact on quality.

Figure 5.6   What can happen to a balloon

SETTING EXPECTATIONS

Identifying project success criteria is a critical step in setting and managing stakeholders' expectations. At times, expectation management may become so important that it becomes a contributor to project success. For example, one project may be considered a success, despite failing to deliver on some of its constraints, but another project may meet most of its constraints and still be deemed a failure. Managing stakeholders' expectations starts by identifying the (often two) most important constraints and confirming them with the sponsor, so that the team can focus on what's really important in the project. When engaging the stakeholders in defining success, PMs may feel pressure to make promises and commitments that are not based on the team's ability to deliver but solely on the stakeholders' wants and needs.

In order to set the right expectations, it is important for PMs to stand strong and not make any unrealistic commitments. PMs who cave under pressure and set unrealistic expectations will ultimately be accountable for the failure and be blamed. When the sponsor or the customer presses for time, budget, or any other commitments on constraints, the PM has three primary options:

1. Say "yes:" There are many situations in which PMs will agree to success criteria, constraints, or commitments without being able to deliver them:

   a. As an attempt to be popular (even though project management is not a popularity contest);

   b. As an attempt to hang onto the role of PM;

   c. To build relationships or a reputation;

   d. As a result of failing to understand what the success criteria are.

   PMs should only say yes to the things they can deliver. One strong indication of a PM's experience is an ability to say no in situations that warrant it (and keep his/her job).

2. Say "no:" When PMs realize they cannot keep the stakeholders happy just by saying yes, they resort to saying no. More often than not, PMs know up-front that certain success criteria cannot be delivered under the existing conditions, although being able to tell the sponsor or the customer this requires a rare combination of courage, credibility, and a solid relationship. Without these conditions in place, refusal may result in the removal of the PM from the project in search of someone who will agree. No one likes a "naysayer," and nobody wants to be one. Unfortunately, stakeholders tend to take it personally and instead of realizing that PMs try to protect their projects, they perceive the PM as the problem. However, replacing the PM will not change the fact that certain constraints cannot be achieved as they are.

3. Say "yes, but:" This is the best option, since it virtually defuses the situation and takes the personal aspect out of the equation. By saying "yes," PMs

position themselves on the same side as the stakeholders involved and not as a threat to the deliverables. By saying "but," "and," or anything else that qualifies the "yes," the PM sets expectations regarding what can be done and specifies the conditions to do it. In addition, it sets the groundwork for making assumptions and specifying the required conditions for success. If there is still a gap in expectations, the PM should urge stakeholders to settle their differences and work toward getting on the same page.

Gaps in Expectations

The PM should have a clear idea of which stakeholders' needs are more important to attend to and deliver value to these stakeholders, manage their expectations, and keep them satisfied. Understanding the stakeholders' needs is a tedious task that needs to take place early in the project, but there are plenty of opportunities to demonstrate what happens when stakeholders' needs are overlooked or when there are differences among stakeholders about their understanding of success. Examples are displayed in Figure 5.7.

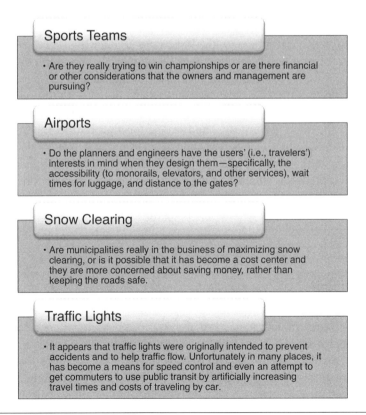

Sports Teams

- Are they really trying to win championships or are there financial or other considerations that the owners and management are pursuing?

Airports

- Do the planners and engineers have the users' (i.e., travelers') interests in mind when they design them—specifically, the accessibility (to monorails, elevators, and other services), wait times for luggage, and distance to the gates?

Snow Clearing

- Are municipalities really in the business of maximizing snow clearing, or is it possible that it has become a cost center and they are more concerned about saving money, rather than keeping the roads safe.

Traffic Lights

- It appears that traffic lights were originally intended to prevent accidents and to help traffic flow. Unfortunately in many places, it has become a means for speed control and even an attempt to get commuters to use public transit by artificially increasing travel times and costs of traveling by car.

Figure 5.7   Success criteria expectation gaps

The list could go on and on, but—when there is a gap between how stakeholders understand success—it is easy to find unhappy users, who are not getting what they need from the product or service they are using.

SUCCESS ACCEPTANCE AND APPROVAL

Regardless of whether stakeholders clearly define the success criteria, the onus is on the PM to pursue that information and have an understanding of what success is and how it is going to be measured. However, beyond defining and articulating success, there are two more things that can help with the delivery of that elusive success: acceptance criteria and approval criteria.

Acceptance Criteria

Acceptance criteria can be understood as the technical aspect of success. For example, during a product release meeting, the customer's representatives refuse to accept the new product release because there are too many defects for their taste. An attempt to push back and say there are only five high-priority defects backfires, since the customer's team toughens up, saying five is too many. There is no real comeback to such a claim because the PM cannot argue with a sentiment or a feeling that the customer has. While the project team may not agree with the customer's view, there is no way to question the legitimacy of the customer's claim.

The lesson to learn from such experiences is to define with the customer what constitutes a defect, then rank and categorize the defects (i.e., low, medium, high, and critical, and what each means) and decide together on the number of defects from each category that will be accepted. For example, if five "high" defects are allowed, then both sides are clear and will not argue about whether a product should be accepted. It is similar to creating a grading scheme breakdown at school, which leaves no room for mood swings or subjective judgment. In essence, this process quantifies the success criteria, saving time and aggravation, and allows both sides to focus on making better products and improving the relationship, instead of arguing about how many defects should be allowed in the product.

Approval Criteria

While seemingly simple and straightforward, too often it is unclear which stakeholder is in charge of acceptance and approval of the various aspects and deliverables of the project. When the need arises for sign-offs and decisions, it is not the time to scramble to figure out who to look for. This information should already be determined during the stakeholder analysis and clearly communicated as part of the communication plan. Knowing who is in charge of approvals and what the specific criteria are for approval can help reduce misunderstandings and set the expectations up-front for what constitutes success and acceptable performance. Unfortunately, in many projects, there is often no clear knowledge of which stakeholders have the authority to approve deliverables.

PROJECT CHARTER

The foundation for defining the project success criteria, its constraints, and its trade-offs is built through the project charter (a more elaborate discussion of the charter will take place in Chapter 7). There is no question about how important the project charter is to authorizing the project, determining the mandate, setting expectations, establishing context, and indicating the authority of the PM. Unfortunately, many stakeholders—as well as PMs—do not sufficiently value its importance, or even misuse the charter altogether. Beyond the traditional elements the charter covers, the PM can use it to help overcome misunderstandings, misalignments, cultural gaps, and adversity.

As a foundation and as a mandate, the charter should be written by the sponsor (but more often it is the PM, together with the sponsor's input) and kept clear and concise (one to three pages). Mark Twain's adage, "If I had more time I would write a shorter letter," illustrates the importance of keeping it brief and the challenge associated with ensuring it contains quality information that—ideally—captures the full story of what the project is about at the high level. Too many projects start their journey with so-called charters, which extend from 5–100 pages. These are more likely plans than charters, but the inability of the sponsors/PMs to articulate the idea of the project within a couple of pages indicates that these projects are not off to a promising start.

The charter provides a set of organizational and project goals and objectives, assumptions, constraints, and high-level success criteria, which serve as a starting point for elaborating, planning, and delivering success and value. Success is put in context for both the organization and the project; by ensuring it captures the essence of the business case, the charter serves as the source for defining what the team will pursue. Throughout the project, as things change—timelines move and commitments adjust—the charter can serve as a point of reference for ensuring that the project is still on track to deliver value. If concise, it can be viewed as the vision and mission statements for the project.

In the likely event that the PM does not have sufficient information to address all aspects of the charter, there is a need to make assumptions and ensure that the gaps are dealt with at a certain point. The assumptions essentially protect the project from stalling due to missing information and help provide the decision makers with options that, even if not correct, will put things into context and trigger feedback, which will help them articulate a valid set of success criteria. Having no charter, a long charter, or an unclear one may build a false sense of security, suggesting that the project has a guiding foundation in place when it does not.

BEYOND SCOPE, TIME, AND COST

So far, the success criteria information in this chapter has dealt with traditional measures of success and provided insights into how to properly define and measure them. There are, however, additional considerations for measuring overall project success, in the form of ensuring project alignment with the business drivers and organizational objectives. While these are not under the control or authority of the PM, the onus is on the PM to ensure that they are looked after. This can be done by alerting the sponsor and the customer, establishing assumptions, and updating the risk register. Failing to do so may lead to delivering success criteria that are not aligned with the organizational needs, adding no value to the business whatsoever.

An argument may rage around why it is the job of the PM to ensure project alignment to organizational objectives and not the organization's senior management or the sponsor; but at the end of the day, if the project fails to deliver value, fingers will point at the PM. It is wise, therefore, to manage the project in accordance with its environment and take the initiative to check whether the project is heading in the right direction. Increasingly, it is not sufficient to careen toward short-term project success, and—with the intention of producing a more sustainable set of outcomes and benefits—PMs need to consider the true impact of the project on the organization.

With no clear set of priorities for success, team members may spend too much time and effort on non-value-adding activities, while neglecting to pursue what they really should. This may lead to inferior results, the need to potentially undo and redo work, and in turn, frustration, strained relationships, and losses. A prioritization scheme can be put together using a set of numbered rankings or the allocation of a pool of points for all the success factors and business goals (awarding more important criteria with more points). It can be enhanced by creating a table, as illustrated in Table 5.1.

The table can be both a guide and a benchmark, asking the appropriate stakeholders to verify that the project is going in the right direction and that the team

Table 5.1 Success criteria table

Success Criteria	Stakeholder Associated	Related Business Objectives	Measurements	Priority	Timelines	Dependencies

has not overlooked or focused too much on any important business drivers or organizational objectives. Discrepancies between this table and previous assessments of the success criteria should serve as a red flag and be brought to the attention of the sponsor. It is important to note that the PM does not define or determine the measures of success but rather, reflects and articulates them. If the PM has difficulty providing a realistic read on the project success criteria, it may be due to unclear or non-transparent measures and serve as an area of concern, since it may impair the project's ability to deliver the intended value.

SUCCESS FACTORS

Let's start the process of creating a meaningful set of success criteria by defining three layers of success:

1. Project objectives: these relate to scope, time, cost, perceived quality, and project deliverables and outputs.
2. Business objectives: these refer to the product, the value it produces or adds to the organization, the overall project outcomes (beyond deliverables), and realized (or to be realized) benefits to the customer and the user.
3. Project organization: this is about the process of delivering and executing the project, the performance of the project team, how conflicts are handled, the lessons learned, and asking whether the team and the organization are better off afterwards. It also examines whether business success and project success are in line with each other. It has been known to happen that although projects were delivered on time and budget, they did not produce the intended benefits to the customer and/or the organization.

The following example can shed light on the matter of aligning the success layers: in the midst of a project with a major bank, the IT manager informs the PM that 36 customers are going to lose their ability to transfer funds electronically into their trading accounts. Since it sounds bizarre that only 36 of nearly 18,000 customers in the project are going to be impacted, further investigation ensues, revealing that everyone will be impacted and the 36 will notice immediately. When the PM tries to push back on the issue, the IT manager clarifies that this is the only way to implement the solution because of system constraints. Luckily, the PM does not find it acceptable to have such a service interruption and insists on ensuring that no customer is impacted by it, despite the additional cost, time, and effort required.

In the short term, the project has to take a hit, but it is the right thing to do for the long term. The PM ensures that the overall benefits are realized, despite being unpopular, and does not allow technical considerations to compromise the service level provided to customers. As a result, the project finishes late and over budget (a form of project failure—layer 1, project objectives) but delivers on its objectives (success in terms of layer 2, business objectives). It is also a partial success in terms of layer 3, project organization, since the project delivers value to the organization. Failure to do this would likely have negative long term impacts on the organization, its reputation, and the relationship with its customer(s).

The PM could have taken the easier road and listened to the advice of the IT manager, but the project would not have met its original success criteria. By the time stakeholders would have realized something was wrong, the PM would have finished the project—with a promotion or a bonus. Project management is not a popularity contest, and at times there is a need to make tough decisions and insist upon unpopular routes. It also involves engaging the appropriate stakeholders for support and buy-in for actions that go beyond the short-term thinking that plagues most organizations.

ENHANCE THE MEASUREMENTS

The journey toward properly defining success beyond the traditional short-term view of scope, time, cost, and a vague sense of quality (to be addressed below) continues by creating variable criteria to measure degrees of success. For example, there are aspects of functionality that if missed, will mean the project cannot deliver value altogether, whereas other scope items may not compromise project value at all. There are questions, as displayed in Figure 5.8, that if answered, can give a clearer picture of what overall project success is about.

The next step in refining the definition and measurements of project success is to break success into parts that can be measured separately. These measurements help ensure there is no gap between the project's success and the value it delivers to the organization. Project success can be measured in two different ways: by **team and process success**, measuring the level of commitment team members demonstrated, and by **organizational success**.

It is easy to find examples of projects that look like colossal failures from the project management perspective but turn out to be quite successful in terms of the benefits they deliver. Some examples that stand out include:

1. The "Big Dig" in Boston:[1] the most expensive underground highway network in the U.S. was plagued by escalating costs, scheduling overruns, leaks, design flaws, and charges of poor execution and use of substandard materials. It was completed in 2007, almost a decade behind schedule. The cost ballooned to $22 billion—almost four times the original inflation-adjusted estimates—and the related interest charges will not be paid off until 2038.

2. The Sydney Opera House:[2] it was formally completed in 1973, having cost $102 million. The original cost estimate in 1957 was $7 million, with a

1	Have we created the right thing?
2	Are customer needs met? Even if not all needs are met, does it matter?
3	Which needs are not addressed?
4	How far are we from addressing the customer's needs?
5	Are we missing functionality? Even if not all functionality is delivered, does it matter to the client?
6	Are the deliverables accepted by both the sponsor/customer and users?
7	What is the overall cost of the project, including bug fixes, warranties and other subsequent costs as a result of not delivering the original functionality?
8	Is the final cost aligned with the target budget?
9	If not, what caused the cost overrun? How far is the final cost from the original baseline budget?
10	Was the project completed on time?
11	If not on time, how late were we? Did it matter that we were late?
12	If we failed to deliver on any of the competing demands, was it critical? How was it addressed? Which other aspect paid for it?

Figure 5.8   Enhance the measurements

Looks great, but almost 1,500% over budget

Image 5.3   Sydney Opera House

completion date set by the government of January 26, 1963. The project was completed ten years late and was nearly 15 times over budget.

Project Failures

With an improved ability to properly measure project success, the team can address and overcome many common causes of project failures. Performing the activities described in Figure 5.9 will clarify the criteria for success, which will increase acceptance and approval rates.

LET'S PUT IT IN ORDER

There are many views and ideas of success: for life, career, entertainment, sports, politics, consumer products, and overall happiness. The same goes for projects: each stakeholder has a different view of success (and how to achieve it), and one of

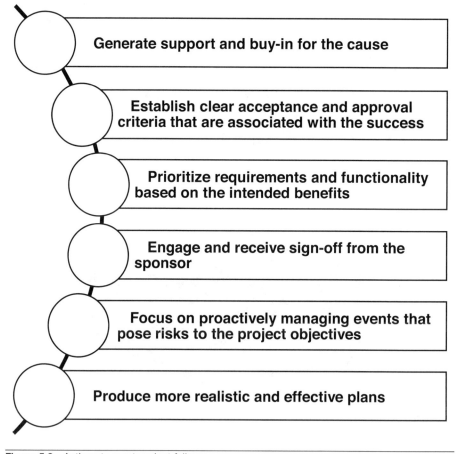

Figure 5.9 Actions to avert project failures

the PM's main tasks is to manage those expectations. With the customer and the sponsor as the most influential and important stakeholders, the success criteria should be aligned with and reflect their needs, while taking into account the business drivers and organizational objectives. As project management methodologies and approaches mature, they evolve from the old focus on scope, time, and cost, to incorporating quality and aligning with stakeholders' needs and expectations.

FINAL THOUGHTS ABOUT QUALITY AND SUCCESS

The final word about improving the ability to define project success criteria speaks to quality. Most PMs have a hard time defining quality, despite it being one of the most critical aspects of success. PMs with time on their hands can break down project quality into a few measureable items that will help define and articulate project success. With the ability to measure the following items, it will be easier to evaluate overall project success from the organization, business drivers, and customer points of view:

- Customer satisfaction: Have a benchmark of project success and break it down into product satisfaction and project process/performance satisfaction.
- Utility: The product needs to work for the users.
- Alignment: Verify that both the customer and the organization view the outcome of the project as a success.
- Defects, changes, and accuracy: This is a common way to measure quality and can be evaluated over time to identify trends in the number of defects and changes that occurred during the project, as compared to the number of requirements.
- In the long term, additional measures and quality attributes may need to be considered, including: maintainability, affordability, flexibility, operability, and reliability.

In conclusion, the task of defining project success criteria can be elusive and confusing, since the project stakeholders are not always clear about what constitutes success. One way to ensure that success is defined properly is to link it with the project constraints and ensure that it is aligned with the needs of the project sponsor and the customer, who are ultimately the stakeholders who sign-off on the project.

REFERENCES

1. Murphy, Sean P., "Big Dig needs $54m light fix," in *The Boston Globe*, on-line at: http://www.boston.com/news/local/massachusetts/articles/2012/04/05/big_dig_tunnels_need_54m_light_replacement_mass_officials_say/ (April 5, 2012).
2. On-line at: http://www.sydneyoperahouse.com/about/house_history_landing.aspx.

6

Assumptions: The Project Manager's Best Friends

Most people don't like assumptions, viewing them as a representation of insufficient planning to make up for a lack of knowledge or laziness. We also have a hard time handling assumptions—we fail to realize that assumptions will change, and we neglect to track them and follow up on their status. Many valid, yet difficult questions come to mind when thinking about assumptions, including the following:

- How to come up with assumptions?
- How to record and document them?
- How to manage and track them?
- What happens if an event occurs that does not conform to the assumption made about it?
- How can a project manager position the idea that assumptions are an important part of planning, so that senior management supports the need to manage assumptions—and remain cognizant of the ongoing need to manage and review assumptions throughout the project?

- How to utilize the assumptions to the benefit of the project, rather than view them as a detriment?
- How to make the assumptions an important part of the risk management process?

WHAT IS AN ASSUMPTION?

Assumptions are "something taken for granted" and "accepted cause and effect relationships, or estimates of the existence of a fact from the known existence of other fact(s)."[1] With this definition comes a word of caution that while assumptions provide a foundation for understanding certain situations, they must go through a thorough examination process before being accepted as reality. Assumptions[2] are conditions, things, and premises we believe to be true, but they offer no confirmation that they will remain the same as they were upon discovery. Assumptions are statements about beliefs related to future events and their outcomes. When considering assumptions, the project manager (PM) wants to keep the project constraints in mind because, under certain conditions, the constraints will limit the project's planned performance.

Assumptions are associated with risks because, in certain situations, they may change from the time we initially plan for them and ultimately pose a threat to the project objectives. As such, a higher number of assumptions indicates an elevated level of project risk. With that said, having a low number of assumptions recorded may not necessarily be a sign of less risk in the project; rather, the project team may have failed to properly record and track the assumptions. This may give the team a false sense of security, thinking they know what they are up against and the project has a low level of risk. Reasons for identifying and managing assumptions are listed in Figure 6.1.

SPECIFY AND RECORD ASSUMPTIONS

Considering how damaging it may be when assumptions are not documented and taken into consideration, it is surprising that many PMs do not give enough attention to doing it properly, or even to doing it at all. As a result, PMs often operate under a premise that may be quite different than the actual project conditions, and they may build plans that turn out to be unrealistic. For example, when people are asked to attend a meeting in one hour, and the meeting is located a one-hour car ride away, they often respond with a "yes"—although, instead of giving an outright yes, they should attach to it a set of conditions or stipulations (a.k.a., assumptions), over which they have little or no control, as listed in Figure 6.2.

1	Ensure that assumptions do not conflict with each other.
2	Provide context and means to record assumptions and identify where they come from.
3	Establish a process for managing assumptions and controlling them downstream.
4	Define follow up or target validation dates for each assumption.
5	Evaluate the level of confidence the team has regarding each assumption.
6	Measure the stability of the assumption's impact on the project's progress and success.

Figure 6.1   Why manage and identify assumptions?

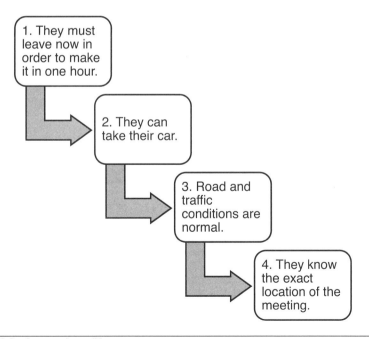

1. They must leave now in order to make it in one hour.

2. They can take their car.

3. Road and traffic conditions are normal.

4. They know the exact location of the meeting.

Figure 6.2   Assumed conditions

It may appear that these things should go without saying, but if any of these conditions are not in place, attendees will not be able to make it to their destination on time.

When PMs know who is going to perform a task, the skills and experience levels of the resources, and the task details (i.e., timelines, risks), it is easier to commit to a certain performance level, similar to the example of arriving to the meeting on time. Despite having this knowledge, there can still be performance issues and unexpected interruptions, but these are part of the inherent project risk. There are additional assumptions that are not necessary to document and manage, since under certain conditions, they may appear to be borderline ridiculous: these are obvious things, which literally go without saying once the project team knows the context of the project work and the people who are to perform it. Using the example of driving to the meeting, some of these assumptions are presented in Figure 6.3.

When there is no information about the task at stake, there may be a need to specify these assumptions, but—once the project team gains context and a basic understanding of the nature of the work and the organizational capabilities—this list becomes a set of preconditions, and its content should not be specified as assumptions. In most projects, it would not be necessary to qualify these items as assumptions, since there is already some level of knowledge and context about who is involved in the project and to what extent they can perform their work.

Why Establish Assumptions?

With the ability to distinguish between assumptions that need to be specified and those that can go without saying, PMs should focus on taking the former type of assumptions and utilizing them for more effective risk management, building

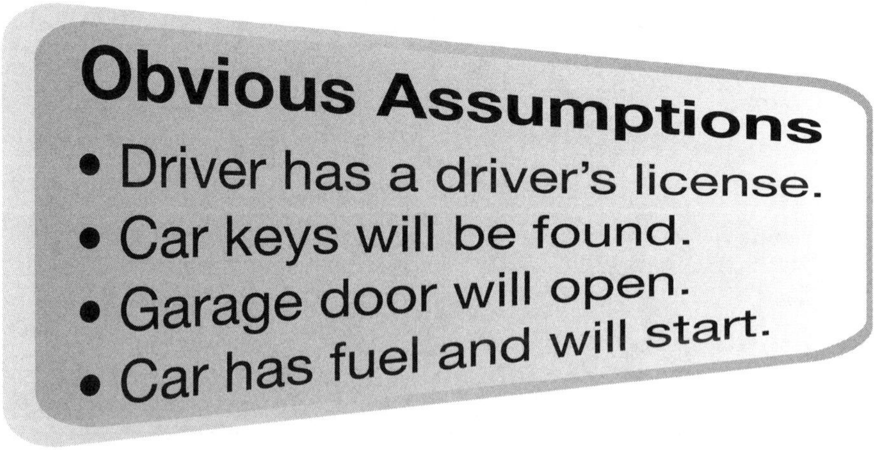

Figure 6.3 Borderline ridiculous assumptions

realistic estimates, and managing stakeholders' expectations. To do it effectively, the assumptions need to not only be defined but also analyzed and reviewed on an ongoing basis. Their status needs to be checked to determine whether stakeholders need to be alerted to potential problems. Project assumptions help define and articulate the conditions of the project environment in the absence of certainty or relevant information, and they help test the validity of plans and estimates.

WHAT MIGHT HAPPEN WITH ASSUMPTIONS

All assumptions follow a similar path throughout their lifecycles but with changing timelines and implications. At first, nothing happens with them. For example, an assumption that a vendor will deliver goods or services on time will remain an assumption until the time of the planned delivery or until there is a clear event that questions the premise of the planning. At that point, one of two things will happen:

1. The delivery is made on time and as planned (after all, somewhere in the universe there is a vendor who delivers what is needed, on time, and to specifications). If the delivery is made as planned, the assumption(s) about it are no longer valid, so they are removed from the assumptions log and business continues according to the project plan.

2. Alternately, in the event that anything does not go as planned with the delivery (e.g., the wrong product or a defective product is delivered, it is not on time, it is incomplete, or there is no delivery at all), then the assumption becomes unsupported and the project faces a risk.

This description of how assumptions may turn out and their link to project risks raises the following questions:

1. **How can the team determine when an assumption becomes a risk?** An assumption becomes a risk when it does not result in what was thought, planned, or hoped for. Therefore, assumptions need to be reviewed on a regular basis—particularly when there are signs they may not materialize as planned and are close to their "maturity" date. The assumption's maturity date refers to the date on which, or by which, a related event will take place that determines whether the assumption is valid. It can also be a date by which there is a need for additional information about the assumption in order to check its validity. Since, by definition, assumptions indicate a chance that events will not take place as planned, assumptions need to be viewed as a precursor to risk management—depending on the stakes associated with them. The extent and rigor the team should apply toward each assumption depends upon:

   a. The nature of the assumption, and how significant it is to the project;

    b. Its impact, in case events do not take place the way they should;

    c. How unlikely it is that events will take place as planned (i.e., how probable it is that the assumption is correct).

2. **What is the difference between assumptions and risk?** An assumption is a condition considered for planning purposes, around which estimates are built. If it does not take place the way it is planned to, it may turn into a risk; once its potential to become a risk is realized, the assumption should go through a risk analysis process, as covered in Chapter 8.

ASSUMPTION CATEGORIES

To make it easier to identify and deal with assumptions, they can be broken down into the following two categories:

1. Assuming something will occur (or not) and planning actions around it.
2. Learning about a condition and making assumptions (for planning purposes) about its consequences.

Breaking down the assumptions into these categories makes it easier to treat them with the appropriate level of rigor. The first category covers events that may or may not happen and helps the team come up with applicable scenarios; the second category concerns events the team knows will happen but has uncertainty about their results or impact. Although it deals with uncertainty, it stops short of being called risk management, since the result of the event may or may not favor the project.

Assuming Something Will Occur and Planning Around It

In this case, an assumption is made about something that needs to occur in a certain fashion as a condition for project success. For example, the PM commits to meeting a deadline based on the assumption that the project will have specific resources allocated to it by a certain time. Although stakeholders may make promises that the resources will be in place in time to do the work, the PM should follow a series of actions, as listed in Figure 6.4.

Making Assumptions About the Consequences of a Condition

For planning purposes, this type of assumption is made in light of a condition the project faces, and it is about possible scenarios that may result. For example, if the project is forced to use a vendor that has notoriously long turnaround times, to prevent the project from stalling until the vendor provides estimates and plans, the team can make an assumption about what the vendor is likely to do. This can give the team a head start in planning around it.

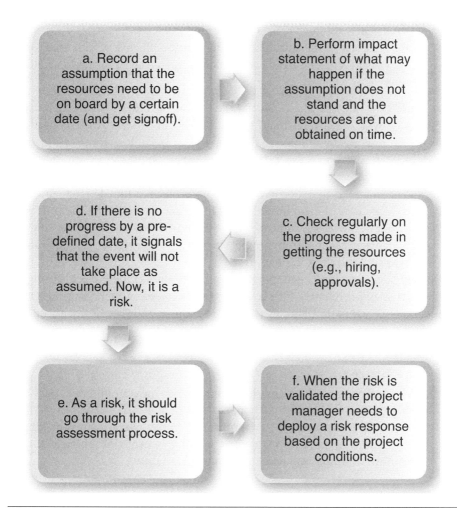

Figure 6.4   Actions to take when facing assumptions

These types of assumptions, which are like educated or informed guesses, require the team to qualify them as risks and plan for the event that things turn out to be different than the assumption predicts. Known as a risk analysis process, it establishes responses and action plans for the possibility that the risks materialize.

DOCUMENT ASSUMPTIONS FROM THE START

It is never too early to start making assumptions and taking them into consideration, since they may produce a series of benefits:

1. Help in the planning and decision-making processes;
2. Help illustrate to the stakeholders that it is an effective way to establish an understanding of the project conditions, even when information is still unknown or when the project faces dependencies.

Assumptions can be established early—while writing the charter—to make sure that stakeholders, who are involved and provide input, understand their obligations, agree on the existing conditions, and establish clear goals. Recording assumptions at such an early stage may also help to obtain greater buy-in from various stakeholders, as the PM instills confidence by keeping them involved, engaging them for input, and giving them an indication that the project team is tuned in to their needs. There is a wide range of assumptions that can be made throughout the process of putting the charter together, some of which are more likely to take place, and lead to multiple benefits, ranging from help in articulating success criteria to identifying dependencies and turnaround time.

In addition to making assumptions prior to the start of the project (during the business case and in charter formation), there is a need to make and document assumptions as part of the planning process that follows and specifically, during two other stages in the project:

1. When managing project change, especially to assess the change's impact on the project;
2. When managing risk: the most common way to measure and rank risks is through their probability and impact assessment, which will be covered in Chapter 8. A major part of the probability-impact assessment is making assumptions and trying to identify missing information—information that once collected, will help resolve the uncertainty.

HOW TO IDENTIFY ASSUMPTIONS

The process of identifying assumptions should yield not only a list of assumptions (a.k.a., the assumptions log) but also several pieces of information about each assumption, as will be specified in this chapter. The assumptions must then be managed as part of a progressive elaboration.[3] According to the Project Management Institute, "progressive elaboration" is "the iterative process of building the level of detail in a project management plan as greater amounts of information and more accurate estimates become available." Additional information is required, and further analysis needs to take place, in order to determine what happens next with each assumption, and whether the assumptions allow the project to continue as planned or any of them need to be treated as risks. For each assumption logged, there is a need to specify a date by which additional information is expected or required to be available for project action to move forward.

Without a recipe for describing how to identify and manage assumptions, the process requires subjective judgment. Most assumptions are made and recorded during the initiation and planning stages, by making observations about the project's conditions and by distinguishing conditions that include sufficient information from those that require additional information. These areas include the project objectives, stakeholders, known issues, and anything about the project environment that may impact the project's success. It would also be valuable to review historical information from similar, previously performed projects and check whether favorable conditions in those projects apply to the existing one, and whether these conditions are likely to facilitate project success.

Some issues and assumptions are more critical to project success than others. Thus, it is necessary to collect sufficient and applicable information from all relevant stakeholders in order to ensure that all points of view are covered, as well as to identify the full range of options associated with each assumption. This may be a simple task in some cases, but with stakeholders' specific views (and at times, agendas) about what and how things should take place in the project, the PM needs to prevent stakeholders from swaying the analysis away from the project's primary objectives. This is important for maintaining objectivity and considering each premise, idea, and assumption in relation to the project objectives and success criteria. Figure 6.5 provides a view of an assumption process flow.

Sources to Review When Identifying Assumptions

The PM should establish a process for identifying and managing assumptions, including assigning roles and responsibilities to team members and stakeholders who are involved in the process. An important part of the process should include reviewing a series of documents that may introduce assumptions. They are listed in Figure 6.6, but they may not all be applicable to every project.

Every assumption should be ranked according to its importance for the project's success and according to how critical it is for it to be true. The scale should include three measures (with a high–medium–low scale of criticality for simplicity). The PM should also determine the level of stability for each assumption as an indication of its likelihood to prove true and remain as planned (once again, with a scale of high, medium, and low to qualify each assumption). Although the PM owns the list of assumptions, the list should also identify stakeholders who should provide information about the assumption (when required).

From the Charter to the Plan

Assumptions that are identified during the formation of the charter can be classified into two types:

1. Assumptions that are recorded as part of the charter: these are major premises about the project and are strategic in nature;

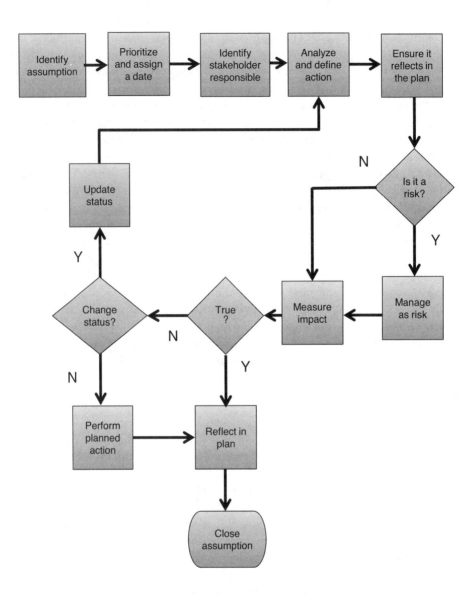

The process flow of an assumption from when it is recorded, through its various assessments, until it is closed.

Figure 6.5 Simplified assumptions flow diagram

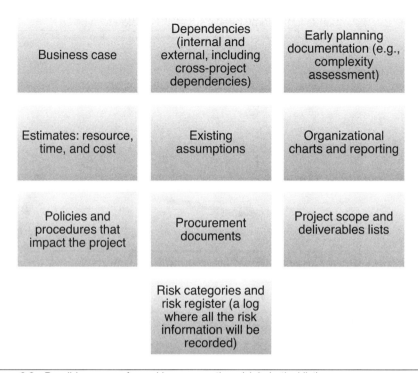

	Dependencies (internal and external, including cross-project dependencies)	Early planning documentation (e.g., complexity assessment)
Business case		
Estimates: resource, time, and cost	Existing assumptions	Organizational charts and reporting
Policies and procedures that impact the project	Procurement documents	Project scope and deliverables lists
	Risk categories and risk register (a log where all the risk information will be recorded)	

Figure 6.6   Possible sources for making assumptions (alphabetical list)

2. Assumptions about missing information in the charter: these are assumptions related to the business case and the organizational project readiness.

Throughout the planning process, additional assumptions will be identified, but they will primarily be tactical and transactional in nature—concerning the processes, the project work, and the resources in it. There is a fine line between too many assumptions and an insufficient number. While more assumptions signal more risks, PMs should avoid trying to artificially reduce the number of assumptions just for the sake of having fewer assumptions. The goal of assumptions management is to address the assumptions and shorten their lifecycles by pursuing the relevant information or by planning in such a way that the impact of a false assumption is reduced.

ASSUMPTION LOG

The assumption log can be a simple list of assumptions or, for a more thorough approach, a spreadsheet listing all assumptions for the project, together with their attributes, which appear as columns in Table 6.1. Depending upon the project's

Table 6.1 Assumptions log column headers and stakeholders involved

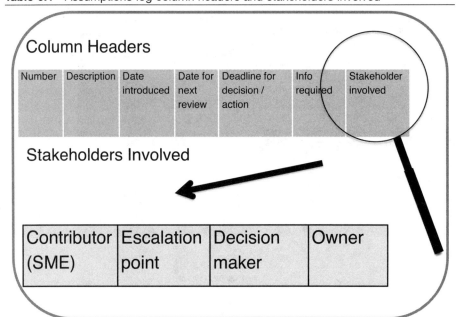

complexity and the nature of the assumptions, PMs need to determine the extent to which they manage the project assumptions. In some projects, it may be sufficient to have a list of assumptions reviewed at certain intervals, whereas a more robust assumption management process will be necessary for others. The assumption log illustrated in the table should contain a list of all the assumptions identified and information about them that adds value to the project planning process.

Keeping cost–benefit considerations in mind, PMs should try to pursue as much information about the project assumptions as possible, but it may not be necessary to have full information for each assumption. Because assumptions involve uncertainty by nature, certain information can be identified as needed at a later date—depending on the time horizon of the assumption—while other assumptions will need a placeholder, which is an assumption within the assumption.

PROJECT ASSUMPTIONS

Assumptions should be based—so far as possible—on facts and on as much information as is available at the time of discovery. Anything that brings the assumption closer to reality should be considered. For example, for a construction project in south Florida, any assumptions made should be based on a low likelihood of frost or snow events. With that said, PMs can make assumptions about anything they believe might happen in the project, as long as the assumptions do not contradict any facts surrounding the project.

It is not enough to come up with general assumptions or sweeping statements, such as "the vendor will deliver the product on time," or "we will be there on time;" rather, there is a need to qualify the assumptions by their areas of impact and their overall context. A better statement would be: "The vendor will deliver the correct version of the product by 3:00 p.m., as planned." When the statement is more specific, or qualified, it is easier to attach a meaning to it and to understand its context and implications in the event that it does not take place as planned. It also provides a timeline for taking action and for looking for information about the assumption.

Project assumptions can be categorized into groups to improve the PM's and the team's ability to focus on identifying the assumptions' impact areas. These categories should focus on the project knowledge areas, as identified by the *Project Management Body of Knowledge (PMBOK® Guide)*,[4] and are: scope, quality and integration, resources and schedule, costs, risks, contracts, communications, and technical considerations.

Technical Assumptions

These assumptions need to be specific to the project and take into consideration integration, transition, scalability, performance, defects, capacities, tools, and methodologies (including code in use, software, programming language). These common types of assumptions provide a foundation for consideration, but depending on the nature and environment of your project, they may not all be relevant. For the assumptions that are categorized as important/critical to success, as well as for those that are unstable, it would also be helpful to consider what part of the project they impact, their relevant history, and how much scrutiny (attention, time, and effort) they require in order to be maintained.

POTENTIAL BACKLASH

For important assumptions, which have the potential to turn into major risks, it is worth documenting them early in the project and approaching the project sponsor or customer for approval. Even if they appear obvious and all stakeholders accept the way things are, it is worth stating them in writing to avoid future misunderstandings. There is also a chance that some stakeholders will mock the assumption management process and deem it a waste of time, ridiculous, or useless. In such cases, PMs should resort to historical information to demonstrate the importance of documenting and managing assumptions and, if possible, provide examples of incidents where assumptions were not properly recorded. Without written assumptions, stakeholders have the tendency to forget commitments, conditions, and promises they have made.

As with other aspects of planning, PMs should resist the urge to take shortcuts with assumptions. With the constant flow of assumptions, issues, and other changes that take place during the project—where even seemingly meaningless events, such as resource availability, may put the project into a completely different situation—and with no proper assumption management, PMs are likely to have difficulty keeping track of the actual impact these events have on the project. Despite these changes—and especially if they appear minor—there is still the expectation that the PM will deliver project success. With documented assumptions, it is easier to provide the sponsor with the reasoning behind the need for more money, time, or people. The sponsor originally agrees to a project under a certain set of conditions, and if conditions change, the PM must try to reset those expectations.

ASSUME AND MONITOR

PMs need to keep in mind that assumptions, even if documented, will not resolve themselves and that there is a need to continuously monitor their status and control any changes or developments related to them. Documenting the assumptions can also be helpful in planning more accurately, with support and input from the appropriate subject matter experts, industry standards, historical information, or other valid and relevant source of information. Once the assumptions are recorded, the PM can flag any change that may impact them and with that, adjust the estimates accordingly and have a paper trail that documents the reasoning. An assumption should be closed (although not deleted, both for documentation purposes and because it may resurface later) only based on merits that satisfy the project criteria and not due to political or other types of pressure that may be applied on the PM.

In extreme cases, when it is difficult to gain agreement on how to move forward, it may be required to take the assumptions management process up a notch and treat it like a plan that needs to have its baseline set.[5] The project's baseline is used to measure how performance deviates from the plan. It is the process of reviewing and approving a plan for performance measurement (specifically scope, time, and cost), so—once a plan is approved—it serves as a benchmark and a standard for measuring performance. It should not go through the same rigor as the process of setting a baseline for the project scope, schedule, and cost, but in the context of assumptions, it should include getting signoff from a decision maker (e.g., sponsor, customer) on the project assumptions. The assumptions baseline ultimately serves to protect the project, and in the process, it also helps protect the PM from unfounded claims.

What If . . . ?

In the event that the assumptions do not turn out to be true or turn out to be less favorable to the project than previously thought, having them documented will help articulate the price the project will have to pay for the change(s) required to mitigate them. In turn, it also helps qualify assumptions as risks when needed for the purposes of impact assessment and response planning. Failing to document and manage assumptions will mean that most changes in the project conditions, when the project is not prepared for them, appear as complete surprises.

KEEP IN MIND

There are a few additional points about assumptions management that may come in handy for the PM to consider to ensure the process is done right and does not end up backfiring:

Sweeping statements—Do not make sweeping statements; try to be specific. It is not enough to say that the decision maker will be available for all signoffs on time; this should be qualified and based on the most likely option, given the available information. An example of a better statement is: "the decision maker will provide a decision on the matter by Friday at 2:00 p.m." Once again, it provides context, gives the team a heads up about when the assumption may become a risk, and helps specify the impact of failing to make a decision on time.

Facts—Do not contradict facts and known conditions. PMs should make any assumptions they need to, as long as they are aligned with known facts and conditions. For example, one can assume that it will take two weeks to hire a new resource, but—if the organization requires one week to post a position and three weeks to handle responses and conduct interviews before extending an offer—it cannot be expected that a resource will report to the project for at least four weeks. Even this timeline must be qualified with the assumption that a suitable resource will be found and will accept the offer.

Making assumptions does not make up for laziness—Do not replace facts with assumptions. Although assumptions are the PM's friends, they are the type of friends that are the result of necessity. Assumptions do not replace the need to look for information, to investigate, or to plan, and they do not justify a set of actions or make up for a lack of effort.

Write them down—Document the assumptions as you discover them. Even with no assumption log, put together a simple list, bring it to the attention of the sponsor, and review it regularly. Even for assumptions that appear to be straightforward, documenting them will help in tracing their rationale later in the project.

Assumptions and risks—Manage assumptions in conjunction with risk: assumptions and risks are related to each other, since both help manage project unknowns. The general progress of an assumption that does not turn out to be true is to turn into a risk that needs to be managed so it will not negatively impact the project success and objectives.

A never-ending job—Assumptions need to be managed throughout the project lifecycle, and on an ongoing basis, to ensure they reflect the latest available information and do not turn stale.

Keep the assumptions manageable—If an assumption is not specific or manageable, or there is no way to measure the type of information it requires, the PM will not be able to act upon it when needed. Under such conditions, the assumption will add no value to the project. Moreover, it may mislead project stakeholders into believing that the team has control over it.

Life is not linear—This concept is applicable to planning, estimating, and assessing risk impact: when there is a one-minute delay in delivering a product, it is likely to result in more than a one-minute delay in the project. Think about missing a commuter train by a minute—the delay is now at least as long as the wait for the next train. PMs should ensure that any impact assessment related to actions or to assumptions takes this ripple effect into consideration.

Hope is not a strategy—Assumptions management is intended to help the PM and the team avoid relying too much on hopes that are not based in reality. Basing plans, estimates, and understandings of project conditions and changes on hope is likely to end with unpleasant surprises and unplanned risks.

Do not over-rely on assumptions—Assumptions should not become the accepted wisdom that guides the project's plans and paradigms; do not ignore facts and actual conditions. Some people do not let facts confuse them and no matter what the reality, always manage to twist the reasoning and explanation to justify their preconceived notion of reality. For example, before Copernicus discovered the earth rotates around the sun, the accepted wisdom had been that the entire universe rotated around the earth. It took over 100 years for the idea of the earth rotating around the sun to become the accepted wisdom, thanks to the work of Galileo.

FINAL THOUGHTS ON ASSUMPTIONS

For the most part, the process of managing assumptions is frustrating, not only due to the headwinds PMs face from various stakeholders but also due to the nature of assumptions themselves: they represent uncertainty. In addition, PMs often face challenges in assessing how much information and analysis about each assumption are needed, which on its own, is a contributor to the frustration involved. Not knowing how much one doesn't know makes it difficult to benchmark the progress made and measure how much more work, if any, is required. With assumptions representing the unknowns in the project, it is nearly impossible to achieve any comfort level with them.

With that said, assumptions are a major contributor to the PM's ability to plan and manage expectations and are not discretionary, but rather an important project undertaking. This chapter has covered several tools and approaches that can be used to manage assumptions in such a way that they will add value to the project, along with the checks and balances to help avoid overusing them.

REFERENCES

1. Based on: http://www.businessdictionary.com/definition/assumption.html.
2. Based on: http://www.businessdictionary.com/definition/assumptions.html.
3. Project Management Institute. *A Guide to the Project Management Body of Knowledge, (PMBOK® Guide—Fifth Edition)*, pp. 553, 2013.
4. Ibid., pp. 61.
5. Based on: http://www.pmhut.com/the-project-baseline-a-project-management -definition.

7

Managing Those Things That Make a Difference

"Don't Come to Me Every Five Minutes for Every Little Thing."

Micromanagement has two parts to it: micromanaging the "what" and micromanaging the "how." Some say Steve Jobs was a micromanager: he was strict and particular about the "what" and left the "how" to his employees. Project managers (PMs) need to develop team members and empower them to be able to make the right decisions and improve at what they do. It is not about making the team overly dependent on the project manager and requiring them to ask about everything they do; rather, it is about bringing them to a level of independence so they become self-directed. This is achieved through effective communication, instilling a culture of collaboration, and taking a risk that comes with building trust and empowering the team. The rewards are well worth the effort.

The Pareto principle, (also known as the 80–20 rule, or the law of the vital few) states that typically 80% of event effects come from only 20% of event causes. Business management consultant, Joseph M. Juran, suggested the principle and named it after Italian economist Vilfredo Pareto, who observed that 80% of the land in Italy was owned by 20% of the population in 1906. He also observed that 20% of the pea pods in his garden contained 80% of the peas. It became a common rule of thumb in business; for example, 80% of a company's sales come from 20% of its clients, meaning that many businesses can easily make dramatic improvements in profitability simply by focusing on their most effective areas and eliminating, ignoring, automating, delegating, or retraining the rest, as appropriate.[1]

When looking at efficiencies and performing value-adding activities in order to lead projects to success, people often refer to the Pareto principle as a way to measure, illustrate, and focus on doing the important things or activities that add value to the creation of the desired product or result. Considering that PMs are typically extremely busy, and their capacities are often spread thin—giving them a limited ability to attend to the constant stream of events, changes, and activities in the project—it is crucial to ensure effective time management and to improve the ability to prioritize what needs to be done first.

Time management and prioritization are related to each other: with a constant stream of project activities, requests, inquiries, issues, meetings, risks, reports, and changes, PMs cannot attend to all of them or even come up with a way to prioritize them. This is why managing time effectively and reducing waste can help one focus on what really matters to the organization's objectives, project success, and stakeholders' priorities.

This chapter examines numerous important considerations for delivering project success. Clearly, not all projects require the same level of rigor and focus, but these items can serve as a checklist for PMs in their efforts to focus on what matters and achieve stakeholder satisfaction. Combined with insights from other chapters (e.g., readiness assessment, organizational politics, defining success, making assumptions), this chapter provides a turnkey style toolkit that can help the PM take control over the project and its destiny.

HOW DO YOU MANAGE YOUR DAY?

There are a few simple ways to measure the effectiveness of time management, starting with the activities listed in Table 7.1 and their associated explanations, which follow.

1. Daily Plan

At the beginning of each day, do you have a plan of what needs to be done during that day? Do you have a clear idea of which deliverables to focus on, activities to perform, and meetings to attend? While it is typical and legitimate to have

Table 7.1 Manage your day

1	Build a daily plan.
2	Set aside time for emergencies.
3	Get busy during the more productive times of the day and the week.
4	Count the number of surprises you have each day.
5	Count the number of emergencies in your project.
6	Track the amount of overtime in your project.

unexpected things to attend to, having a daily plan reduces the risk of surprises. With no plan, you may end up wasting time figuring out what to do, reacting to situations rather than leading them, and performing non-value-adding activities.

2. Set Time Aside

Do you have time set aside for unexpected events, emergencies, and risks? Prioritizing what you need to perform each day reduces the need to make time for emergencies, since it is easy to bump some of the lower-priority activities to give way to emergencies. The time set aside needs to be conceptual (through reprioritization of planned activities) rather than a physical block of time set aside; after all, there may be days with no emergencies.

3. Productive Times

You should set your day and plan activities and deliverables for the team in a way that leverages and takes advantage of the more productive parts of the day and the week, in the following fashion:

1. Try to avoid setting meeting times for the first thing in the morning. Various circumstances and traffic problems are likely to cause at least one team member to be late to the meeting.
2. The morning hours are when people are generally more focused and likely to be more productive.
3. When calling meetings for the later parts of the afternoon, remember that team members may be distracted by efforts to produce deliverables and finish things that are due by the end of the day.
4. The same goes for considerations about the days of the week: typically, Mondays will suffer from emergencies formed during the weekend or spilled over from the previous week, and Fridays will have team members scrambling to complete things before the weekend. The most productive and effective days for most team members seem to be Tuesdays and Thursdays, followed by Wednesday. This does not imply the office should be shut down on the other days of the week, but—if you have flexibility in arranging timing of deliverables—try to capitalize on the more productive times of the day and the week.

4. Count the Surprises

To what extent does your day look the way you planned it? If at the end of the day, you retrospectively look at how your day shaped up—as compared to how you thought it would be—and they are two completely different days, there is room for improvement in how you plan your days, or in how you manage your project and how much control you have over the project's course.

5. Count the Emergencies

How many emergencies does your project go through, and how often do they occur? The more often you need to attend to emergencies, the less organized your time is. Emergencies can take place for a variety of reasons, as illustrated in Figure 7.1.

Emergencies are part of reality, but PMs should strive to reduce their frequency and total number by following these steps:

1. To fix something, it must first have a measure, so PMs need to establish a mechanism to count how many emergencies are "declared" throughout the projects.

Figure 7.1   Sources of emergencies

2. Before even setting a reduced target number, PMs need to identify how many of the "declared" emergencies are real against how many are false alarms. At this point, PMs should form two plans:

   - Educate the team to minimize the number of false alarms;
   - Take ownership of the project and tighten the communication ground rules to clarify what constitutes an emergency, and reiterate the project objectives and success criteria to refocus the team on the right target.

It is also important to keep in mind that when reacting to emergencies, team members often rush through activities. They may take shortcuts and are more likely to not follow processes and best practices, resulting in mistakes. At some point, the team may become oblivious to the term "emergency" and its synonyms.

6. Overtime

How much overtime is needed in your project? It is normal to require some overtime when approaching deadlines, but when teams heavily and regularly rely on overtime, it may indicate challenges in the PM's ability to create realistic plans, manage time effectively, and properly lead the project. Depending upon the organizational culture, overtime should raise an alarm: it is likely to cause cumulative and long-term damage to team morale, ultimately leading to more performance problems and retention issues. Since some stakeholders believe that those who stay overtime actually work harder or better, some team members may view overtime as a goal in itself, rather than as a means to catch up on urgent work.

PMs need to look first at their own leadership and style to check their potential contributions to the need for overtime. However, there is a strong possibility that it might be an organizational cultural issue that is beyond the scope and capabilities of the PM. Regardless of the cause, the issue must be addressed, since overtime burdens team members and will negatively impact their performance over time.

WHAT TO MANAGE

Another attempt to effectively manage time and prioritization can be done by breaking down the types of activities that need to take place: transactional and transformational.

- Transactional activities involve daily chores, and although important to the project, they are tactical in nature. They include schedules, budgets, requirements, ongoing reporting, and deliverables.
- Transformational activities involve managing things that make a difference and help to manage the project more effectively. Overall, they are more influential to the project than transactional activities and include

change control, communication, risk, quality, project health, lessons learned, and relationship management.

The Chief and the Deputy

Ideally, the PM should perform the transformational activities; that is, act as the leader and manage the project to success by setting expectations, defining guidelines for the transactional activities, and empowering team members to define their activities and generate realistic estimates. Often however, PMs do not have the capacity to manage the important transformational aspects and get consumed by troubleshooting and following up on transactional activities. In order to allow PMs to perform their work at an ideal capacity, companies should post openings for two people to fill the role of PM—they would combine forces and act in the following roles: a chief PM for the transformational activities and a deputy PM for everything else.

Unfortunately, this type of ideal job will not be posted anywhere anytime soon; the idea is to help stakeholders realize that in order to maximize the value PMs produce, the organization needs to give them a chance to do it by providing them with the tools/resources they need. When PMs are consumed by daily transactional troubleshooting, it limits their ability to provide a meaningful contribution to the project and to actually manage it. Limited in this way, PMs are sucked into the vortex of events. They become reactive, and lose their edge in controlling the course of the project.

TRANSFORMATIONAL FOCUS

This section details areas where PMs should ensure a sufficient amount of focus throughout the project. Strong performance by the PM in these areas significantly contributes to project success; failing to control these areas is often the preamble to project failure.

Change Control

PMs should facilitate a process to ensure that every change in the project is captured, assessed, and evaluated in a way that prevents scope creep, ensures realistic estimates, and reduces the number of unnecessary change requests; in short, the process should be formal yet effective. It should also be proactive, so the PM can work with the stakeholders who are more likely to introduce changes to reduce the number of requests submitted. It can also serve as an educational process, so that all stakeholders know what constitutes a change and when a change request should be submitted.

Since change is closely integrated with risk, the process should enforce proper evaluation of risk for every change. Lowering the number of change requests allowed is about protecting the project and allowing only really necessary changes to go through. This is essential to protecting the project and the team from distractions and allowing resources to perform their work according to the plan. Establishing the change control process early in the planning stage and enforcing it throughout the project is effective in keeping scope creep to a minimum and with it, the need to scramble to undo damage.

Communication

The role of the PM includes many activities that are "very important;" however, *the* most important thing for the PM to manage is communication. PMs should spend the majority of their time communicating, as it has a substantial impact on project success. Communication management is comprised of a few areas of focus, as demonstrated in Figure 7.2.

Conflict Management

While an aspect of communication, conflict is so abundant in projects and influential to their outcomes that it is a stand-alone item to manage. The most effective

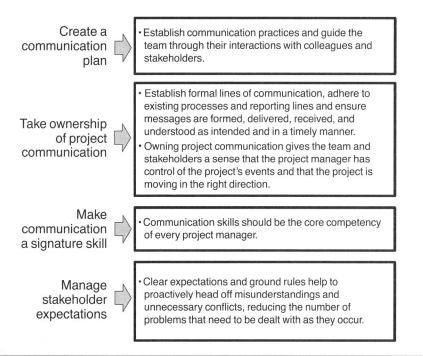

Figure 7.2 Communication management areas of focus

ways to measure whether conflicts are managed effectively are to check whether the same conflict tends to resurface later in the project, or whether the same team members or stakeholders repeatedly engage in conflicts. One of the measures of good leadership is how effectively conflict is managed throughout the project. While it is a routine occurrence, projects will fare better when their issues and conflicts are brought to a resolution and do not reemerge.

Risk

A negative risk is an event that if it were to take place, it would be likely to compromise the ability of the project to achieve its objectives. As a precondition to managing the right risks (including: understanding what risks are; identifying, analyzing, and thinking of responses to them; and controlling and acting upon them), the project team must know and be able to articulate the project success criteria. Without clearly understanding the success criteria, the team will not know which risks to focus on or how to manage the risks that impact project success.

Although managing risks effectively does not guarantee successful delivery, proactive risk management (as described in Chapter 8) favorably positions the team to prevent risks from happening, rather than reactively scrambling and being surprised by unexpected events. It also helps the team to reach the project's destination faster, more efficiently, and with less cost and fewer aggravations than teams that simply react to risks as they happen.

Quality

Corporate leaders often refer to quality and customer satisfaction as their top organizational priorities. However, in practice, the message does not always trickle down to all levels of the organization, and significant gaps form between the good intentions and the (less than satisfactory) results. Ensuring quality is everyone's role, but the onus lies on the PM to ensure that project quality, product quality, and overall customer satisfaction are delivered, along with meeting organizational objectives.

Success and customer satisfaction can only be achieved through hands-on project quality management and by putting together a quality management plan (as detailed in Chapter 9). The quality management plan specifies all activities that must take place on the journey toward delivering a quality product and customer satisfaction.

Project quality is also about ensuring that the competing demands (a.k.a., project constraints) balance each other out, and that both project risks and business risks are considered and do not clash with one another. An example of such a clash is when the project team tries to perform the work faster or at a lower cost—at the expense of product features, functionality, usability, or quality. This may lead to a faster turnaround time or cheaper delivery, but it may also result in producing an inferior product or service and ultimately, customer dissatisfaction. In the long run, it is more expensive and frustrating to undo project results and redo them to specification than it is to plan quality into the project from the start.

Project Health

Many PMs do not really know the true state of their project health, or how well their project is doing. In some cases, even if they get an accurate read on the project's health, it is solely through a review of the project deliverables. However, learning about problems by reviewing deliverables may make it too late to allow a proper and cost-effective fix.

PMs need to establish and utilize a series of indicators that allow them to identify the true state of a project at any given point—prior to producing any major project deliverables. This should be done through reviewing plans, processes, resources' performances, and eventually, deliverables. Project health checks can help identify areas of potential problems long before they turn into performance issues; health checks are an important part of the prevention, as a proactive process.

Lessons Learned

Many people and organizations do not learn from their mistakes and tend to make the same mistakes repeatedly, stumbling upon similar types of problems without managing to fix them. Whether it involves a professional or a personal matter, we need to learn from our actions (both successes and mistakes) so we put ourselves into a better position moving forward. The future always brings new challenges, but at the very least, we should not stumble upon the exact same hurdles as we did before.

For various reasons, most PMs do not identify lessons learned on their projects, which leads to a failure to capitalize on successes and get better at what they do and to repeated mistakes. While costly (time, resources, money) and requiring planning up front, conducting a lessons learned exercise at the end of a project is critical to organizational improvement and should become a mandatory part of every project.

Following the lessons learned exercise, there should be a post-implementation review (PIR) that takes place three to six months after the end of the project. While the lessons learned is about making the team better and improving processes, the PIR ensures product success and focuses on the final product and the benefits it yields. Additional information about these two elements appears in Chapter 12 which deals with organizational influences.

Customer Relationship Management

While the team is in the process of producing the project deliverables, one of the most important roles of the PM is to manage the relationship with the customer and the other stakeholders, along with their expectations. Beyond ensuring that the product is produced to quality specifications, relationship and expectations management involve the way things are done—including handling, reporting, style, pace, and processes and their transparency. The customer pays the project's bills, and as such, it is important to keep the customer happy. It is not about gold plating (i.e., giving the customer more than asked for), but about making sure the customer feels comfortable with the amount of information shared and its nature.

Early in my career, I was working in retail banking when a famous customer of high net worth entered the branch. It appeared that there was an error on a form the bank had issued for him, and as a result, he was going to lose roughly $200 from exchange rate differences. The customer was less worried about the loss than frustrated with the error and its associated inconvenience. My efforts to rectify the situation took longer than I initially thought as the process was complicated and required multiple overrides—including one from the branch manager. Eventually, I resolved the issue and gave the customer his money back. He shook my hand, sincerely thanked me, and said, "there should be more people like you in this organization." I felt good about doing the right thing and making the customer happy, but shortly after he left the branch, my manager made it clear to me that I should not have made an effort to recover the $200 for the customer and advised me not to do anything like this again. She also added that this particular customer had so much money that he should not care about such a small amount. My attempts to remind her that it was the right thing to do, that the customer should not have had to pay for the bank's technical error, and that he was happy with the level of service he had received fell on deaf ears. For the manager, it was a waste of time, effort, and $200, and she had no regard for the goodwill and the positive message it gave the customer about our level of care.

My rationale for treating the customer the way that I did was driven by the concern that he may take his business elsewhere because he felt mistreated. It is not that high net worth customers should be treated differently, but that organizations need to make a genuine effort to satisfy all customers as much as possible, within their service level agreements. Unfortunately, many organizations forget about the importance of customer relationship management and the ongoing need to ensure that customers get the value they expect.

Stakeholders' Expectations Management

When both project milestones and deliverables are achieved as planned, but when they fail to meet the targets set by the plan, it is important to continually manage the customers' expectations, specifically focusing on the areas that appear in Figure 7.3.

A concerned, unhappy customer can be devastating to a project, whereas a customer who feels informed and involved is easy to deal and collaborate with, even in difficult times. Expectations should not only be set for project objectives and deliverables but also for the process, communication, and transparency levels that

Keep them informed

Fix issues that arise

Address any of their concerns

Make them feel they are being heard

Ensure that they are satisfied with the information they receive

Figure 7.3   Stakeholder expectations management

are to take place within the project. For example, when a senior executive asks for a report concerning a specific aspect of the project, the PM needs to specify a clear set of expectations around the report's structure, format, and details. Otherwise, the focus of the task may shift, from examining the merits and substance of the report to its structure, color, or format.

Setting expectations is also important when handling plans and estimates. When the PM cannot produce a plan that promises an on time/on budget delivery on all intended objectives, senior management should not put the blame entirely on the PM. The onus, however, is on the PM to clarify that the anticipated delays or overruns are not results of choices made, but reflect the reality the project faces. The PM, through expectations management and communication, should position the situation in a way that brings stakeholders to the same side of the problem. Working from the same side—not viewing each other as the problem—will allow the stakeholders and the PM to come up with options to overcome the problem together. This philosophy can be summed up as, "Let's argue about the plan now, so we do not need to fight over failing to meet expectations later."

TIME WASTED

Wasting time does not necessarily come in the form of browsing the web, updating one's status on social networks, or taking care of personal matters. It can also be the result of doing work-related things that simply do not add value or performing value-adding activities in a slow, cumbersome, or inefficient manner. Ironically, due to the fast pace of work and project events, most of us do not get a chance to look back and review how much time we actually spent on particular activities during the project, which prevents us from improving the way we utilize our time in the future.

When we do get to look back, we are likely to discover that we spend the better part of our days on transactional activities that appeared to add value to the project but actually added less value than the effort and time invested in them. This inevitably results in failing to spend sufficient amounts of time on value-adding activities. Value-adding activities are the transformational items discussed earlier in the chapter (communication, risk, quality, and change control). Additional details about them appear in their respective chapters in this book.

Waste Categories

The amount of time that can be categorized as waste typically paints a staggering picture and can be broken down into three types:

1. Non-work-related activities: These are personal matters that we attend to while at work and include anything from conversations with colleagues to running personal errands, phone calls, e-mails, online shopping, checking the news, and checking social media sites. These activities account for roughly 15% of the workday. Not all of it is a complete waste, since it is important to interact and socialize with colleagues, but in this context, it is time spent in the office that cannot be utilized towards adding tangible progress.

2. Work-related distractions: Emergencies, changes in priorities and work assignments, work-related discussions, (the majority of) meetings, and help and advice to/from colleagues typically take up about 15% of the remaining time spent at work.

3. Doing non-value-adding items: Even while working on things that are related to the project and that need to take place, there is still a chance that they may not be done correctly or that they do not add value to the project. In addition, there are activities that are almost a matter of a daily routine for most of us, yet they add no value to the project. Examples are listed in Figure 7.4.

Too many of these events are part of most projects' realities, and any attempt to evaluate where time is spent will usually reveal that most PMs have only a few minutes a day to add value to the project and the organization.

a. Engaging in unnecessary arguments

b. Taking shortcuts and failing to follow processes

c. Involving too many stakeholders in communications or decisions

d. Communicating inefficiently (overuse of e-mails and text messaging)

e. Reacting to risks and changes instead of managing them proactively

f. Producing defects and then having to fix them

g. Spending time on bottlenecks and inefficiencies

h. Stumbling on communication breakdowns and misunderstandings

Figure 7.4 Non-value-adding activities

MORE TRANSFORMATIONAL AREAS OF FOCUS

The PM needs to ensure that the team has what it takes to perform the work and is presented with as few distractions as possible. In addition to the items already discussed, areas the PM needs to proactively manage are identified in the following discussion.

The Big Picture

The PM needs to make sure that organizational objectives are taken into consideration and that any impact on operations or on other outside projects is taken into account. Although it should go without saying, PMs need to always keep in mind that projects do not take place in isolation: anything produced needs to be integrated into organizational operations.

This also applies to dependencies on other projects' deliverables and resource management: working together with fellow PMs and with those who share resources with the project helps develop constructive relations that are more likely to produce realistic options. Furthermore, communicating with other projects allows issues to be addressed in a proactive and collaborative fashion. Such cooperation is less costly and more intuitive than waiting for deliverables to fail or scrambling for resources at the last minute.

Manage the People

It is no secret that project management success is about managing the people—the team, the customer, and the stakeholders. Part of managing people includes: developing rapport, engaging them, having one-on-one conversations, buying them coffee (if they drink coffee), addressing issues, listening, giving advice (when appropriate), offering support, empathizing, providing constructive feedback, being candid, discussing challenges, paying attention to their needs, tuning in to their emotions, learning what motivates them, and giving compliments when deserved. While project performance is measured through deliverables, these activities serve as the building blocks for success. Through these informal forms of communication and people management, the PM builds relationships, identifies underlying issues, proactively works with the team, measures trends, influences, motivates, and leads.

Connecting with people is the result of a genuine effort to engage them, and necessitates spending time walking around, sensing when and to what extent team members are in need of support, showing interest in what they're doing and how they feel, and asking them for their views, opinions, and reactions to situations. Quite often, this occurs over a cup of coffee or in an informal conversation outside of the office.

Many PMs do not see the value in spending time on these activities and categorize themselves as task-oriented, with a focus on achieving results. While everyone wants to achieve results, it is more likely to happen with effective people management and relationship building. PMs who are people-oriented are more likely to make team members and stakeholders feel better, which ultimately leads to more sustainable performances with better results. An atmosphere of support and collaboration is more likely to create a happier and more cohesive team that will conform to the project's objectives. While it may sound idealistic, this effort has been proven to pay off and produce results that are superior to those from teams that are all about business and are led in a cold and remote fashion, which only focuses on work and results.

Project Charter

The project charter serves many purposes, but it should be viewed as the birth certificate of the project. It is common to encounter projects with long and vague charters or with no charters at all (along with the excuse that only large and high profile projects have charters). It is understandable for organizations to focus on producing charters for larger projects, engaging in a more robust and effective risk management process, and delivering sufficient rigor and scrutiny to ensure they are successful. For smaller projects, organizations commonly do not require the same kind of focus or rigor, which unfortunately comes at a price: the smaller projects are often mismanaged, and their increased likelihood to fail may end up costing more in time, resources, money, and aggravation to the organization.

Aside from the fact that each large project is typically the size of several smaller projects, the question of why organizations do not produce charters for smaller projects comes down to their organizational philosophy and attitudes toward risk and quality. While the overall stake of all smaller projects is usually lower than that of a single large project, the cumulative impact of many small project failures may be significant for the organization. Neglecting to produce a charter for a project is not usually pinpointed as the cause of a project's failure, but it can be viewed as a contributing factor and an early sign of potential failure.

In short, the charter is critical to project success. It needs to be short (up to three pages), and it serves as an opportunity to show the organization and the team how important the project is, the project's focus, and the potential value it brings to the organization. It is a combination of a legal document (to authorize the project), a marketing tool (to show the value it brings), a means to address cultural gaps (providing context that connects the business case to the project), and a way to set expectations (a short and articulate review of what the project is about).

The charter should ideally be written by the project sponsor, but it is common for the PM to write it. It is important that the PM does it in collaboration with the sponsor for input, as a point of reference and information. It is easy to create a list of items to include in the charter, but populating the document with quality information is a challenge, especially when it must be done within a couple of pages.

Even when a PM is appointed to a project later in its lifecycle, this does not preclude the PM from needing to review the charter. In the event that there is no charter, the PM does not necessarily need to put one together but does need to ask questions. The content of the charter can serve as a checklist of things to ask in order to get a clear and correct picture of the project. The phrase "better late than never" applies here, since the PM can gain valuable information just by asking questions that should have been asked at the outset.

There is one more thing to keep in mind when putting a charter together, or when tracing back to create one: there will be many unknowns, and they should not prevent the PM from moving forward to the estimating and planning stages. Unknowns should be recorded as assumptions.

Alignment to Business Objectives

The senior leadership of the organization is in charge of selecting and initiating projects, and it is the responsibility of the PM to ensure, along the way, that the project produces deliverables that are in line both with its mandate and with the business objectives. Anything the project produces that is not aligned with the business objectives, or that compromises the performance of other parts of the organization in any way, should be addressed quickly and reported to the project sponsor.

Many PMs think in silos and pursue their project goals to their own benefit, with no regard for the overall business and organizational objectives. It is fair to expect that someone at the senior level of the organization should notice this, but it is likely such misalignment may go unnoticed. When PMs suspect silo thinking, they should alert the sponsor. It is safer to raise a red flag that turns out to be a false alarm than to continue producing project deliverables that ultimately damage the performance of the overall organization. A silo-thinking PM is set for failure.

Out of Scope

During the requirements and scoping process, the project team typically identifies areas that are out of scope for the project. When an item is out of scope, it is not within the responsibility of the project team to action it. However, it can get confusing, as there are three types of items that can be out of scope:

1. Unnecessary items: They are not included in the scope of the project.
2. Procurement items: These deliverables are part of the project scope but will be built by a third-party vendor or supplier and not the project team. The project team still needs to engage the vendor and manage procurement.
3. Dependencies: Items that need to be done or take place as part of the project but are performed by a different project team within the organization. Although these items are not part of the project scope and the team is not responsible for them, attention should be paid to their production—since any delays, risks, or problems will negatively affect the project.

Misunderstandings about what is in or out of scope are common and often lead to arguments and problems with customers who have different views of the project's inclusions and exclusions. One way to combat this (beyond performing an effective scoping process) is to write a "sweeping statement" on the top of the scope and requirements document that states, "If it is not explicitly mentioned here, it is implicitly out of scope." This can help stakeholders realize that if they do not see it written down, then it is not going to happen. The requirements document and scope statement are similar to any contract, as with the sales or lease agreement a car dealer gives a customer: if it is not written on that piece of paper, it will not be included with the car, even if the dealer verbally promised it would be.

Priority vs. Urgency

There is much confusion concerning the meanings of "priority" and "urgency" and their contexts. Project priority refers to the overall priority level the project is given by the organization. High priority means the project is regarded as strategically important; it produces visible products or results that are critical to business success. Projects viewed as high priority tend to receive more organizational attention: formal processes, project charter, rigor, senior stakeholder involvement, a robust decision-making process, and the right of way for resources and dependencies. Priority level does not typically change during the lifecycle of a project.

With that said, many people use the term "high priority" in a context that can better be described as urgency. In light of troubles, delays, and other pressing situations, stakeholders are forced to ask for more resources and special treatment, reasoning from the project's high priority. However, because the project priority remains the same throughout its lifecycle, it is the measure of urgency that changes and is likely to change multiple times over the project's lifecycle. It is possible that, at certain times, high priority projects take a back seat in urgency to other projects, and smaller and lower priority projects require more urgent attention.

PMs do not determine the project's priority, since it is set (and hopefully communicated) by senior management, but PMs should be able to label their project's level of urgency. This activity should take place on an ongoing basis and in collaboration with other PMs and stakeholders, who compete for the same organizational resources.

Project urgency levels change according to the project's performance and the nature of its deliverables. To help with the process, Figure 7.5 provides a set of criteria for determining a project's urgency. PMs can measure these criteria in relation to other projects and organizational initiatives, adjusting the relative weight of each item based on the specific conditions and environment.

The level of project urgency can help the organization identify the project that requires more attention or resources. Therefore, it is not enough to measure each project's level of urgency in isolation: each project must be put in context and compared to all other projects that compete for the same resources. Since it is common to have multiple projects competing over the same organizational resources (e.g., people, environments, tools, machines, money), a measurement of relative urgency will help to determine which one(s) gets the right of way.

A practical way to measure urgency is to use the cross-project urgency face-off technique illustrated in Figure 7.6. This is where PMs who compete for the same resources meet every week or two to discuss the relative levels of their projects' urgencies for the upcoming reporting period. The aim is to help stakeholders figure out and agree upon an action plan that will serve all of the projects' needs to the best level the organization can accommodate. A project that is deemed more urgent than

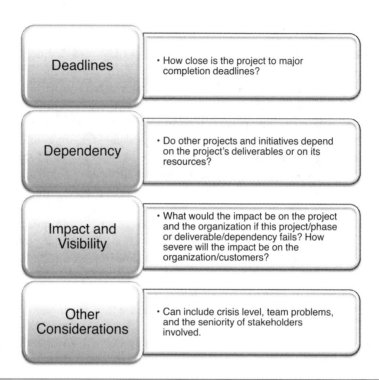

Figure 7.5 Criteria to determine urgency

its counterpart will be able to get priority for shared resources when both projects need them. By that, the urgent project may push the other one into crisis mode, and the next time the PMs convene to discuss their respective projects' urgencies, the ranking will be adjusted to reflect the new conditions.

This mutual consultation is an effective and constructive method that involves collaboration, as opposed to the way most projects handle competition for resources—through arguments, maneuvering, stress, and aggravation. The meeting should bring forward all projects' considerations into their respective bids for urgency; each project will then be compared with the others to determine the most urgent project for that reporting period.

The face-off mechanism is not an exact science, but it can help avoid situations in which all projects constantly try to be positioned as the most urgent. Based on the ranking, if the need arises, it will allow the organization to divert resources and shift its focus from one project to another as needed. Projects that get the right of way will probably manage to get their urgency levels down, while projects labeled as lower priority that give up resources to the higher priority projects are likely to be pushed further into crisis mode and become more urgent by the next assessment.

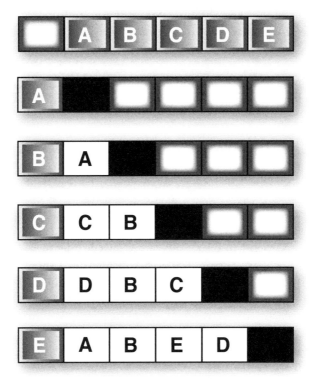

The projects compete for urgency based
on a set of pre-determined criteria that
take into consideration deadlines,
dependencies, impact, and level of crisis.

Figure 7.6   Cross-project urgency face-off

Projects are still likely to suffer from a shortage of resources, but this structured process is more efficient than a series of ad hoc conversations, arguments, and trade-offs that inherently, do not take the multitude of relevant considerations into account. The collaboration is likely to ease the symptoms of a culture of alligators (introduced in Chapter 1) and create momentum for effective teamwork and collaboration.

Negotiate on Merits

When assessing change, having discussions with customers, or looking for ways to add features and functionality, the negotiation process about the impact of the changes has to remain focused on the project merits and trade-offs, as defined by the project constraints and success criteria. PMs need to make sure that the conversation does not veer towards incentives, penalties, threats, or promises that are outside the consideration of the competing demands (scope, time, cost, resources, risk, and quality). It is important to explain to all stakeholders that PMs are on their side and have the same interests.

FINAL THOUGHTS ABOUT MANAGING WHAT MATTERS

Scarce resources, continuously growing demands, a need to do more with less, and an ongoing squeeze on costs are the realities with which most PMs contend. As a result, most projects do not operate within best case scenario conditions from the very start, and their focus turns towards cutting losses and providing the next-best set of values and benefits to the stakeholders. This chapter has examined multiple important considerations for project success, which PMs should focus on. With little time and limited capacity, PMs must manage their time effectively and channel their focus toward the relatively few things they can (partially) control—the transformational activities.

REFERENCE

1. Based on Wikipedia: http://en.wikipedia.org/wiki/Pareto_principle.

8

Managing Risk Effectively:
What's Missing from
Current Risk Management
Methodologies

"Let's Mitigate."

Mitigation is the most common strategy for dealing with project threats and can be done through any one or more of the following techniques: reduce the probability of the event taking place, reduce its impact, improve the ability to detect it, and get ready for it. With that said, the popularity of the mitigation strategy should not come from loving the word "mitigate." Risk response planning begins with coming up with strategies for dealing with risks, but must be followed with devising a specific set of actions that execute the response strategies. Identifying the need to mitigate but stopping short of coming up with specific actions may help explain why project risks are often poorly managed.

Managing project risks is one of the most important ingredients for project success. It is easy to follow a process for risk management, yet most project managers (PMs) do not like talking about it or doing it and have no time for it. The result is a reactive and at times insufficient risk analysis, which is reflected in project results. There are many project practitioners who are on the lookout for new tools, techniques, and templates to help manage project risks; however, there is really no need for more tools. What is needed is to effectively utilize existing methodologies to help PMs, instead of trying to make the tools think for PMs.

Table 8.1 Risk terminology

Term	Definition
Risk	A measure of uncertainty; associated with the chance (measured by probability) and the consequence (impact) that an event would affect project objectives and success criteria.
Risk Event	A specific episode or occurrence that may have a positive or negative impact on project success.
Uncertainty	The lack of information to forecast and predict future events and the ambiguity of information and data to support the planning and forecasting of future events.
Risk Trigger	An indication that a risk has occurred, is taking place, or is about to happen.
Detectability	A measure of the ability to sense, notice, or recognize that a risk has happened or is imminent.
Probability	The chance or the likelihood that an event will occur.
Impact	The potential consequence or outcome that a risk may have on project success criteria.
Response-Ability	The aptitude, capacity, and desire that a project team and the organization have to respond to a risk event.

Risk terms are quite simple to define, however they may cause confusion among some stakeholders.

Risk management is not about figuring out everything about the project risks or about eliminating all risks; it is about managing the risks, controlling them, and making informed decisions about which risks need to be further addressed and attended to. Although most risk-related terms are simple to define, Table 8.1 provides basic risk terminology to ensure there is a common understanding of these terms moving forward.

CHARACTERISTICS OF RISK

A risk is an event that may happen; if it does, it may have an impact (positive or negative) on the project. Risks are generally referred to as known-unknowns or unknown-unknowns.

- Known-unknowns are events that may take place and have an unknown aspect to their probability or impact. We are not sure whether and how they may affect us, and they are the responsibility of the project team to identify and address.
- Unknown-unknowns are unlikely events stemming from outside of the organization and can be potentially game changing (for example, pandemics or environmental issues). Under certain conditions, unknown-unknowns can become known-unknowns. For example, when moving

from one region to another events that may be unlikely in one region may be likely in a different region (e.g., types of natural disasters, climate, geo-political situations). Often, their existence has not been encountered before, and they may be part of organizational business continuity or disaster recovery plans. The PM does not have the authority, access to information, or capacity to consider these on the project level.

WHAT TO AIM FOR

There is a growing recognition among PMs and senior management of the need to invest more in project risk management. Unfortunately, recognition alone does not give risk management the attention it needs, and many organization's risk management practices are at best, not sufficient and at worst, practically nonexistent. Risk management should be done effectively, efficiently, in a timely manner, and proactively. Let's take a look at what these words really mean:

Effective—Effective risk management refers to identifying events that may pose a threat (or introduce an opportunity), which will impact the project's success criteria, and making sure no additional risks are overlooked. Failing to plan for and manage risks may give stakeholders a false sense of security that the project is on the right track, but looking the other way will not make risks disappear.

Efficient—Efficiency is about not wasting time, resources, or money on irrelevant events and risks that have no impact on project success. Wasting time on managing irrelevant risks, or missing newly-introduced risks, yields similar results to not managing risks at all—with one difference: the wasted time adds no value.

Timely—"Timely" means performing risk analysis early in the project and revisiting it systematically and regularly. Although there is never enough time for managing risks properly—due to multiple project emergencies, deliverables, constraints, and issues—sufficient risk management will directly contribute to fewer emergencies and more time to produce the intended value and benefits. "Timely" also refers to learning about the time proximity of each risk and dealing with risks before it is too late.

Proactive—A definition for "proactive" is more challenging: by nature, part of a risk response strategy is reactive, since it is about responding to an event that has already occurred. This is also known as "corrective action," which means taking something that is broken and trying to fix it. Time, money, planning, and resources have been spent on performing activities and producing deliverables that now need to be fixed, undone, or redone—at an additional cost—simply to bring them to their intended levels. Proactive risk management is about taking action up front—before the risk event occurs—working on the root causes and sources of risk, and taking preventive action. That being said, it is difficult to justify and obtain buy-in for prevention.

RISK METHODOLOGIES

There are many approaches and methodologies for managing risks, but none of them can do the PM's thinking. The challenge is to utilize a methodology that is applicable for the project and the organization and tailor it to the circumstances at hand. The risk management approach outlined by the Project Management Institute (PMI) can serve as a foundation for managing project risks, and this chapter complements it by focusing on areas that require additional attention. This is an example of why the PMI refers to it as "good practice:" PMs should not use it as a prescription to follow closely, but rather as a toolbox of ideas and options. PMs should pick whatever works for their specific project, context, environment, and situation, keeping in mind that no two projects or organizations are alike.

Risk and Communication

PMs struggling with how to tackle project risks should go back to the stakeholder analysis and use it as a starting point for their risk management process. The information in the stakeholder analysis, including stakeholders' risk tolerance levels, can provide the PM with valuable insight about areas related to each stakeholder that may produce project risks. For example, stakeholders who are risk averse (a.k.a., risk haters) may require more hand-holding, and identifying their needs early on can help the PM prepare appropriately.

The next place to visit is the area of communication management, where any component of the communication management plan that is overlooked or mishandled may result in elevating the project risks. The stakeholders' styles and positions about the project have the potential to significantly impact project risks, and Table 8.2 shows the link between various communication considerations and potential risks they may lead to. Chapter 11 deals with the connection between risk and communication extensively.

WHERE TO START

The one thing that precedes the stakeholder analysis is the project charter, which is where risk management begins, since it provides a review of what the project is up against. In the event that information in the charter is unclear or missing, the

Table 8.2   Risk and communication considerations

Communication considerations	Associated questions that may indicate risk areas
Relationships, team's make-up and dynamic conflict level and style, and interactions among stakeholders	Are there political issues that may become road-blocks?
	Are there power struggles around the project?
	Are roles and responsibilities defined and understood?
	Do the conditions, relationship history, dynamic, or team members predispose the project to conflict?
Framework, ground rules, expectations, and best practices	How effectively does communication in the project flow?
	Do team members and stakeholders understand each other?
	Does information in the project flow or are there blocks?
	Are reporting lines clear?
	Is there a feeling that the project manager owns the communication and that stakeholders get the information that they need in a timely manner?
	Is there a set of escalation procedures?
	Are priority settings and decisions communicated properly?

project team should come up with a list of questions to ask the sponsor and the customer in order to fill in the blanks. From here, managing risks is mostly about project integration—ensuring that risks are considered and managed in the context of the environment, market conditions, organizational needs, and project specifics.

Unfortunately, despite recognizing the need to follow these steps, many PMs find themselves with no clear idea of how to define project success (beyond delivering everything on time and on budget) and with no specific questions to ask the sponsor. If information is still missing, or in the event that project priorities are not clear, it is time to make assumptions, document them, and make sure to revisit them on an ongoing basis. Assumptions are a source of risk, and as illustrated in Chapter 6, properly managing them is closely tied to project success.

Emotional Resilience

Managing risks requires the PM to demonstrate emotional resilience. While risk methodologies are straightforward to follow, project stakeholders and team members have different sets of drivers, priorities, and interpretations of the project, which require PMs to stand strong and maintain focus on protecting the project success criteria—despite multiple viewpoints and agendas. Stakeholders constantly try to promote their interests and points of view, competing for the limited project resources, and often conflicting with the project objectives and priorities.

Not every event that raises concerns among certain stakeholders needs to be addressed at the project level, and not every loud stakeholder who presses a specific agenda or has influence on decision makers should dictate the project risk management strategy. Emotional resilience also involves dealing with resistance and conflicting priorities firmly, but professionally, with sensitivity to stakeholders' egos, and trying to influence and reason with them while maintaining healthy relationships.

DO NOT WAIT UNTIL THE WHEELS FALL OFF

It is normal to believe that things are fine, even when there are signs things are not heading in the right direction, given the combination of PMs' limited capacities and the preventive nature of project risk management. It is one of the sources of incorporating hope into a risk management strategy. It is also common to wait until something goes wrong, view it as a wakeup call, and scramble to address the risk events and consequences. For many organizations, risk management can be equated to calling a life insurance agent for a quote—when they hear the elevator cable snapping overhead while on the 50th floor of a high-rise building.

Risk management involves the need to anticipate what might happen in the future. It is not about making pure guesses, but it is an attempt to plan for events— based on the likelihood and possible outcome and impact on the project. It also involves an effort to gather sufficient information about these events for planning purposes. For the risk management process to be effective, it must involve open communication, where stakeholders are not afraid to discuss potential risks, and the team culture promotes collaboration—not "shooting the messenger."

RISK PLANNING AND APPROACH

Despite the fact that most PMs and stakeholders understand the need to manage risks, in many organizations it is hard to find a clear methodology or plan for risk management. Other organizations engage in sufficient risk management for larger projects, while the majority of their smaller projects end up with ineffective—or no—risk management planning altogether. A risk management plan jumpstarts the thinking process toward handling project risks and covers a few basic elements, as listed in Figure 8.1.

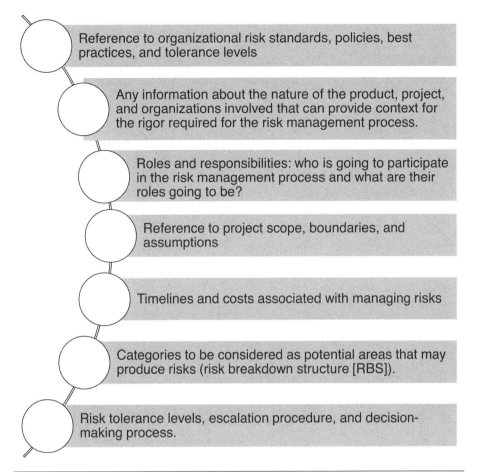

Reference to organizational risk standards, policies, best practices, and tolerance levels

Any information about the nature of the product, project, and organizations involved that can provide context for the rigor required for the risk management process.

Roles and responsibilities: who is going to participate in the risk management process and what are their roles going to be?

Reference to project scope, boundaries, and assumptions

Timelines and costs associated with managing risks

Categories to be considered as potential areas that may produce risks (risk breakdown structure [RBS]).

Risk tolerance levels, escalation procedure, and decision-making process.

Figure 8.1   Elements of the risk management plan

RISK REGISTER

The risk register (or risk log, illustrated in Tables 8.3a–d) is a table that lists all the project's risks and their corresponding information as it becomes available throughout the process. There is no guideline for the level of detail it should include, but detail is a reflection of the level of due diligence in the risk process. It is easy to overdo it and dive into unnecessary levels of detail; hence, the importance of maintaining a balance between a sufficient amount of information and too much of a good thing. Overdoing the risk process is a waste that yields little-to-no benefit to the project or the organization. The following discussion identifies fields that may be included in the risk register (the order in which the fields are listed here is not necessarily the order in which the information is to be obtained).

Table 8.3a   Risk register content headings: Risk identification

Risk identification

ID	Risk category/source	Date raised	Raised by	Date last reviewed	Risk statement	Risk description	Triggers (events, other projects, other risks)	Expected trigger time	Ability to detect

Table 8.3b   Risk register content headings: Risk analysis

Risk analysis

Overall impact	Probability	P-I score	Impact areas (success criteria, stakeholders, other risks)	Monetary impact (EMV)	Urgency, proximity, timing of impact

Table 8.3c   Risk register content headings: Risk response planning

Response planning

Response-ability	Response strategy	Contingency plan	Fallback plan	Response actions and plans	Actionee (respond to risk, cleanup)

Table 8.3d   Risk register content headings: Risk control

Risk control

Owner (monitor the risk, update)	Status	Trigger date	Notes

SWOT ANALYSIS

Analyzing the strengths, weaknesses, opportunities, and threats (SWOT analysis) to a project (see Figure 8.2) often takes place on the organizational level, but it could be useful for risk planning. It gives the project team a chance to review its internal capabilities (strengths) and flaws (weaknesses) against the external conditions (opportunities and threats) the project will face.

There are a few simple guidelines that can transform the SWOT analysis from an exercise that does not create further value into a meaningful tool in the risk identification and planning process:

- Strengths and weaknesses are mutually exclusive. A condition the project faces cannot be labeled as a strength and a weakness at the same time. There could be, however, different aspects of the same condition that can be perceived as one or the other. For example, if a team's strength is its ability to focus maximum effort on a risk that happens, it is not a weakness that they do so and let other tasks due at the same time slip. The level of effort required must be determined and controlled by the PM. The

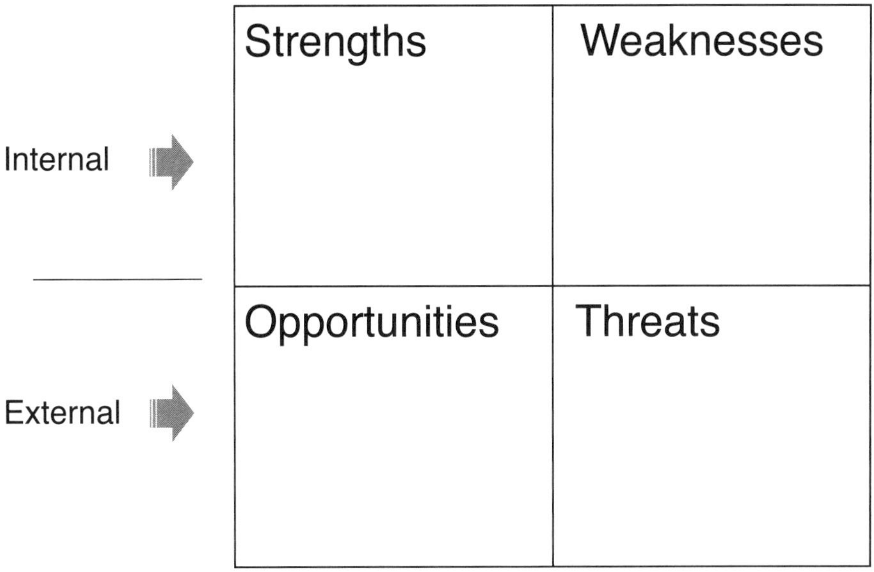

	Strengths	Weaknesses
Internal ⇒		
External ⇒	Opportunities	Threats

SWOT analysis is commonly used as part of strategic planning and for risk management. It is a promising exercise that is often not followed up with an action plan, which reduces the exercise's value to the project organization.

Figure 8.2   SWOT analysis

same rule applies to the external factors represented by opportunities and threats.

- Generally, there should be no more than a handful of items in each one of the four categories of the SWOT analysis (i.e., strengths, weaknesses, opportunities and threats).
- The goal of the SWOT analysis is to engage the team and other stakeholders in an effort to objectively identify their strengths and weaknesses.
- It can help the team examine its ability to respond to risks, and even determine whether there are any risks it cannot respond to.

Examples of strengths include: resources, capabilities, team dynamic, conflict resolution, communications and ground rules, technical knowledge, reputation, access (to information, decision making, capital), or any competitive advantage (efficiencies, economies of scale). Weaknesses can be deficiencies or challenges in any of these areas. It is important to maintain a sense of objectivity and be realistic about the extent of the strength and avoid discounting weaknesses. We generally have the tendency to overstate our assets and ignore more challenging areas.

Opportunities may include: unfulfilled customer needs, new technologies, favorable changes in regulations or market conditions, organizationally related opportunities, and new markets. Threats may include any reversal of opportunities, shifts of consumer or public tastes away from the company's products and services, emergences of substitute products, new regulations, and other environmental challenges and restrictions. Here too, it is important to remain realistic and not list items that are generic, too sweeping, theoretical, or meaningless—things that appear to be opportunities but are not.

SWOT ON STEROIDS

SWOT analysis presents a great deal of promise but may produce little value: it often ends up being a square with four quadrants on a Power Point slide, with no follow-up on the findings. To make it meaningful, the team needs to consider the intersections between the internal and external aspects of the SWOT analysis, and the potential strategies they can yield,[1] as illustrated in Figure 8.3.

Strengths and Opportunities: Offensive Strategies

The project team should not necessarily pursue all (or any) of the opportunities it faces, but it should try to develop and enhance its strengths, capabilities, and core competencies by identifying a fit between its assets and identified opportunities. The connection point between strengths and opportunities will help the team propose or formulate applicable strategies, which should be called offensive strategies. With

	Strengths	Weaknesses
Opportunities	Offensive Strategies	Flanking Strategies (Workarounds)
Threats	Defensive Strategies	Blocking Strategies

An extended SWOT includes strategies that may be available as a result of the intersections of the internal and the external factors. It can serve as a source of information for risk identification and risk response planning.

Figure 8.3   SWOT on Steroids

a handful of items in each category of the original SWOT, the team may come up with multiple strategies; although, quite often, only few will turn out to be feasible.

Weaknesses and Opportunities: Flanking Strategies

In an attempt to capture an opportunity by overcoming weaknesses, or alternatively, to try to overcome a weakness in order to prepare for capturing an opportunity, the team may come up with flanking strategies or workarounds. For example, when there is an opportunity to deliver a product on time, but it still has defects, the team can define workarounds for these defects that will make the product functional, and help capture the opportunity by delivering the product on time.

Strengths and Threats: Defensive Strategies

The same line of thinking is applicable to threats: try to utilize strengths (typically a defense, but potentially an offensive mechanism as well) to reduce the probability and impact of threats. For example, form strategic alliances to defend against a threat from a competitor.

Weaknesses and Threats: Blocking Strategies

A blocking strategy is an attempt to overcome weaknesses that may give way to threats, or alternatively, to try to block threats in order to reduce the project's vulnerability, despite its weaknesses. This blocking technique may help reduce the chance the weaknesses will make the project and the team susceptible to external threats.

Closing Thoughts

"SWOT on Steroids" not only challenges the team and other stakeholders to create lists of items that are perceived in certain ways but also helps generate extra thinking around the team's capabilities and putting the risks the project may face into context. The result is the gateway to risk response planning; however, it does not replace the need for further response planning and analysis.

RISK IDENTIFICATION

Once a framework is in place, it is time to start identifying risks that may occur in the project, keeping in mind that not all identified risks will require further action. When facing simpler projects with little uncertainty, the risks may be kept as a list of red flag items to track, but on more complex projects, the risk identification process is the foundation of the process of assessment, analysis, and response for further action and monitoring. During the risk identification process, focus should be given to identification only—no further action (e.g., analysis) should be taken at this point.

The PM should facilitate the identification process from the outset by providing relevant stakeholders and those who are involved in the process with context and materials to review. The PM should then hold a risk identification meeting, with all of these stakeholders, that involves creative thinking, brainstorming, and leveraging previous experience and knowledge to create a list of risks for further consideration.

Throughout the risk identification process, the PM needs to consider:

Missing Information—When the project team is missing information for the planning process (about resources, capabilities, deliverables, objectives, stakeholders, or decisions) this is a potential risk that may be remedied, at least partially, by making assumptions.

Quality of Data—Even with information in place, there are times when the sources of information may not be knowledgeable or credible. When relying on this information, the team needs to verify whether the information is correct and relevant and consider the risks associated with not having the correct information.

Risk Breakdown Structure

The risk breakdown structure (RBS) (displayed in Figure 8.4) lists categories that represent areas that can produce risks, and gives the team an opportunity to address these areas and work with their associated stakeholders on prevention. Within the categories of the RBS,[2] there are subcategories that help focus efforts toward identifying where risks may emerge from. Not every one of its subcategories will necessarily end up producing risks, but all are worthy of consideration. The RBS also gives the PM the opportunity to engage stakeholders, who are associated with areas that may produce risks, and work with them on taking preventive measures. There are additional items that should be considered under each subcategory, with specific considerations and areas to look at as likely producers of risks.

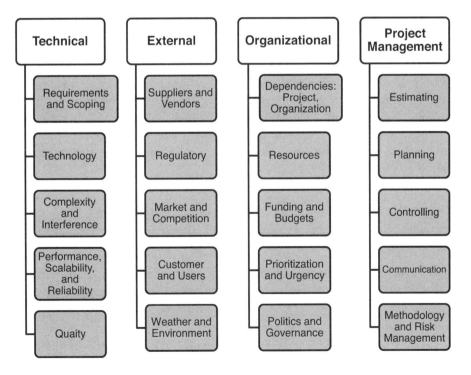

This RBS example is based on the RBS presented in the *PMBOK® Guide* and is refined with slightly different names and additional subcategories to articulate areas of focus.

Figure 8.4 Risk breakdown structure (RBS)

THE RISK IDENTIFICATION PROCESS

With the list of items to consider under the Risk Planning and Approach section of this chapter and the bank of categories that may produce risks (as outlined in the RBS) to look at, the next step is to put together a straightforward risk identification process. To make it easier and more intuitive for everyone involved, it is recommended to perform due diligence and provide stakeholders with as much context as possible. The categories and considerations can serve as checklists to ensure that all items are taken into account. Although not all of the items considered will actually produce risks, this extra effort is better than the alternative of missing risk-producing items.

Incorporating the categories into the risk identification process also helps to approach (at least some) risk areas in a proactive manner. If there is an indication that certain categories (or stakeholders) tend to produce more risks than others, it allows the PM to direct extra effort and focus toward these areas and work with the stakeholders to proactively address or avoid risks—at a lower cost and by potentially introducing fewer secondary risks.

A structured risk identification process helps reduce bias, allows the team to maintain focus, and decreases distractions created by loud, influential, or other stakeholders with agendas and drivers that may not be aligned with those of the project. A structured risk identification process is more organized and systematic than an unstructured one, where team members and stakeholders randomly come up with risks based on their areas of focus. As a result of the haphazard approach, certain points of view or considerations may not represent the process, and the associated risks may not be identified. A structured approach can help reduce and defuse the negative impact of, and the wasted time and effort in, addressing events that—although legitimate concerns for certain stakeholders—are not relevant for the project objectives.

Things to Include in the Process

The following list contains a set of recommended steps for conducting the risk identification process:

1. Begin by compiling the project's risk events through an examination of issues and concerns created by the stakeholders—possible sources are: the project description, cost and schedule estimate, procurement plans, risk checklists, and the work breakdown structure (WBS). The PMI views the WBS as an important piece in the planning process and as a foundation for estimating. The PMI defines the WBS as "a hierarchical decomposition of the total scope of the work to be carried out by the project team . . . ;"[3]

2. Examine and identify project deliverables and milestones and break them down into a level of detail that permits the evaluation of the significance of any risk they may be affected by;

3. Consider the project change control mechanism: assess stakeholders' support, disposition, and loudness about issues. Consider the impact of change on all constraints and objectives and on project risks, including the impact on other projects and operations;

4. Check assumptions, risk dependencies, urgency, and timing: although it is not time to analyze risks yet, it may be worth noting any items that may make a risk stand out;

5. Review project documents, including: contracts (with clients, vendors, business partners) and other procurement documents, historical information (risk documentation, lessons learned), the business case, charter, readiness assessment, complexity assessment, schedule management plan, and cost management plan. Not all of these documents (especially the historical information) may be available or contain credible information, but they may give the PM insight into things that might happen or have happened on previous projects;

6. Assess the communication plan and stakeholder analysis information: these can help identify gaps in communication needs and stakeholder expectations, as well as areas of potential conflict of interest or friction among team members and stakeholders. For PMs who were not part of initiating and early planning of the project, it can also provide an indication of the level of transparency and the communication process, style, and efficiency, including potential bottlenecks, redundancies, and areas that are underserved or might turn explosive. If not handled with care and in the context of stakeholders' needs and project objectives, these items may become sources of potential risks.

For many of the risks identified, the project team may decide to take no action—due to various reasons, capabilities, restrictions, and considerations (mainly cost–benefit related). This serves as a reminder that part of managing risks is allowing some risks to occur and realizing that not all risks can, or should, be addressed or avoided.

It is advisable to ensure that communication lines with stakeholders are open and clear for exchanges of ideas, concerns, decisions, and other information about the risk identification (and subsequent analysis) process. This also helps develop rapport and relationships with stakeholders and clarifies that the PM's role is to help articulate the reality about the project risks and to provide input and recommendations for the risk management process. Unfortunately, it is common to find stakeholders who associate PMs with certain risks, just because the PMs bring up those risks.

RISK ANALYSIS

Analyzing risks is a natural progression from the identification process, and the PMI breaks it into two types: qualitative and quantitative analysis. The following is a brief discussion of the two types of analysis, along with additional insights that can help make the analysis meaningful:

- Qualitative risk analysis is foundational and includes a review and assessment of all identified risks to measure whether they are worth further analysis and a proactive response;
- Quantitative analysis is an attempt to numerically determine the probabilities of various (adverse) events and the potential extent of losses from those events. It comes after the qualitative analysis and is performed only for risks that are deemed severe or significant. This type of analysis is meticulous and detailed in nature, and it requires specific expertise and extra time and costs to perform.

The risk analysis process is intended to produce a reading on each risk's overall severity, score, and magnitude, along with the ability of the project team to rank risks in relation to each other. It involves a series of activities that start with combining the basic measurements of probability and impact.

Probability and Impact: Start With Impact

Although probability appears before impact in the probability-impact formula (P × I), it is recommended to measure the risk impact first, to reduce any potential bias by the probability value, which is particularly applicable when the probability of a given risk is perceived as low. This practice may help prevent stakeholders from discounting the overall magnitude of the risk, thinking that a risk's low probability implies its low importance.

A risk impact measurement refers to the overall consequences, results, and costs associated with a risk if it happens, regardless of its probability. There are numerous examples of low probability risks with significant or potentially devastating impacts, and it is important to not let low probability mislead PMs into believing a risk is not important. A fire, for example, may be low in probability but have extremely severe consequences; therefore, it is important to consider, analyze, prepare for, and take all possible measures to prevent one.

The impact assessment measures the overall effect a risk might have on the project's success and objectives. Standing strong against any bias may sound obvious and simple, but it requires emotional resilience and focus on the project goals, considering that some stakeholders may try to promote their points of view with tactics that are not necessarily aligned with the merits and success of the project, including:

- Being loud and vocal with their positions;
- Being intimidating—insinuating negative consequences if the PM does not pursue their agendas;
- Exploiting political power and relationships.

Rank the Impact

There are a number of ways to express the measure of impact:

- Throughout the early planning stages, it can be expressed by using a high-medium-low scale;
- As the planning process progresses, it can (and should) be refined to numerical values, on scales of any range that makes sense for the stakeholders and team members involved; for example, 1–4, or 1–10.

Once the impact values are in place, the project team should then try to associate a cost and a schedule impact to each risk. Although no two projects are alike, and the cost and/or schedule impacts are specific to each project, it is possible to assign generic impact values as a percentage of the total project (usually measured in money or time). Table 8.4 provides a risk impact scale (in this example, a scale of 1–9, where 9 is high) that can serve as a guideline and, if necessary, should be adjusted to the specifics of each project.

Table 8.4   Values and their associated impact for the RIBT

1 Minor impact	• Budget impact: around 1–2% interruption (of the remaining resources and budget) • Ability to maintain budget: contained by contingency • Schedule impact: no impact on critical path
3 Limited impact	• Budget impact: up to 5% interruption • Ability to maintain budget: contained by contingency • Schedule impact: may affect interim deliverables and milestones
5 Considerable impact	• Budget impact: up to 8% interruption • Ability to maintain budget: likely to lead to an impact on scope (remove scope items or reduce functionality within existing scope) • Should not reduce testing • Schedule impact: overall project delays
7 Major impact	• Budget impact: up to 10% interruption • Ability to maintain budget: need to remove chunks of scope. Should not consider reducing testing; in need of major trade-offs • Schedule impact: significant delays of major deliverables
9 Devastating impact	• Budget impact: more than 10% interruption • Ability to maintain budget: find more money or go back to the drawing board for major scope reductions • Schedule impact: main deliverables unrealistic

Refine the Impact Ranking

The next step is to refine the impact numbers and express them in terms of the project constraints and success criteria. This includes providing an indication of each risk's impact on functionality, schedule, budget, quality, and any other measure of success. Certain risks may have a more severe impact on one project success criterion over the other risks; depending on the impact areas, these will determine the overall severity of the risk.

For example, in the middle of a project, the heads of the IT and Finance departments warn the PM about equipment failure. They present two options in relation to a major equipment failure:

1. Fix the equipment, which is technically possible but will take a significant amount of time;
2. Buy new equipment, which will be expensive and take the project over budget.

The finance manager is adamant about fixing the equipment, which would translate into saving money. However, this is in direct conflict with the project mandate to deliver on time, no matter what. With time as the most important constraint (and success criterion), the decision is quite easy (despite the resistance from the finance manager): buy new equipment, go over budget, and deliver on time.

A Combination of Considerations

This example demonstrates a typical situation of conflicting stakeholders' priorities; it integrates stakeholder analysis, an understanding of success criteria, and a focus on managing risks in such a way that will not hinder project success. Ideally, all stakeholders' needs should be met, but as with many projects, when risks materialize, the project no longer faces the best case scenario, and it becomes quite clear that whatever the decision, someone will be unhappy.

Knowing each stakeholder's drivers and motivations and staying focused on project success help the PM to prioritize risks. In this example, the PM should build a quick business case to justify the decision and illustrate to the finance manager that spending more money now and delivering the project on time (assuming it is on track), will save money in the long term. In addition, a case should be made for the importance of maintaining a positive relationship with the customer.

Risk Impact Breakdown

Table 8.5 supports these risk findings, provides illustrations of risk significance, specifies their full impact, and helps compare them to each other. Filling in all fields of the risk impact breakdown table (RIBT) helps build a risk statement, which helps

Table 8.5 Risk impact breakdown table (RIBT): A one-stop view for risk impact areas and context

Risk description (condition)	Generic areas of impact (may cause)	Quantifiable description of consequences (may result in quantifiable impact)	Risk timing	Impact (1-9)				Factored impact (weighted average)	Escalation (name a stakeholder to approach with the problem)
				Scope	Schedule	Cost	Quality		
Poor scope and multiple change requests (CRs)	Costs of CRs Time to process CRs Impact on objectives and benefits	$72,000 8 business days Optimization benefits realized Value created	Early or late implementation	3	3	7	4		

identify and communicate the risk and should be done, at a minimum, for all high profile risks.

As part of a risk impact assessment, the PM should be cognizant of, and alert stakeholders to, additional nonquantifiable impact areas that high level risks have. These areas include: morale, churn, conflicts, and misunderstandings that may surface as a result of the risk event. These items are difficult to identify and measure, but with experience, the PM should be able to prepare stakeholders for them.

Probability

Determining the probability of a risk occurring is not an easy task and needs to involve historical information, lessons learned, expert opinions, and sometimes some gut feelings. Team discussions about probabilities should not be settled through arguments and power struggles, related to who says what, but on merits and empirical information. In the event that there is a significant gap in an event probability estimate, the team should not compromise on a middle-of-the-road value because it will be meaningless and will not provide a realistic assessment of the probability. Instead, the team needs to deliberate and determine which value presented is valid. It may be useful to utilize Agile-like card estimation techniques, known as Planning Poker,[4] for the risk probabilities, which will also help reduce bias. In Planning Poker, team members express their estimates and simultaneously flash a card that represents their estimate's probability value.

Measuring a risk's probability goes through a refining process that is similar to that for impact measurements:

- Start with a high-medium-low likelihood scale for each risk;
- Refine it into numeric probability values. Scales to measure the probability can be 1–4, 1–5, or 1–10, which are the most commonly-used scales;
- A measure of percentage points is the most intuitive and ranges from 0.1 (for the lowest) to 0.9 (for the highest). Expressing probability in percentage points value offers an additional advantage: since it is different from the impact scale (1–10), it prevents confusion.

Zero, Fifty, and One Hundred Percent

The numbers 0 and 1 should not be part of the percentage point's values, since if there is zero chance that something might happen, it should not be part of the risk analysis because it is not a risk. Similarly, 1 (representing 100%) is not a risk either. If there is a 100% chance for something to happen, it should not be part of the risk assessment but part of the project scope and WBS.

Another number that should not be allowed to represent probability is 50% (0.5). Even if the probability assessment indicates that a risk has a 50% chance of occurring, it should be further investigated, as this is insufficient. While it may be the case mathematically, it could simply be due to a lack of information on the subject matter; either way, it is a sign that additional information is needed. Even if there is a 50% chance for a risk to happen based on historical events (for example, the vendor has delivered 5 of the last 10 deliveries late), there is always a way to gather more information and further refine the estimate. Stating that there is a 50% chance is not an indication of knowledge; anyone can make a guess on anything with that level of confidence.

Use a Range

When it is difficult to determine a specific value for the probability (in percentage points), it may be sufficient to use a range as a placeholder, keeping in mind the need to refine it moving forward and narrow it down to a more specific probability value (for a quantitative assessment and risk rating that is based on multiplying probability by impact, $P \times I$). Proposed values for a risk probability scale are displayed in Figure 8.5.

Probability and Impact Matrix

With a probability measure of 0.1 to 0.9 and an impact measure of 1 to 9, the project team now has the ability to combine the two factors and place risks on the probability and impact matrix (Figure 8.6), where the location of each risk is determined by multiplying probability by impact.

The probability and impact matrix helps illustrate the severity of identified risks. The probability is presented on the Y axis and should be presented in percentages, ranging from 1% to 99%. The impact is presented on the X axis and should reflect the overall impact the risk will have on the project, if it materializes. As the estimates are refined, the PM should also try to measure each risk's impact on the

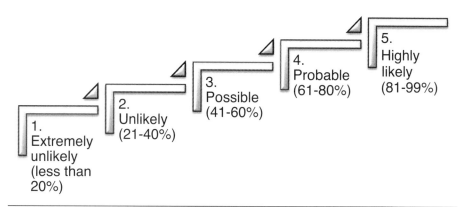

Figure 8.5   Values for probability measures

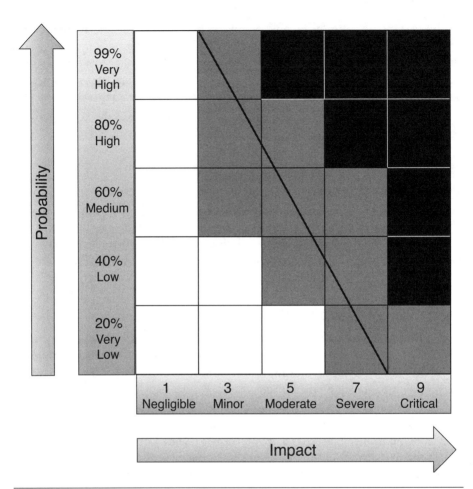

Figure 8.6 Probability and impact matrix

specific success criteria of the project. It is important to ensure that both the probability and the impact ratings are based on quality (i.e., credible) information and are not arbitrary. There should be a line crossing the matrix from the top left to the bottom right, to reflect the risk tolerance level of the project. Risks placed on the top right hand side of the line are more severe, while risks on the lower left hand side are of a lesser combination of probability and impact and, hence, will require less focus (but should not be ignored).

The threshold line should represent the actual tolerance level and approach to risk the project has. If the line is in a position that does not fully reflect the true risk tolerance level of the project, it may result in paying extra attention to risks that are not meaningful or significant to project success. Alternately, it may also lead to paying insufficient attention to risks that are significant and compromise the project success.

The tolerance line should then be split into two, creating a red zone on the top right hand side of the matrix; a yellow zone in the middle; and a green zone on the lower left hand side. The position of each line and the corresponding size of each zone provide guidance for whether to respond and how to respond to the risks in these areas. A detailed discussion about approaches to risk response is included later in this chapter.

When two risks have the same score (P × I), priority should be given to the risk with the higher impact over the one with the higher probability. Intuitively, the risk that may inflict more damage to the project is more important to attend to, but project distractions and stakeholders' agendas may cause PMs to lose track and spend project resources on irrelevant risks.

RISK URGENCY: BEYOND PROBABILITY AND IMPACT

When there are two or more risks of a similar magnitude, the project may not have the capacity to attend to both of them, and a decision needs to be made regarding which risk is more urgent to attend to. A risk face-off comparison, as demonstrated in Figure 8.7, can help in this matter, comparing the risks to each other—apples to

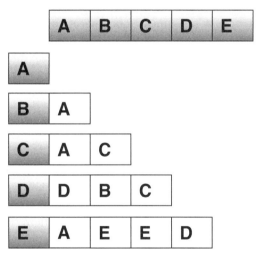

This paired comparison of risks helps determine which risk is more urgent. Consider impact time, risk dependency, stakeholders impacted, success areas impacted, and critical path impact.

Figure 8.7 Cross risk paired analysis

apples—to determine the more pressing one. For example, if one of the risks hits the critical path, it will be more urgent to respond to than to a risk that does not impact the critical path.

Expected Monetary Value—Financial Impact

The next step in refining the risk analysis is to incorporate a quantitative measure to determine the overall financial impact of each risk. Each risk (or, at the very least, each high profile risk) has to be measured by its overall financial impact on the project (and on the organization), which involves looking at the probability of the risk and factoring it by its overall estimated financial impact. This is a challenging task, since it is difficult to accurately estimate the projected monetary value associated with each risk. The financial measure is called expected monetary value (EMV) and is calculated by the probability of the risk times the overall dollar value of its financial impact.

When calculating the costs of risks, it is important to look into how the costs of the risk management process should be labeled. The efforts involved in managing risks add up to large amounts of (time and) money, and some stakeholders may argue that these costs should be included in the overall EMV for all the project's risks. This amount should include the overall cost that goes toward risks up front, plus the overall cost impact assessment. Looking at this figure for severe risks can help justify the risk management process. However, with limited capacities to manage risks, such a calculation adds an additional load that most projects cannot afford.

RISK ASSESSMENT

Part of the risk analysis process should include risk assessment, where existing physical and environmental controls are evaluated to assess whether they are sufficient to handle project risks. It should also include another look at the business impact assessment to identify business areas that may be impacted by project risks, including: service levels, customer relations, support functions, warranties, service calls, and internal operations—both legal and financial.

For projects with sensitive stakeholder relations, extra attention should be given to checking which stakeholder may be directly impacted by project risks to help the PM prepare for a range of possible reactions stakeholders may have. It also helps reduce the bias in the analysis process from agenda-driven pressures stakeholders may apply. Extreme types of stakeholder reactions may turn into new risks, and effective stakeholder management strategies and relationship management is important in these situations.

The analysis and assessment results may surprise some stakeholders and upset others, since they may disagree on whether the findings that the risks they are associated with are important for the project objectives. This will likely trigger challenging responses and behaviors and, once again, requires a strong command of project communication and relationship management. Special focus should be given to maintaining good relationships with these stakeholders by showing respect for their points of view—never questioning the legitimacy of their concerns.

NEXT STEP: TRIGGERS AND DETECTABILITY

Risk management is perceived to be reactive in nature, and with this perception comes the temptation to procrastinate and to sit on problems until they are urgent and cannot be ignored. This procrastination turns risk management into an uphill battle to get senior management's buy-in to take preventive and proactive measures—and the longer one procrastinates, the worse it gets. It is often difficult for the PM to justify taking preventive actions, and there are always stakeholders who prefer to sit and wait for problems to occur. Even organizations that have a risk management process often neglect to look for what might precede or lead to risks and to examine the team's ability to detect such events. There are two things that can help project teams cope better with risk events, just by getting a heads up and recognizing that a risk is imminent, emerging, or taking place: understanding risk triggers and their detectability.

Triggers

A trigger is an event or an indication that a risk is imminent or has already happened. A simple example of a trigger is: clouds are a trigger for rain and serve as an indication that it might rain (although it does not rain every time it is cloudy). When it is cloudy, there is a better chance for rain and depending on the circumstances—and metaphorically speaking, the project team may need to take measures to prepare for rain.

Some triggers may be events that, if they take place, will trigger risk events. When identifying these trigger events, it is important to verify that the trigger has a causal effect on the risk event and that the relationship between them is not merely casual or coincidental. For example, it may be true that each time someone coughs, it rains later in the day; however, a correlation between events means that one event actually leads to and causes the other one. If two events happen to take place around the same time, it does not follow that they have a causal relationship. This example illustrates the need to carefully check for causal relations between events, so the project team does not waste its limited resources on preventing events that make no difference to the project or do not result from the "cues."

Detectability

Detectability is a measure of an organization's or a team's ability to sense, notice, or recognize that a risk has happened or is imminent. It is about looking for events or conditions that may lead to (i.e., trigger) risks and for ways to improve the ability to detect them. There are more advanced ways to detect (or forecast) rain than looking for clouds: it can be done with radars, satellite images, and other forecasting models. To the untrained eye, on a clear day it is easy to determine whether it will rain, but on a hot and humid day with hazy skies, it is difficult to determine whether a thunderstorm may be approaching. After identifying triggers for risks, the project team needs to determine its ability to detect these triggers, which in turn, may impact the overall severity of the risk.

The Importance of Triggers and Detectability

When looking at risk categories and identifying the source of each potential risk, the PM should check to see if conditions are conducive for the risk event to take place. Based on this assessment, the team can direct its focus toward more urgent events and threats (time proximity, severity, dependency, impact areas), than toward risk events that are not severe or imminent. Taking an umbrella every morning when heading out may not be the most efficient thing to do, since a quick look out the window or at the weather forecast (to identify triggers) may be sufficient to make the right decision and save you from taking an umbrella when it is not necessary.

Early detection of risks may help combat them more effectively, prepare to deal with their impact, and even avoid them. It can also buy time for the team to better position itself for the upcoming risk event. Given the importance of risk triggers and detectability, PMs must keep in mind that an easy-to-detect risk is not necessarily a low priority or an easy risk to manage.

RISK RESPONSE PLANNING

The position of the risks on the probability and impact matrix determines whether they require further action. Such action is response planning, and it must be proportionate in cost and effort to the type, magnitude, and severity of the risk event. It would be pointless to spend more on eliminating a risk than the total cost of the risk impact (with the exception of health and safety).

Although the word "response" is reactive in nature, risk response planning predominantly involves taking proactive steps prior to the risk event materializing. While this chapter focuses on how to handle and manage negative risks, PMs should always be on the lookout for and get the project ready to capture any opportunity it may come across. Opportunities generally do not appear out of nowhere—they may present themselves in untimely and vague ways—hence, project teams need to be prepared. For example, the only prerequisite for winning the lottery is to play the lottery, but without playing, there is no chance of winning. It sounds so simple, but in a similar fashion, organizations may not be in a position to capture opportunities as they present themselves.

Steps for Risk Response Planning

Risk response planning should follow these steps:

1. Identify a response strategy: this is often not a choice between several options. In most cases, the project team is forced into a limited set of options, depending on the situation at stake;
2. Define specific response action(s) to apply to the selected strategy;
3. Think of a contingency plan, in the event that the risk takes place despite response planning efforts (e.g., an attempt to reduce the probability of the risk occurring);
4. For significant risks, prepare a fallback plan (or "plan B"), in case the contingency plan also fails.

Response Strategies

The SWOT analysis helps articulate a project's internal capabilities (i.e., strengths and weaknesses) and supports the risk identification process by listing opportunities (positive risks) and threats (negative risks). SWOT on Steroids enhances the analysis and proposes potential risk responses, by offering response options within the context of the project's capabilities. When considering response strategies, there are four response options, as illustrated in Figure 8.8.

Response to Threats

Avoidance is about removing a specific threat by reducing its probability or impact to zero. At the end of the process, the risk event will not take place. Avoidance is a strategy against major risks with unbearable consequences to the project (often known as "show stoppers"). It is recommended to identify the need and apply this response as early as possible, since the cost to eliminate a risk is likely to grow dramatically as the project progresses.

Mitigation is the most common risk response strategy and is about taking action before a risk is triggered in order to reduce its probability and/or its impact and EMV. It can be done by adopting one or more of the following techniques:

1. Reduce the probability of the risk occurrence;

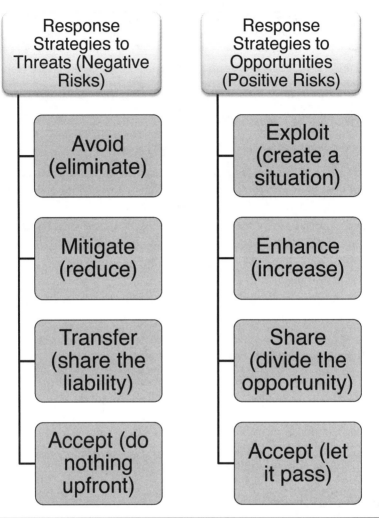

Figure 8.8 Risk response strategies

2. Reduce the impact of the risk event, should it take place;
3. Improve the ability to detect the risk or its trigger(s) before it happens. (Even though this option does not reduce the risk impact, it may help the team prepare for it or take special measures.)

Transference can be viewed as a form of mitigation, since it is about finding a third party who can share part of the financial impact of the risk event, should it take place. Transferring a risk converts the unknown risk impact into a known effect (usually a cost). Unfortunately, transferring is not free, since the third party accepting the risk will demand compensation for it. Naturally, the lower the project team's ability to respond to the risk, the more it will cost. Risk transference can be done on the front end (probability) or the back end (impact):

- Front end: an example of front end risk transference is selecting a type of contract with a lower risk, or including provisions to avoid additional costs. This is an attempt to transfer the risk to the other party before it actually occurs, but not all parties will agree to assume some of these risks;
- Back end: purchasing insurance is a common form of transferring risk to the back end. Since fire may lead to damages and dramatic project over-runs, the insurance will get a third party (insurer) to assume the costs associated with the damages from the fire—with the potential to include (for additional cost) special arrangements, such as an alternate location, should the project site no longer be usable.

Transferring is not about blaming others or shirking responsibilities, and it does not eliminate the overall risk impact. Therefore, using this method is often done as part of a mitigation strategy, or when the ability to reduce the probability of a risk event is limited.

For Both Threats and Opportunities

Acceptance is about accepting and bearing the consequences of the risk. It means the project team does not have one or more of the following: ability, money, time, resources, desire, or interest to do anything about the risk. Accepting a risk can be active, which involves developing a contingency plan (a form of mitigation), or passive, which means accepting the fact that the risk event might take place (assuming the risk) and with it, there will be an impact. By accepting a risk, the team essentially determines that the risk is small enough that the project can live with its consequences. Alternately, acceptance may be the response strategy chosen (i.e., a decision to do nothing) when there is no ability to respond to a risk.

Response to Opportunities

Sharing is about dividing an opportunity and sharing it with another party, so it improves the project's chance of benefiting from it. This strategy is most appropriate when an organization does not have the ability to capture the opportunity on its own and must resort to accepting help from another organization (through connections, access to resources, knowledge/capital, skills, or expertise).

Enhancing is about increasing the chance that something good is going to take place. It can be done through increasing the probability, increasing the impact of a positive risk event, or improving the ability of the project team to detect an opportunity in a timely manner.

Exploiting is about creating the conditions for a situation to take place, since it would otherwise simply not occur. It is illustrated by the example of increasing the chance of winning the lottery by playing it.

Beyond Response Strategies

Once the strategies are in place, the team should move to planning what action(s) to take for each response strategy, with the likelihood that more than one action will be required for each strategy. The team should conduct a cost–benefit analysis in search of the most appropriate actions.

Part of the risk response plan is identifying a person who will own the risk (known as the owner) for the purpose of monitoring it and initiating action. In the event that a risk occurs, it is also important to identify an actionee, who will step up in an attempt to respond to the risk, undo the damage, or fix the damage that results from the risk event.

> **Response Costs**—The team needs to keep track of the response costs, which are associated with developing and implementing the risk response, as well as with the costs of the response itself (e.g., the cost of insurance).
>
> **Response Timing**—Similar to knowing the time a risk is expected to take place, it is important to identify and keep track of the date by which a response should be implemented. A good response may be deemed useless if delivered too late, since it will not address the risk as intended.
>
> **Adjusted Probability and Impact**—Upon completion of any round of risk response planning (there should be multiple rounds throughout the project, as risks are discovered or change), the team needs to determine the new probability and impact levels of each risk, in light of the response strategies and actions selected. It will also yield a reevaluated risk priority level and provide insight into whether the risk has been sufficiently reduced to an acceptable level, or whether additional response actions may be required.

CONTINGENCY

Contingency planning is about preparing to respond in an orderly fashion when an unplanned event takes place. It can also be viewed as an alternative to action, if certain conditions materialize. Contingency planning is an extension of risk response planning and is about what the team needs to do if a risk event that is above the accepted threshold level takes place.

To determine the total value of the contingency (the EMV), the project team needs to identify all the remaining risks (accepted, and those left after being reduced) that are above the project's tolerance level. This EMV determines the funding the PM should request from the sponsor to allocate as the contingency reserve. The contingency reserve is a pool of funds that should be identified by the PM and allocated to the project (as a commitment or as part of the budget) to cover the known-unknowns (accepted or reduced risks), which remain after the efforts to manage and reduce risks. At a minimum, the total amount of the reserve should be higher than the full impact amount of any single risk within it—otherwise one risk can become a show stopper.

In addition to the contingency reserve, the PM should identify team members and other stakeholders as actionees, who should be made available and apply their experience and knowledge toward recovering from the impact of the risk event, should it materialize. Time reserve should also be allocated, based on estimates of how long it will take the project team (and specifically the actionees) to clean up or recover from the risk event.

In the event that there is no valid contingency plan in place, a workaround can bypass situations that are introduced as a result of risk events occurring. It essentially tries to deal with each situation, specifically in an attempt to reduce the losses associated with it. PMs must keep in mind that when there is a strong workaround (or a good fallback plan), it may serve as a deterrent to fixing the problem, since it allows a false sense of routine and success.

Sometimes PMs need to execute a response plan that includes recalling a resource that is no longer reporting to the project. Before doing so, the PM needs to consult with the sponsor, and possibly with other stakeholders, to ensure that this is the right way to maximize value for the organization as a whole. Although, instinctively, PMs try to salvage their own projects to avoid becoming part of the culture of alligators (as discussed in Chapter 1), they do need to check whether pulling a resource from a different engagement is the right thing to do.

S.W.A.T. Teams

Some organizations resort to a form of S.W.A.T. team (they may use a different cool and catchy name) as their contingency plan. It is a team of skilled and experienced employees—not assigned to any project's critical path—that is deployed in the event of a crisis in the organization in order to swiftly and effectively clean up the mess caused by the risk event. It is a decision that costs more on the front end (training and salaries for a team of qualified individuals who do not add value to a specific project). However, as with readiness, communication, and quality planning, deploying this team to address a crisis (not for trivial risks) is likely to make financial sense, since it will be able to resolve situations that may otherwise deteriorate into outright disasters.

SECONDARY AND RESIDUAL RISKS

Any selected response strategy and its actions may trigger additional risks, known as secondary and residual risks. Secondary and residual risks should not be ignored or undermined.

Secondary Risks

Secondary risks (Figure 8.9) are risks that are triggered or introduced as a result of a risk response; as such, they should be treated in a similar fashion to the side effects from consuming a product or taking a medication. Planning for and implementing a risk response may help address or reduce a specific risk, but it may also trigger one or more new risks, which would not have been introduced otherwise. Failing to consider secondary risks may leave the project team unprepared for them.

For every response strategy and action plan, the team should think of the potential secondary risk(s) it may trigger (this needs to be done while planning the

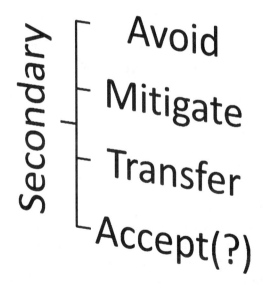

When selecting any response strategy, it may trigger secondary risks as a result of the actions taken in the risk response process. Arguably, even no action (i.e., accepting a risk) may lead to secondary risks if the current risk is not addressed.

Figure 8.9 Secondary risks

response). It is possible that when reviewing the response options to a risk, the team may deem them unrealistic or infeasible, thereby making the risk "non-response-able" and possibly requiring additional actions or changes to the plan. Any action taken may trigger new risks, by either increasing the probability of other risks or introducing new risk events with their own impact areas. Accepting a risk may also trigger secondary risks, if the team fails to address the existing risk to some extent.

Residual Risks

Residual risks are risks that remain in the system after performing the risk response planning. They should not be ignored; rather they should be placed on a "watch list," which includes all of the risks that are below the threshold tolerance line (to the lower left hand side of the probability and impact matrix, often in the green zone). This list includes the following response strategies (also in Figure 8.10):

- Mitigated risks that have been reduced to an acceptable level;
- Transferred risks;
- Accepted risks.

When selecting a response strategy for risks (except for avoidance) it will leave the team with residual risks. These are risks that remain even after the risk response planning.

Figure 8.10   Residual risks

Even though no additional action is required for these risks, they may still occur. At the very least, the team should review the watch list in a timely manner (at regular intervals, as part of risk monitoring and control, in addition to when specific risk conditions change). If the team takes action as part of the avoidance response strategy, there will be no residual risks for this event, since it should eliminate the specific risk event by reducing its probability or its impact to zero.

CONTROLLING RISK

The process of controlling risks is straightforward but faces one major challenge: people simply do not perform it properly, or they fail to do it altogether. Whether because of time constraints or, ironically, due to being consumed by unexpected risks that materialize from weak risk management practices, the results are the same: project teams often neglect to follow up on what really happens with risks. Project risk control activities, reviews, and reassessments should be prescheduled and performed regularly, as part of the risk management plan. Controlling risk involves two main actions: checking what is going on to determine if and what action needs to take place, and taking action based on the situation. PMs can put together a checklist of items to ensure they know what needs to take place as part of the risk control process.

    Review Identified Risks and the Watch List—Previously identified risks need to be checked regularly for any changes they may go through, including accepted risks and ones that were reduced to an acceptable level. Both types of risks should be reviewed at regular intervals to check whether the risks, or their related conditions, have changed (i.e., trigger, rating, priority, probability, impact, ability to detect, ability to respond, timing) and whether any risks require further action or can be retired (are no longer relevant).

    Review Changes—When change requests are accepted, or if project conditions change, there is a need to review the new conditions for additional risk analysis or risk response planning. Additional information about change requests and risks can be found in Chapter 12.

    Execute Contingency or Fallback Plan—For risk events that materialize, the control process serves to execute and implement the contingency plan, to ensure the project recovers from the risk with minimal damage. Execution of contingency plans is also about recognizing that the project no longer operates under the best case scenario. It includes managing stakeholders' expectations, so they realize that corrective actions and changes to the plan (baseline) follow the risk plan and that the recovery efforts are about bringing the project performance to an acceptable and agreed-upon level, rather than to the pre-risk performance level.

    Identify New Risks—With changing project conditions (assumptions, constraints, and issues), changing requests, changing risk conditions, and varying performance levels, the project team should be on the lookout for new risks on an ongoing basis. New risks may also be introduced by any categories on the RBS, so the team needs to track these areas regularly. Failing to identify new risks may make the risk register stale, which means it will fail to address upcoming challenges.

Update Lessons Learned and Risk Plans—There may be a need to update lessons learned to ensure that the organization does not stumble into the same risks in the future, or in the event that there is a need to update processes and practices with vendors, relationships, response actions, or risk tolerance levels. The goal is to provide the organization with better risk management practices for future projects. As part of the lessons learned process, project teams need to ask themselves—at the end of the project—how effective the risk management process and results have been. Referring to it as the merits test, the team and the organization should look at the bottom line and check whether the risk management process produced the desired results.

Review Response Strategies and Actions—The team needs to review the response strategies and actions performed for risks that have occurred to ensure that they are effective. There should also be a review of risk response strategies and action plans for risks that have not materialized—to ensure that the plans are still relevant and to consider whether an alternative strategy or action plan needs to be formed.

Evaluate Risk Process Effectiveness—Evaluating the effectiveness of the risk management process should take place at predetermined intervals. This review is not about the risks but about how effective the process of managing them has been. It should cover the following areas:

- Review budgets, timelines, roles and responsibilities, tolerance levels, and any other procedural aspect of risk management to check whether it is effective, efficient, cost effective, and timely;
- Look into whether there is a need to change the way risks are managed;
- Review data sources, to determine the reliability and quality of information and whether the sources of data need to be changed.

Report Risk—Risk tracking and reporting needs to follow the risk plan and must be done in a way that adds value to the project and its stakeholders. Beyond the need to produce meaningful, relevant, and clear reports that produce a complete, timely, and accurate set of data, PMs need to ensure that the reports satisfy the stakeholders' needs. Part of risk reporting is to provide sufficient and timely information for the appropriate project stakeholders, and PMs should ensure that each stakeholder gets all the information needed—and nothing beyond what is needed. When stakeholders come across information they are not supposed to be exposed to, it opens the door for misunderstandings and additional burdens on project communication that on their own may introduce new risks.

Perform Throughout the Lifecycle—Risk control starts with risk identification and occurs throughout the project lifecycle. It includes a set of activities that are not complicated to perform, but do require finding the time to do them properly. The PM must find time and capacity for controlling risks, and it is advisable to plan for it up front, during the project planning stage, to avoid the need to scramble for resources and take shortcuts later in the project.

ADDITIONAL RISK CONSIDERATIONS

Risk Dependencies—the Cascading Effect

Risk dependencies are difficult to identify and comprehend, since they are about events that may come from outside of the organization. They may appear within two different settings—cross project risk dependencies and cross risk dependencies:

1. Cross project risk dependencies: these are risk events that are triggered by events (and risks) in other projects. For example, when project A depends upon processes, deliverables, or products that are produced by project B, problems at project B are out of project A's control but will negatively impact project A. Alternately, risk dependency can also take place when two projects share a resource, and a situation in project B may prevent the resource from reporting to project A on time. Even for projects in which risks are properly managed, there may be external events that have significant impact on the project. They mainly come from other projects and are mostly related to resources and deliverables. This topic is further elaborated in Chapter 12.

2. Cross risk dependencies (within the project): these are risk events that may trigger other risks within the project. For example, a small delay in completing a construction deliverable may push the project into the winter season, resulting in extra costs and the need for specific tools and expertise because the concrete must now be poured in subzero temperatures.

Nonlinear

The construction example further demonstrates how risks and delays are nonlinear in nature, as a slight delay in completing the deliverable creates a greater delay in actual construction. This is similar to the previous case of arriving at the train station mere seconds after the commuter train has left: regardless of the size of the delay, its actual impact depends upon how long it will take for the next train to arrive. Such situations occur in projects where seemingly minor risks trigger more significant ones, which have a much more severe impact on the project objectives. Once again, effective communication allows the team to conduct candid risk assessments that look at the risks' impacts downstream—all the way to the project objectives and success criteria.

Show Stoppers

Some risk events have a combination of probability and impact that make them severe enough to be called show stoppers. They pose such strong negative impacts on the project that if they take place, they can cause the project to fail outright. An example of a show stopper is funding approval for a new initiative: in the event that the funding request is not approved, the project cannot move forward and will need to stop.

Identifying risk timelines is important for all risks, but it is critical for show stoppers, so the project team can identify a point in time by which a decision or a reference to an event needs to be made. When the project reaches that moment, there are two options:

1. The risk materializes and the project stops;
2. The risk does not happen and the project can proceed as planned. Besides updating the outcome on the risk/issue log, there is no need for further action.

Proactive Risk Management and Communication

Identifying categories, performing stakeholder analysis, making assumptions, and working toward recognizing triggers are the main components of proactive risk management. When a risk materializes, there is no more uncertainty about it, and the need for corrective action is clear. However, risk management is much more cost effective when it focuses on prevention and working with the sources of risks in an effort to prevent them from happening. By doing so, the project team is able to channel its efforts more efficiently and utilize its excess capacity toward other value-adding activities in the project, rather than reactively responding to risks that could have been averted.

Despite the advantages associated with early alert and detection of risks, it is known to be a tough sell, since preventive action and a thorough risk management process are expensive and hard to justify. It involves the difficult task of identifying what might happen, or trying to predict the future. In order to achieve buy-in from senior management, the PM needs to build a business case and demonstrate why it makes sense to consume additional resources for something that may not happen. Stakeholder analysis and communication planning are critical for the project risk management process. They can help PMs approach stakeholders in the appropriate context and express the justification in sufficient detail, appropriate language, and rigor for the stakeholders' needs.

Risk Statement: Choose Appropriate Wording

Another area that illustrates the touch-point between project risk and communication is the ability of the PM to articulate the risk in such a way that is clear and easy to understand by most stakeholders. It is common to see gaps in the perception and understanding of risks among various team members and stakeholders, and the ability to clearly articulate risks and their impacts is critical for determining how to handle them. The wording of the risk or the risk statement is about capturing the risk event into one sentence that clarifies it for everyone involved. A simple structure of a risk statement reads:

"If a certain condition occurs, then consequences might happen, resulting in a quantifiable result."

This kind of statement describes any risk the project may encounter and puts the risk results into the context of the project objectives. As risks evolve during the project lifecycle, there will be a need to adjust the risk statement to reflect the current conditions associated with the risk. At first, the risk statement may not include the full quantifiable results details, as more information may be needed, but having the statement in place helps the team identify areas that require additional information or due diligence. The team also needs to keep in mind that there may be more than one area to mention in the quantifiable results. Wording a risk properly and in a way that is clear to all relevant stakeholders is a difficult task, but once done, it should clearly illustrate what the actual risk event is and its trigger(s) or consequence(s).

Do Not Overdo It

A common question many PMs have concerns knowing how much risk planning is too much and how much is sufficient. While there is no single answer for all projects, the following factors should be considered when determining when to stop: project complexity, project cost, the level of risk in the project, dependencies on the project, the overall visibility and stake for the organization, and historical information. Unfortunately, most PMs only realize they have overdone risk management after the fact.

Gut feel, a sense of comfort about the risk management performed, and a check of the risk management rigor against the issues, constraints, and assumptions can become proprietary indicators. These help PMs know when to stop, since they can compare their projects with previous projects within the organization.

Another Type of Risk: The 100% Probability Event

When thinking about risks, project teams look for events that have a certain probability of occurring, but "probability" suggests an event has less than a 100 percent guarantee. Events that are guaranteed to happen need to be part of the project scope and not on the risk log. However, there are events that are not part of the project plan but are guaranteed to happen. The question about them is not IF they are going to take place, but WHEN, and WHAT their impact will be. These are major events—such as security breaches, extreme weather events, public health events (e.g., a flu pandemic), and system failures. A more specific example, related to extreme weather events, is: a "once in a hundred years" rainfall event that may cause flooding of a facility, leading to leakage of hazardous materials into water supplies.

Organizations need to have plans in place for when these types of events strike—such as Disaster Recovery Plans (DRPs) or Business Continuity Plans (BCPs). Their funding is typically part of the management reserve, not from the project funding or contingency reserve. It is not the job of the PM to put these plans together for a specific project, but—if there is a chance these events will impact the project—the PM needs to make a reference to the DRPs and the BCPs that are in place. At times, it is difficult to determine the risk tolerance level and the attitude toward risk that an organization has, and a look at the DRP and the BCP can serve as a strong indicator of how an organization views risks. Even though these disasters are not project risks, the way organizations treat them is a strong indication of what a PM should expect when dealing with project risks.

Honey and Vinegar

When managing risks and trying to alert stakeholders about dangers and negative events, there is a fine line between appearing difficult and giving the impression of being realistic. Stakeholder analysis and engagement plans can help the PM determine how to engage stakeholders, and which reasoning to use, so that stakeholders view the PM as part of the solution and not the problem. The PM should also remain positive and provide options and alternatives that point to a potential solution, which is aligned with the project objectives, rather than simply stating what cannot be done. It is crucial to price the risk's consequences in currency, values, and terms that matter to each stakeholder and resonate with individual objectives and drivers.

Care—Even If You Have No Control Over It

If there is an area in the risk response plan that is not under the control of the PM (e.g., dependence on resources, or actions and decisions by others) the PM still needs to make sure it is recorded, that the appropriate stakeholders know about it, and if needed, to qualify it as a secondary risk. Even events the PM cannot control may inflict damage on the project, and it is worth the effort to manage them properly.

Risk and Politics

Politics in the organization affects every aspect of the project—including risk management—and it is not a choice PMs make, but a reality they have to face and deal with. Recognizing politics in risk management and dealing with it requires the PM to stand strong and maintain focus on the project objectives, while trying to educate stakeholders and communicate with them in meaningful terms and values that resonate with them. Standing strong also means quantifying to these stakeholders the impacts their requests would have on the project. Sometimes, little can be done about these things, but effectively communicating the impact to the stakeholders may bring them back to their senses. Here are examples of the politicization of risk:

- When stakeholders try to promote certain risks to get special attention, but the attention is misaligned with the severity of the risk;
- When senior stakeholders request that the PM remove a risk from the risk log, only so other stakeholders (e.g., the steering committee) do not see it;
- When response plans get stripped of their resources, actionees, or subject matter experts—but the expectation remains that they will be executed as planned.

Escalation

Organizations should include clear escalation procedures for risks. These procedures provide guidelines for the types of events that require escalation, the forms of the escalation, the messages to communicate, and the recipients. Having the right escalation process in place directs team members and stakeholders to do the right thing and reduces risk, by serving as a turnkey solution that lessens the need to scramble to find out who needs to be notified and what the message is. Following these procedures allows PMs and team members to maximize their focus on addressing the problem at stake.

Risk Meetings

Dedicated risk meetings should take place on a regular basis (in most cases, once a week, depending on the project velocity). These are not meetings in which risks appear as line items on their agendas, along with other topics; rather, they are special meetings that deal solely with project risks. The highlights of these meetings, along with information about risks' urgencies, timeliness, or other items that require the project's focus should be extrapolated and discussed in the project status meeting.

FINAL THOUGHTS ON RISK

Managing risk does not help the PM win any popularity contests. Stakeholders may not like certain events or conditions, and they may have a hard time realizing that managing risks is not a matter of choice, but part of reality—no pressure they apply or argument they make can change it. The only things that can change risks are a change in the plan, a proper risk management process, or a change in expectations, which includes concessions between competing demands. Failure to identify or to properly manage and track risks will impact project success and the quality perceived by the customer. PMs must also keep in mind that there may be post-implementation risks, which—in a similar fashion to business risks—may impact the organization beyond the completion of the project. PMs need to ensure that the risk log is made available to a program office or to other stakeholders, with the suggested plans to respond to these risks, as appropriate.

REFERENCES

1. Inspired by Robert W. Bradford, Peter J. Duncan, and Brian Tarcy, *Simplified Strategic Planning: The No-Nonsense Guide for Busy People Who Want Results Fast* (Worcester: Chandler House Press, 2000).
2. Adapted from: Project Management Institute, *A Guide to the Project Management Body of Knowledge*, (*PMBOK® Guide—Fifth Edition*), 60–61 (Sylva: Project Management Institute, 2013).
3. Ibid., 567.
4. Based on: Mike Cohn, *Agile Estimating and Planning*, 1st Edition (Stoughton: Pearson Education, Inc., 2005).

9

Learn What Quality Means

"The User Will Figure It Out;" "We Don't Need UAT;"
or "Testing? Don't You Have Good Developers?"

These comments may seem technical in nature, but their impact on the project and the organization can get deeper and more severe since they indicate a disturbing view of quality. The reality of constant time and money constraints leads stakeholders to search for ways to shorten schedules, some of which are more creative than others. Since there may be little-to-no flexibility in adjusting project constraints (specifically scope, time, cost, and resources), project managers are under pressure to deliver on these constraints, leaving no choice but to assume more risks and make decisions that adversely affect quality. From a quality management perspective, this option is unacceptable, and while no one will ever admit this is the approach they choose, it happens quite often: reducing the time, effort, or scope of testing. The attitude, that the customer or the user will figure it out or find the problems with no testing or without training, is borderline ludicrous. Project managers must understand the trade-off relationship between constraints and articulate the price of failing to balance them to senior stakeholders.

There is a major disconnect between what people and organizations say about quality and what they actually do about it. As one of the four competing demands, which serve as project success criteria (along with scope, time, and cost), it is clear that quality should not be compromised, but less flexible constraints (often time and cost) usually get priority over quality. One way to measure project quality is to look at the number of recalls, errors, defects, and warranty calls that users need to contend with and the costs associated with them.

To make matters worse, many organizations consciously choose to sacrifice quality in order to focus on other success criteria. For example, when there is no time/money to include a feature, the project team may suggest delivery of the product without it and have it included in the warranty for the customer. In this case, they make a clear decision that time or cost considerations prevail over quality. It also speaks volumes about the organization's philosophy on quality. Although a warranty offers customers repairs or adjustments executed and paid for by the performing organization, it also means that the organization passes the onus and the hassle to the customer, including time, aggravation, and inconvenience. The gap between words and actions illustrates that values about quality cannot be expressed only in words; they must also be evident in the actions and conduct of the organization and its employees.

MANAGEMENT RESPONSIBILITY

In 1945, Joseph Juran said, "It is most important that top management be Quality-Minded. In the absence of sincere manifestation of interest at the top, little will happen below."[1] If management has the aptitude for it, a passion for quality will eventually spread, like a domino effect, to the entire team and the organization. There are, however, plenty of examples of large organizations that are not only failing to follow this concept but also acting in exactly the opposite way: when cost-saving initiatives preside, quality deteriorates—with all the negative consequences that may follow.

To achieve project quality, it is the job of the project manager (PM) to demonstrate people skills (leadership) first and project management and technical skills (management) second. In fact, leadership starts with the sponsor, who should act as the overall leader of the project, ensure the project vision is accurately articulated, and translate it into actions that inspire and motivate the team. It is not only about the goal of producing deliverables but also about the means of getting there (accomplishing success for the customer together). This kind of healthy environment instills trust within the team, encouraging them to share ideas and challenge processes without fear. When team members are driven by fear, their innovation and ideas for improvement are stifled, and they shirk responsibility, refrain from sharing feedback and ideas, and hide mistakes. This inevitably leads to team members failing to learn from previous mistakes and avoiding making decisions altogether.

The Next Process is the Customer[2]

W. Edwards Deming introduced the concept that meeting customers' requirements is the task of everyone within an organization; by that, he expanded the definition of "customer" to include both internal and external customers. According to this view, every person or step in any business process has to be treated like a customer and provided with exactly what is needed, when it is needed. This is the principle that "the next process is the customer."

Offshoring

Offshoring provides an example of how actions represent organizations' views of the importance of quality, and the full impact of these actions. The idea behind offshoring is to introduce cost savings that are intended to free up funds, so they can be reassigned to improving quality and service. However, at some point, this concept went awry—for many organizations, saving costs has become the ultimate goal, rather than the means to achieving quality and service improvements. It is a known fact that the outsourcing of jobs to lower wage regions (known as offshoring) does not add value to the customers or to the organization. Differences that are related to colocation, time zones, cultures, language, communication, and values add up to higher costs, slower processes, and more hassle for both team members and customers.

With the constant need to reduce costs and (seemingly) improve efficiencies, large organizations up the ante of offshoring by negotiating "better" deals with their overseas partners. These deals mean that the outsourced service providers deliver more services for lower costs, further negatively impacting service levels, customer satisfaction, and productivity within the organization. With layoffs and reductions occurring in large numbers in North American operations, the remaining employees already need to do more with less, and they now need to contend with the latest trend in outsourcing and offshoring, which is the opposite of "the next process is the customer." Documents are received with typos, spelling mistakes, punctuation and factual errors; figures and reports are missing information and produced without references to data sources; shortcuts are made in information gathering and fact checking; and questions and follow-up inquiries are not addressed properly or in a timely manner.

Waste

These poor standards, which are common to offshoring, lead to significant waste, which forces the already-stretched North American workforce to contend with the poor quality of the work delivered by these service providers—spending time, energy, and resources (including frustration) on bringing the work up to minimal standards. These professionals need to spend their scarce time doing their own work, not on fixing substandard work delivered by others. It is not cost-effective to have the higher-skilled North American workforce spending time correcting the work of the lower-skilled offshore workforce because it reduces the time they have for their own tasks.

In offshoring, the organization chooses to save money on the front end, by paying less to the service providers and having local talent fix broken work and take on this new responsibility at the same pay. It sounds simple and straightforward, yet it is not always apparent to the decision makers. This chapter provides readers with information on how to make the right decision at the outset, and what to look for when trying to manage quality.

ABOUT QUALITY

Quality is misunderstood by many, who think it only relates to the end product or final deliverable and do not realize that it also involves processes, efficiencies, innovation, and continuous improvement. To ensure these are done right requires a quality management culture in all levels of the organization, from senior management through to the project team members. There are many reasons why organizational improvements often do not manage to sustain themselves, but one common reason is that team members try to avoid pointing out problems and challenges so that they are not associated with them and are not assigned to fix them. It is easy to blame employees for this, but the management responsibility concept, along with the 85:15 rule, show that it results from management's attitude towards quality. The 85:15 rule (introduced by W. Edwards Deming) states, 85% of the problems in any organization are system-related and hence, are under the control of management, while only 15% are worker-related.

Through quality management, PMs not only are influenced by their organizational culture but also have the ability to play an instrumental role in shaping the culture of their projects. It is up to the PM to attempt to build a project culture that is quality-driven and to explain to the organizational leadership the impact of not doing it right. Standing strong on these quality principles also provides the PM with a great opportunity to leave a positive mark on the organization—one that promotes a culture of collaboration, open communication, transparency, long-term thinking, training, information sharing, and quality decision making. This is the best way for the PM to avoid falling into the stereotypical role that many stakeholders have of PMs: as a funnel, through which stakeholders seek to promote their agendas to the front burner of the organization.

WHAT IS QUALITY?

Quality is the degree to which a set of inherent characteristics fulfills requirements.[3] It can be defined as a set of activities that is planned to help achieve project quality and to meet or exceed customers' expectations. Two additional definitions complement each other (details in Table 9.1): conformance to requirements and fitness for use.

Quality Planning

Quality planning serves as a reference to the organization's overall philosophy of quality. It is about determining and designing the organization's quality standards and associated policies and procedures. Project quality plans use existing organizational policies—if there are no applicable policies, they need to create new ones and identify new standards. The project quality plan defines the activities that need to

Table 9.1 Defining quality

Definition	Conformance to requirements	Fitness for use
Introduced by	Phillip Crosby[a]	Joseph Juran[b]
Explanation	How well a product or service meets the targets and tolerances determined by its designers	A definition of quality that evaluates how well the product performs for its intended use
Focus area	The managerial aspect of quality—quality assurance: process reviews, walkthroughs, and audits	The technical aspect of quality—quality control: testing and inspection
Answers	Are we doing the right thing?	Are we doing the right thing right?

This table expands on the two sub-definitions of quality: conformance to requirements and fitness for use. It presents their origins and illustrates their focus areas.
(a) Crosby, Phillip (1979). *Quality is Free*. New York: McGraw-Hill.
(b) Juran, Joseph (1986). *The Quality Trilogy*, Quality Progress 10, no. 8, 19–24.

take place in order to deliver the product and achieve the customer's quality expectations. These activities also determine how to meet the quality standards that are relevant to the project, which quality events need to take place, and what information and tools they need to utilize. These events utilize checklists, standards, and templates, and include reviews, walkthroughs, and inspections to follow up on the quality assurance and control processes.

The results of quality planning include checklists to make the quality management process easier and less risky, along with quality metrics and measurements to measure the project's performance. The measurements will also serve as the foundation for continuous improvement (in Japanese, *kaizen*) and as an input to the lessons learned process. Obtaining approval for the quality plan is the last step in finalizing it.

Quality Assurance

According to the Project Management Institute (PMI) and the quality concepts introduced by the likes of Deming, Juran, and Crosby, quality assurance is not about testing and inspection—even though it is often referred to as such in many organizations. Quality assurance is the management aspect of quality. With the targets defined in the quality plan, the project team needs to evaluate whether the project complies with the organization's project processes and policies. In essence, there are two questions to ask as part of this process:

- "Are the processes correct?"
- "Are we doing the right things?"

Quality assurance should take place throughout the project and involve periodic quality audits, walkthroughs, process reviews, and process analyses of repeatable activities to validate that the project activities comply with the organization's and the project's standards and policies. Quality assurance is about reviewing and assessing whether plans, processes, and in turn, results meet the standards. The quality assurance process should result in executing the continuous improvement plan, making recommendations for changes (for improvement, not scope-driven changes), and for corrective and preventative actions, as needed.

Quality Control

Quality control is the technical aspect of quality. The team measures the results against the standards and takes corrective actions (recalibration, adjustments), answering the following questions:

- "Is everything alright with the deliverables?"
- "Are we doing the right things right?"

The results of the quality control process should include identification of quality improvements, a list of quality control measurements (to be assessed and analyzed throughout the quality assurance process), validated deliverables, and if needed, defects for repair, corrective, and preventive action.

COST OF QUALITY

"Cost of quality" is widely used but often misunderstood. Like any good thing in life, quality comes with a cost; as articulated by Phillip Crosby, in his book *Quality Is Free*,[4] it is not a gift, but it is free—conceptually. The actual cost of quality was first articulated by Joseph Juran as the "cost of poor quality:"[5] any cost that would not have been expended if quality were perfect contributes to the cost of quality. Quality costs are the sum total of: the costs incurred by investing in the prevention of nonconformance to requirements, appraising a product or service for conformance to requirements, and failing to meet requirements.

The goal of quality processes is not to do them simply because they are the right thing to do, but because the return on the investment in quality has a dramatic impact on the organization. A 2002 study reported that software bugs cost the U.S. economy $59.6 billion each year, and that one third of the bugs could be eliminated by improved testing infrastructure.[6] This is in line with other research findings, which indicate not only that the cost of poor quality can exceed 20–30% of sales but also that most businesses are not aware of their actual spending on quality, as they do not keep track of it properly. Many people believe their organizations spend no more than 5% of their total sales on quality. There is a notion that the cost an organization incurs in an effort to obtain a new customer is, by far, higher than the cost to retain an existing one. Similarly, the cost to eliminate a failure after the customer gets the product (a.k.a., external failures) is significantly higher than it is at the development phase. Effective quality management is about early detection of errors in an effort to reduce costs.

Cost of quality consists of four elements, presented in Table 9.2: prevention, appraisal, internal failure, and external failure. The total cost of quality comprises the cost of conformance (including prevention and appraisal) and the cost of non-conformance (including both types of failure costs). The measure of the cost of quality is not the actual price the organization pays for building a quality product, but rather the cost of failing to create one.[7]

By nature, prevention costs are the lowest quality cost per item, while appraisal costs are relatively more expensive (albeit the total spending on prevention should be higher than the total spending on appraisal). Failure costs can be much higher per item, with external failures potentially becoming dramatically more expensive than internal failure. Unfortunately, the most common way of measuring failure only includes the common costs, such as warranty, scrap, and rework. However, true failure costs also include hidden costs, such as management time, downtime, increased inventory, decreased capacity, delivery problems, and lost orders.[8]

Table 9.2 Quality cost components

Cost type	Category	Details	Examples
Cost of conformance Money spent during project to avoid failure	Prevention costs	Up-front costs to meet customer requirements. Cost incurred to prevent poor quality and to reduce appraisal and failure costs. This is the cost to "design" the quality into the product.	Design plans, new product review, quality planning, supplier surveys, quality improvement plans, preventive auditing, and process improvement implementation, education, and training.
	Appraisal costs	Costs incurred to determine the degree of conformance to quality requirements through measuring, auditing, or evaluating.	Inspection, testing, process reviews, service audits, calibration, compliance audits, and investigations.
Cost of non-conformance Money spent during and after project due to failure	Internal failure	Costs associated with defects found within the organization (as a result of testing, inspections, and reviews) before the customer receives the product or service.	Scraps, rejects, rework, design flaws, repairs, reinspection, retesting, material review, defect evaluation, and downgrades.
	External failure	Cost associated with defects found after the customer receives the product or service.	Processing customer complaints, customer returns, evaluation of customer complaints, corrective actions, maintenance, warranty claims, product recalls, and possibly legal costs.

The cost of quality includes costs of conformance and cost of nonconformance to requirements.

There are many ways to view the desired ratio between the various costs of quality—as illustrated in Figure 9.1, which illustrates the difference between the actual cost of quality and the way it should (and should be perceived to) be. However when measuring the true failure costs—including internal, external, and

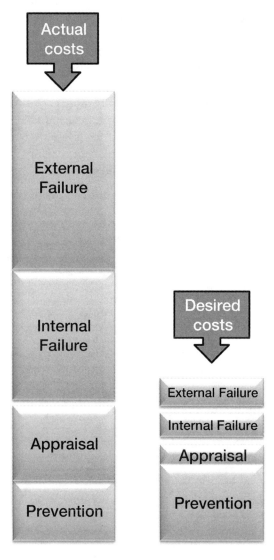

On the left, the actual level of cost allocated to quality may range around or above 20-30% of total sales, while on the right, the desired portion of sales that should be allocated to quality if done properly is 5%.

Figure 9.1 Simplified depiction: actual vs. desired cost of quality

hidden—it is safe to say that one dollar not spent, or misspent, on prevention may translate to a multiplier of 2, 3, or even 5 going forward, through each of the other three categories of quality. It is not unheard of that this one misspent dollar ends up as $100 in external failure costs, which includes compensations, penalties, litigation, and damages. The timing of incurring the different types of quality costs is demonstrated in Figure 9.2.

QUALITY MANAGEMENT PLAN

The project quality management plan is a document that records the information needed to effectively manage the quality of the entire project from start to finish. It should define the project's quality policies, processes, procedures, and criteria, or refer to the relevant items in the organization that are applicable to the project. The plan should address the items listed in Figure 9.3. The plan is created during the planning phase of the project and should include the section headings as they appear in Figure 9.4.

The quality management plan document should also include a few supporting items:

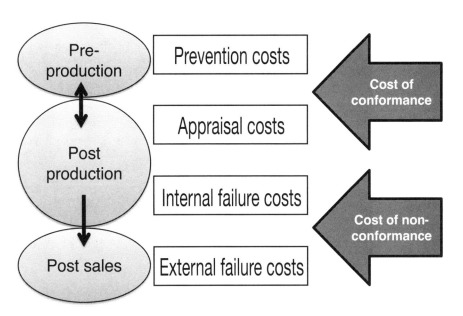

The categories of quality costs are shown in reference to a timeline and broken into cost of conformance.

Figure 9.2 The timing of incurring quality-related costs

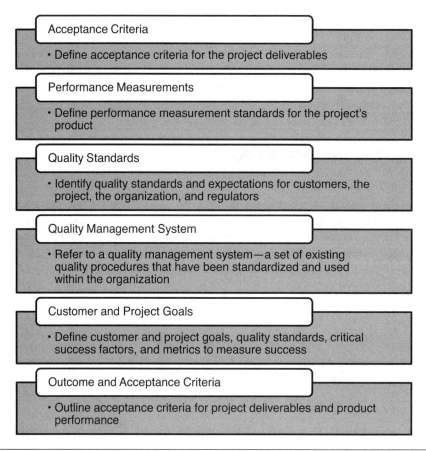

Figure 9.3 Things to address in the quality management plan

- Section for approvals/signatures by the main stakeholders involved;
- References to documents and their locations;
- Glossary for quality-related terminology, in the event that there is no other glossary for the project;
- Version management and document control section.

QUALITY CONSIDERATIONS

When putting the quality plan together, PMs need to keep in mind that quality is about customer satisfaction and that decisions related to quality should be geared towards achieving customer satisfaction. The effort should be driven by prevention, which means incorporating quality into the project processes and activities, rather

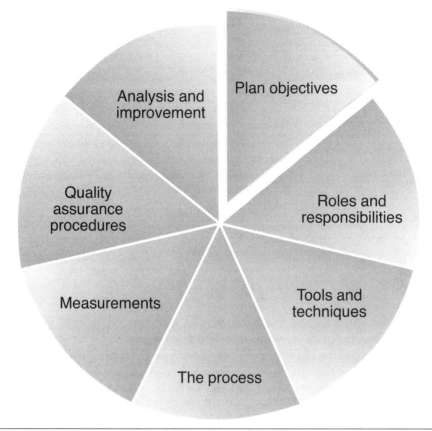

Figure 9.4 Quality plan section headings

than ensuring quality through inspection alone. While quality is the job of everyone in the organization, attention should be given to the responsibility of management to ensure quality and to inform all stakeholders of their roles in project quality.

Guidelines to Consider When Writing a Project Quality Plan

The project quality plan is geared towards providing the project and its stakeholders with easy access to quality requirements. When putting the plan together, the PM should ensure that the items in Table 9.3 are addressed.

POKA-YOKE

Poka-yoke, also referred to as "mistake proofing," is widely used; while people benefit from it, they are often unaware of its existence. The term was coined in Japan during the 1960's by Shigeo Shingo,[9] who was an industrial engineer at Toyota. The initial term was baka-yoke (or "fool-proofing"), but this was perceived to be

Table 9.3 Quality plan guidelines

☑	Nonconformance	Outline procedures to handle any type of nonconformance in the project processes or deliverables, address roles and responsibilities, describe conditions and measurements, and specify relevant resources and document availability.
☑	Corrective actions	List the criteria, guidelines, and procedures for taking corrective actions for problems encountered during project execution.
☑	Procurement	Define quality requirements and control for subcontracting or outsourcing parts of the project.
☑	Audits	Define criteria, goals, format, and timing for quality audits, including criteria and needs for internal vs. external audits.
☑	Inspection and testing	Detail the plans for all types of testing.
☑	Records management	Define procedures for maintaining quality records, including: metrics, measurements, variance reports, improvement plans, and checklists throughout the project lifecycle and afterward.
☑	Training	Specify training requirements for the project team.
Ensure these items are addressed in the quality plan.		

dishonorable and offensive and was, therefore, changed to poka-yoke. Poka-yoke is a simple method for preventing defects in business processes and helping people and processes work right the first time. Poka-yoke can substantially improve quality and reliability by having products designed in such a way that users are forced to use them as intended or at a minimum are prevented from making mistakes. The results are fewer errors, mishaps, damages, and possible injuries. Examples can be found nearly everywhere, as shown in Figure 9.5.

PROJECT HEALTH

Beyond the many measures proposed by a variety of quality concepts (e.g., the seven basic tools of quality), there are ways for PMs to measure their project health through "proprietary" measures. Proprietary measures are indicators the team can collect information for and track, but since they are situation-specific and organization-specific, any data they provide is meaningless on its own—unless data is collected over time so it can be benchmarked and compared against other projects within the organization for trends and context.

These indicators relate to quality in two primary ways, and many of them can be used both during and after the project:

1. **They provide an indication of project health**—These are interim reads of the state, process, progress, and general health of the project throughout its lifecycle, which provide indications about where it is trending. These measures provide a comprehensive analysis of the project, through

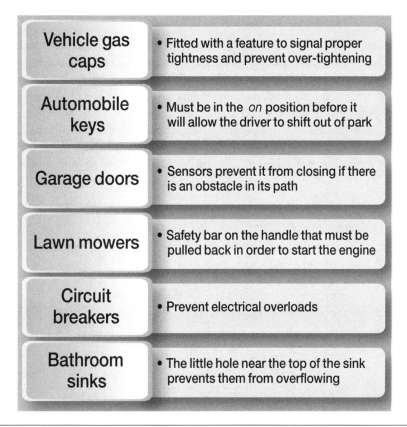

Vehicle gas caps	• Fitted with a feature to signal proper tightness and prevent over-tightening
Automobile keys	• Must be in the *on* position before it will allow the driver to shift out of park
Garage doors	• Sensors prevent it from closing if there is an obstacle in its path
Lawn mowers	• Safety bar on the handle that must be pulled back in order to start the engine
Circuit breakers	• Prevent electrical overloads
Bathroom sinks	• The little hole near the top of the sink prevents them from overflowing

Figure 9.5 Poka-yoke examples

an instant summary of the current situation, indications of weakness, identification of best practices, and an opportunity for equal comparisons of projects to each other. They also provide an insight into project governance and management oversight.

2. **They act as post-project indicators**—Beyond the validated deliverables and the project's results, there are a variety of measures that can point at performance levels of the team, processes, and the project as a whole. Even when the project delivers its results and they are accepted by the customer, there may be performance issues that if addressed, will lead to future benefits and opportunities to avert future problems.

These indicators and measures serve, in part, as a proactive mitigation measure and a lessons learned process, which needs to take place as part of the continuous improvement process (*kaizen*)—with the intention of capitalizing on benefits and improving weaknesses going forward. A discussion of lessons learned appears in Chapter 12.

Benefits

Conducting periodic project health checks provides the PM with real-time findings on areas for improvement, along with a chance to review ideas for improvement of processes and deliverables. Although the collection and interpretation of the data consumes time and resources, the investment pays off—by engaging the team and providing an opportunity for exchanging information and expertise. The project sponsor, other stakeholders, and the organization as a whole also benefit from a real-time option to mitigate risk and an ability to address findings about the project management practices quickly in the event that action at the organizational level is needed.

HEALTH MEASUREMENTS

There are multiple ways to measure project health, and no two organizations will benefit from exactly the same set of health-check items. Presented here is a list of potential measures; however, this discussion does not offer values for benchmarking, since every project and organization can develop a set of these values on its

Image 9.1 Project health

own, relative to other projects within the organization. PMs should be mindful of the costs and efforts associated with collecting, assessing, and communicating the data, and should conduct a cost–benefit analysis to ensure that the measures add value to the project and the organization. The list includes types of project health measurements, along with a short explanation of what they mean, as presented in Figures 9.6–9.8 and Tables 9.4–9.6. Some measurements may not be valuable for certain environments, and in every situation, project teams should stand guard

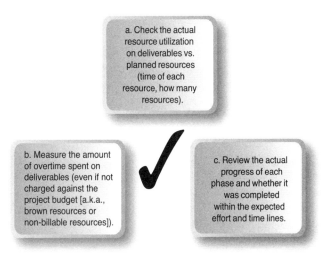

Figure 9.6 Results and deliverables

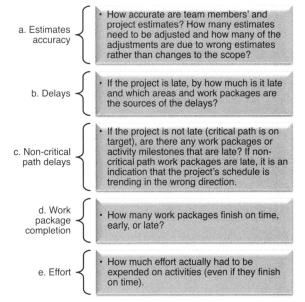

Figure 9.7 Estimating and scheduling

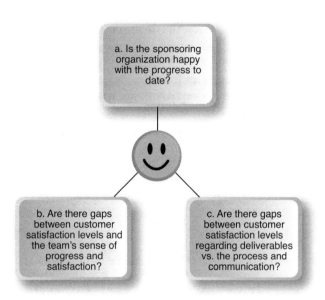

Figure 9.8 Customer satisfaction

Table 9.4(a) Scope, requirements, defects, and change

	Health measure	Explanation
A	Requirements stability	Number of changes submitted per requirement and how much the project's goals changed over the course of each phase. Many changes may signal that the project's goals are not clear.
B	Defects per requirement	The number of defects discovered per requirement.
C	Defect discovery	Trends in defects discovery and who discovers them: project team vs. the customer (include timing, costs, and impact).
D	Defect fix	Time, effort, and cost required to fix defects and how many defects are fixed vs. defects that require multiple fixes or are not fixed at all.
E	Defects per change	The number of defects discovered per implemented change request along with the measure above for defect fix.
F	Changes acceptance rate	Tally how many of the change requests submitted were actually accepted and to what extent.
G	Change per stakeholder	Which stakeholders submitted each change request and identify trends in the rate of acceptance vs. rejection per stakeholder.

Table 9.4(b) Scope, requirements, defects, and change

	Health measure	Explanation
H	Cause for change	The number of change requests submitted as a result of scope addition/change and the number of changes triggered by risks and performance issues that require changes to the baselines.
I	Change implementation	Number of changes implemented as intended.
J	Change control process effectiveness	Quantify how effective the change control process is. Is it clear? Does it produce realistic estimates and impact assessment? How long is the process?
K	Change control process adherence	Check whether the change control process is followed (if not, implement poka-yoke).
L	Risk and change	The nature and the number of risks associated with change requests.
M	Final deliverable vs. original goal	Compare the final deliverables to the original scope to assess variance against the original targets (even for accepted change requests); this allows a chance to check how effective and realistic the initial scoping process of the project was.

Table 9.5 Issues and risks

	Health measure	Explanation
A	Number of issues	The number of issues at various milestones against other projects (compare the number of issues generated vs. the number and the speed of issue resolution). Having more issues at a given point than in a previous project is not necessarily a negative trend but it may indicate that the project is facing more challenges than previous, similar projects.
B	Issues resolution time	How many of the issues became stale and were not resolved in a timely manner and became a crisis or a risk that materialized.
C	Risk process effectiveness and efficiency	How much time and money does the team spend on risk management and for each risk? Are the risks identified at realistic probability and impact rates? How many new, unplanned risks are introduced throughout the project? How prepared is the team for risks that emerge? Are the previously planned responses valid and do they solve the risk?
D	Response effectiveness	The number of events for which the response plan was inadequate.
E	Escalation	The number of times issues have to be escalated to the sponsor.
F	Risk stability rate	Compare at specific points in time whether the team still discovers significant risks and at what rate.
G	Assumptions remaining	The more assumptions, the more potential for risks to materialize.

Table 9.6 The human factors: conflict and team dynamic

	Health measure	Explanation
A	Conflict	The number of conflicts within the team that requires escalation.
B	Sources of conflict	The number of conflicts due to behaviors, misunderstandings, miscommunication, processes, or practices vs. the number of conflicts due to performance or work. More conflicts of the former type indicate that the team is distracted. Disagreements about merits and substance are an indication that team members care and that they are involved but there is a need to check whether they escalate and if they get personal.
C	Troubleshoot with the client	The number of special calls/troubleshooting with the client that are unscheduled or urgent. It indicates a weak plan or communication problems.
D	Conflict resolution process	Assess the conflict resolution techniques used and check how effective they are. This can be done by examining whether the same conflicts tend to reintroduce themselves within the project and how many times people are engaged in conflict with each other. It may indicate that the project manager's preferred conflict resolution technique is not effective.
E	Staff turnover rate	This cannot be isolated from environmental factors such as the organization and the market, but it may still signal trouble with the project team.
F	Team morale	Is the project team happy with the progress made and chances for success?
G	Meetings	One of many indications of leadership. How many team members are late or do not attend meetings? How many meetings start late? How many meetings go over time? How effective is the team in achieving the meeting's goals? What is the number of participants in meetings?

against taking the measurements out of context. Under no circumstances should PMs try to use too many of these project health measures. One to a handful should be sufficient to measure meaningful aspects of the project's health. Overdoing it may backfire—in the form of too much information, too many numbers, and no ability to extrapolate meaningful information from them.

FINAL THOUGHTS ON QUALITY

Quality is not a difficult thing to explain, do, comprehend, or implement. People realize the importance and criticality of delivering quality, and the main challenge is to find the time and priority for it. With so many fires raging in the project, issues piling up, and unrealistic expectations and estimates, this translates into performance issues, conflicts that consume the team, miscommunication and misunderstandings, and unexpected events. Overall, this vortex of events makes the PM reactive, at best—with little time and energy to pursue quality.

Quality is often perceived as something farther into the future, not urgent, of a conceptual nature, and at times, utopic and wishful thinking. Furthermore, two other worrisome thoughts about quality occur in: 1) those who genuinely believe it is not their job to think quality, and 2) those who believe quality is the job of management. These mindsets are either the result of misinterpreting the 85-15 rule or of failing to see that quality is everyone's job. Quality does not just concern small things, which will go away on their own. PMs need to proactively address these perceptions, reaching out to stakeholders in an attempt to get buy-in on the importance of quality and on the fact that it is everyone's job.

Reaching out to stakeholders for this purpose should take a one-on-one approach—in an informal and non-antagonizing manner—and be based on insights obtained from the stakeholder analysis to ensure appropriate handling, which is conducive to collaboration and based on the stakeholders' motivations, drivers, and priorities. Chapter 11 provides additional insights on how to deal with this challenge.

It is the responsibility of the PM to reach out to management and inform them of the importance of quality, in the event that it does not get the front seat treatment it requires. While the PM has little control over organizational priorities and senior management's decisions, it is within the PM's power and authority to reach out and alert senior management about areas of challenge related to quality. Once again, stakeholder analysis provides the PM with valuable insight into how to approach senior managers about this matter. The most effective way to get the message across is to price the potential impact of the challenging quality areas in terms, currencies, and values that resonate with those of the corresponding stakeholder in a way that will provide motivation to do the right thing for the project and organization. In many organizations, it will also be necessary to translate every success criterion, constraint, defect, and feature into a monetary value, so it is important to keep the concept of the cost of quality in mind.

The PMI mentions that "Every project should have a quality management plan;"[10] however, the PMI's previous decision, in the *A Guide to the Project Management Body of Knowledge* (PMBOK® *Guide—4th Edition*), to remove the need for a quality plan baseline does not quite support the notion of focusing on quality. Removing the need for a baseline came from a pragmatic point of view, since many projects do not even have a quality plan. Regardless of whether there is a need for a quality plan baseline, it is clear that the PM should ensure, and even insist, that there is a quality plan in place. If there is no support for it, the PM should identify it as an assumption and as a risk, along with the associated potential impact.

Quality management is not about pointing fingers or looking for excuses; it is about making sure things are done to the appropriate extent within project circumstances. If quality does not receive the right amount of organizational attention, failing to send out an alert about it makes the PM part of the problem. This chapter has provided information that can help PMs build a meaningful quality plan, and ensure that the information in it pertains to the needs of the project and the organization as a whole.

REFERENCES

1. J. M. Juran, *Juran's Quality Control Handbook*, 4th Edition (New York: McGraw-Hill, 1988).
2. Henry R. Neave, the British Deming Association, *A Brief History of Dr. W. Edwards Deming*. (Knoxville: SPC Press, Inc., 1992).
3. International Organization for Standardization (ISO), *ISO Standard 9000/2005*: "Quality management systems—Fundamentals and vocabulary" (Geneva: Prentice Hall, 2005).
4. Philip Crosby, *Quality is Free* (New York: McGraw-Hill, 1979).
5. J. M. Juran, *Juran's Quality Handbook*, 5th Edition (New York: McGraw-Hill, 1999).
6. RTI International (formerly Research Triangle Institute), "Software Bugs Cost U.S. Economy $59.6 Billion Annually, RTI Study Finds" (July 1, 2002).
7. Based on the American Society for Quality (ASQ), *Principles of Quality Costs: Principles, Implementation, and Use*, 3rd Edition, ed. Jack Campanella, 3–5 (Milwaukee: ASQ Quality Press, 1999).
8. Ibid.
9. Shigeo Shingo, *Zero Quality Control: Source Inspection and the Poka-Yoke System* (Portland: Productivity Press, 1986).
10. Project Management Institute (PMI), *A Guide to the Project Management Body of Knowledge*, (*PMBOK® Guide—Fifth Edition*), 228 (Sylva: Project Management Institute, 2013).

10

Managing Project Change

> **"We Don't Need a Change Request. This Is a Small and Easy Thing To Do."**
>
> This is a special request for change, where stakeholders expect the change to go through without taking it through the change control process altogether. Whether due to time constraints, an attempt to funnel in items that should be out of scope, or simply a disregard of the process, project managers (PMs) must stand strong and ensure that any change is appropriately channeled through the change control process. No pressure, promises, or even implied threats should sway project managers from enforcing the proper handling of change requests through a formal process. Failing to stand strong will lead to scope creep, which will directly cause schedule and budget overruns, as well as indirectly lead to morale, quality, and performance problems.

Change in projects is inevitable. While change can be viewed as exciting, it involves uncertainty and can be difficult to handle. From the point of view of both product and customer, change is a good thing: it moves the product from its unrealized state in the plan to (closer to) what it is intended to be. From the project team's perspective, change is not favorable, as it requires changes to the plan and to the way work is performed. Change leads to uncertainty and causes team members to get out of their comfort zones. Simply, it is one of the most challenging things a project needs to go through. It is the cause of a significant part of total project uncertainty and, in the majority of projects, change is mishandled and ineffectively managed.

CHANGE CONTROL

The good news about change control is that it can be compared to planning. The differences are that in a change, there is a perceived sense of urgency, and it is required at various points throughout the project—while work is taking place and not only at the start. The similarities are that it requires the ability to estimate, to assess the impact of taking or not taking actions, and to think about the risks, resources, and integration of the change items in question. With the change control process and project planning so similar to each other, one question comes to mind: why is it that change control is so problematic and challenging? This chapter offers a few ideas to make the project change control process easier to manage and more successful.

Comparing change control to project planning may not be such good news to many project managers, since in many projects, the planning process does not yield a realistic plan that can lead the project to success. However, the ingredients of realistic and effective planning are clear and well-known (as outlined throughout this book), namely: spend a sufficient amount of time, involve the right stakeholders, check readiness and complexity levels, define roles and responsibilities, make assumptions, plan for risks, set realistic expectations, focus on what matters, and plan for change. Knowing what change control involves does not always mean that PMs do it properly—but at least it is a starting point.

Agile and Change

Agile methodologies offer an alternative to the need to go through project change, by eliminating it from within the iteration (e.g., phase, cycle) and handling any need for change between iterations. With realistic plans and shorter time horizons, there is a freeze on requirements during the current iteration, and changes take place at gate points—not while work is getting done. This freeze gives the project team and stakeholders a chance to review the work done in the current iteration, and—if there is a need for change (i.e., add, remove, fix, or change existing features and directions)—a decision is made prior to the start of the next iteration. It protects the project and the team from "real-time changes," which occur while the work takes place, and gives the team a chance to prepare for the next iteration and properly assess the change's impact prior to performing the work.

Since the main challenges with project change are related to the assessment of the impacts and risks associated with changes, considering and assessing changes only between iterations reduces risk and gives the team a chance to conduct a realistic change impact assessment, free from having work performed in the background. Regardless of when project changes take place, the need to assess the impacts and risks of potential changes requires a change control mechanism to be in place.

PROACTIVE PROJECT CHANGE MANAGEMENT

The first thing to do when planning the change control process is to take a proactive approach. Although project change is predominantly handled in a reactive manner, there are ways to look for areas of potential change and to work with stakeholders who are likely to request and introduce change before a project change takes place. Early setup and planning to address areas of the project that may produce change—before the change takes place—are key to effective project change management. While the effort consumes time and money—considering the pain and trouble that can be introduced from mishandled project changes—this investment makes sense and will pay off later in the project.

Managing project change is not about suppressing and eliminating every potential change; it is about acknowledging the importance of managing the change in its stages of evolution throughout the project lifecycle:

1. Recognize that project requirements will evolve and build a mechanism to manage these changes;
2. Identify areas that may produce change;
3. Prevent unnecessary change from occurring;
4. When change is accepted, manage it effectively and ensure that accepted changes are treated like any other requirement;
5. And one more thing: change is not only about requirements and scope; change requests can be made for a variety of reasons in the project, as will be illustrated later in this chapter.

Proactively managing change requires going back to the early planning activities of the project:

Project Objectives and Scope Stability—Reviewing the project objectives and inquiring about the details are the first steps in an effort to detect the stability of a proposed project idea. While changes may arise in any situation, this process can provide the first indication of the likelihood of significant changes in project direction. While the results of this process may not be scientific or quantifiable, there is a good chance that reason for concern at this stage will likely translate into changes later in the project.

Project Readiness Assessment—When the organization does not appear to be ready for the project undertaking, (i.e., lack of any of the following: clarity of objectives, understanding of needs, resources, scoping, prioritization), it is an indication that changes are likely to take place throughout the project.

Project Complexity Assessment—Understanding the expected project complexity is an extension of the readiness assessment. The higher the level of complexity, the more likely the project is to encounter challenges and risks, and potentially face additional changes.

Stakeholder Analysis—Learning about stakeholders' characteristics, interests, abilities to influence, levels of involvement, dispositions, tendencies, capabilities, influences, and interests in the project is key to managing most aspects of the project—from defining success criteria to managing risks and change. Every bit of information the PM can gain about stakeholders will provide insight into what to expect from them and into the likelihood that any given stakeholder will serve as a source, trigger, or catalyst of change. Relationships, states of mind, conflicts, and rapport may also be contributing factors to stakeholders seeking project change.

Requirements Management Process Assessment

There is a strong correlation between the requirements management process and the change management process: the latter cannot be planned effectively without an understanding of the former. To ensure the requirements process is effective and relevant to project needs, the PM and the business analyst should conduct a requirements process review, which should take place at the start of the project, as well as during and at the end of the requirements management process. Input to this assessment should include a review of historical information in an effort to gain insight into the requirements process as a whole so the process is not only clear to all involved but also fosters collaboration, clear communication, and the articulation of benefits that are sufficient without being too burdensome. A simplified requirements process is presented in Figure 10.1.

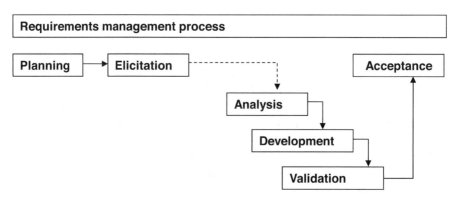

A clear process for requirements management does not guarantee effectiveness but serves as the first step toward it.

Figure 10.1 Simplified requirements process

A review of the items in the process assessment should provide an indication of how effective and relevant the process is for the project's needs. In addition to the generic items listed in Figure 10.1, an inclusion of items in Figure 10.2 will enhance the assessment.

There is no right or wrong value for any of these items, since they all need to be assessed in relation to the project environment, the project methodology (e.g., waterfall, incremental, or iterative), and the track record for managing requirements within the organization. An indicator of overall requirements success is a lower number of changes in the project scope. The requirements process and historical information review should also include the following items:

- Requirements quality criteria: set up a list of items that each requirement should adhere to as success criteria (see Table 10.1);

For an effective requirements management process, review historical information from previously performed projects, along with existing processes for this project.

Figure 10.2 Requirements process and historical information review

Table 10.1 Requirements quality criteria

Complete	Contains all information needed by developers
Consistent	Does not conflict with other requirements
Correct	States a customer or external need accurately
Feasible	Can be implemented within known constraints
Independent	Self-contained as much as possible
Negotiable	Can be changed when necessary
Necessary	Documents something that customers really need
Prioritized	Ranked by importance
Testable	Can be proven by testing, inspection, analysis, or demonstration
Traceable	Linked to customer needs and to designs, codes, and tests
Unambiguous	Has only one possible meaning
Valuable	Adds value and benefits to the customer

Every requirement should qualify for all items on the list. If they are not in place it means that the requirement is not properly defined and that it needs additional analysis.

- Requirements risks: examine the complete set of requirements for risk factors, related to the product development, and manage risks that are associated with the requirements, including the following:
  - How strongly the project is tied to business objectives;
  - The relationship of errors and defects to potential safety issues and losses;
  - Whether the project deals with new products, services, or user types;
  - Complexity of the requirements;
  - Potential requirements change.

Communication Planning

An effective communication plan includes information, ground rules, and boundaries that go beyond specifying the lines for reporting and information flow. The communication plan should address areas related to: criteria for the type of information that needs to go through formal channels, the methods and formats to be used to communicate change, and a clearly described change control mechanism that should be followed. It should also specify escalation procedures and decision-making processes in relation to change management.

Project Risk Management

Project changes and project risks are closely linked. While project changes inherently involve risks, project risks may trigger changes and the need to formalize them by creating a new baseline for the project constraints. This chapter discusses this topic.

Change Control Process Planning

The change control process is a combination of project scope management, integration, communication planning, and risk management. It involves addressing quality management considerations and estimates (of time, resources, and costs) to make an impact assessment.

THE CHANGE CONTROL PROCESS

Project conditions, existing processes, and management will determine how PMs handle project change requests. Large projects often mandate a formal process, which dictates how change requests are submitted, assessed, and managed. Regardless of the project size, PMs should follow a process that is clear, effective, and formal and that includes communication considerations, such as setting expectations about the process and defining the process and its turnaround times.

Change requests need to be submitted in writing—preferably using an agreed-upon form that requires requesters to include a specific set of information about the change request. The form should produce a set of benefits and due diligence measures from the outset, including the ones listed in Figure 10.3.

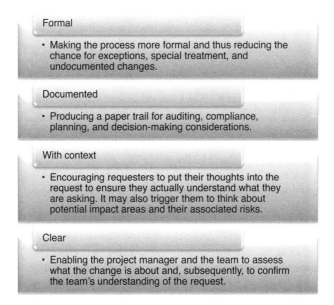

Formal
- Making the process more formal and thus reducing the chance for exceptions, special treatment, and undocumented changes.

Documented
- Producing a paper trail for auditing, compliance, planning, and decision-making considerations.

With context
- Encouraging requesters to put their thoughts into the request to ensure they actually understand what they are asking. It may also trigger them to think about potential impact areas and their associated risks.

Clear
- Enabling the project manager and the team to assess what the change is about and, subsequently, to confirm the team's understanding of the request.

Figure 10.3 Due diligence

Identify or Realize a Change

The first step in handling a change is to realize that a change is taking place. There are three ways in which changes are introduced into the project:

1. A change request (CR) has been submitted by a stakeholder. Most likely related to a scope and requirements change, it may involve adding new functionality or modifying/removing existing functionality. A variety of reasons may lead to a stakeholder submitting a CR, including: a change of mind, a change in needs, a need for a feature or a solution, changes in conditions and markets, forgotten items, or a change in priorities. Regardless of the source of change, there is a need to process and handle the CR effectively and in a timely manner.

2. A scope change has occurred: at times, the PM simply realizes that a scope change has occurred. It could be a result of "scope creep," where functionality somehow ends up making it into the project scope, or a mis-handled CR, where there is no proper impact assessment for the proposed change. Whatever its source, scope creep is an indication of mishandled communication and at times, weak project management practices. When a scope change occurs, the PM is the one who needs to submit a CR; this CR is not for approval, but rather for an impact assessment. Unlike a typical CR, which should be submitted by the requesting stakeholder, a change-in-scope CR is requested by the PM and can be viewed as an administrative CR for the purpose of impact assessment.

3. Any other type of change in project conditions has occurred, which jus-tifies a CR. These types of changes can be viewed as project configura-tion changes, involving anything that will have an impact on the project constraints, success criteria, and baseline. Mainly, they involve changes in resources, but they also include other changes that are related to schedul-ing, costing, and procurement.

Figure 10.4 presents a change control flow: once a change is identified, there is a need to understand what it is about and its potential meaning for the project—before assessing it. The process should be formal and effective; once an approval is made, the team needs to implement it. The last step is for the PM to ensure that the change was made, as intended, and that it integrated into the rest of the product or result.

Understand the Change

Understanding what the change is all about is the next thing that needs to take place, and it should occur before the change impact assessment is conducted. The process of understanding what the change is all about consists of two elements:

From the project manager's point of view, the change control
process should be simple to manage.

Figure 10.4   Change control process

1. Understand what the change is all about: The PM needs to gain an understanding of the purpose of the proposed change and what it represents.
   Regardless of the change impact or how the project is faring, understanding what the change is about is an important piece of information for
   making decisions about the change later in the process.

2. Preliminary impact assessment: With an understanding of what the
   change represents, the PM should arrange for an abbreviated impact
   assessment, which reviews the change in the context of the project objectives and produces a high-level preliminary impact assessment, similar
   to a "smoke test" that may determine whether the change is even worth
   the effort of looking into. The preliminary assessment considers both the
   change objectives and its projected complexity to measure whether this
   particular "fruit is worth picking."

Assess and Analyze

With the initial understanding of what the change is about, and a decision that the change is worth assessment, it is time to take it through the process of impact assessment and analysis. The goal is to identify the impact of the change on the project as a whole and on any of its success criteria and constraints—including scope, timeline, budget, resources, risk, and quality.

The impact assessment process should be planned for and defined in advance, so that it sets expectations for stakeholders about what change analysis involves. It should include turnaround time and goals and identify the stakeholders to be involved in it, including relevant reviewers, team members, and subject matter experts. It is also recommended to appoint a change owner (often a business analyst), who will facilitate the process from start to finish and ensure there are no gaps or bottlenecks and that assessment is handled as planned. The goal of the process is to gain sufficient understanding of the change impact, to put together recommendations for a plan to implement the change if it is approved, and to have all this information organized for presentation to the change control committee. Change impact assessment should be formal and clear so expectations around it are also clear. It should also be effective so that it produces a realistic impact assessment, including risks, plans, and recommended actions, as well as potential downstream impacts on other projects or parts of the organization.

The assessment and analysis of the CR should consider the potential effects of the change on all aspects of the project and should include the implications of the change not taking place. The consideration of whether to implement a change should include both the impact of the change if implemented and the impact of all the other associated options (as described in the approval section of this chapter). Not performing the change, delaying its implementation, or doing it in a different way than requested will each have corresponding implications on the project, the organization, and various stakeholders. These implications, including their associated risks, costs, and timelines, must be taken into consideration.

Change Scale Review

Regardless of the type of change or its technical aspects, the project team should be able to assess every proposed change from a generic point of view. A generic review of this type provides the project team with two benefits:

1. Consideration of the impact the proposed change might have on a list of project characteristics and capturing the level of uncertainty involved with each;
2. Performing a cross change comparison, or "apples to apples." In the event that two proposed changes compete for the same resources, a review of

this type can provide insight into which one may pose more risk to the project overall.

The change scale review presented in Table 10.2 provides a system-wide view of the change's impact on the project and the organization, by assessing a set of characteristics and the potential uncertainty that each change is likely to produce. The project team can come up with a scale of 1 (low) to 5 (high), where 5 signals more risk and uncertainty for the project and the organization and an overall higher level of change complexity. This measure can help compare project changes—both if they compete for the same resources and as a retrospective, to evaluate the change control process during a lessons learned exercise. The cross project view of proposed changes can be used for approval purposes, as well as for a lessons learned exercise, where high change scores signal more complexity and the risks associated with it.

Make a Decision: Approve or Reject

With the change impact assessment concluded, the change should be ready for discussion and decision making by the change control committee. This committee considers all available information about the proposed change, reviews recommendations that have been made in the process, and makes one of the following decisions about the CR:

1. Accept the change as is and proceed to implementation;
2. Accept the change with modifications;

Table 10.2 Change scale review

Project considerations	Level of uncertainty
Approval level required	
Urgency of the change	
Impact on end user	
Financial impact	
Organizational visibility and impact areas	
Scope of the change	
Experience in change area (i.e., new technology, first time?)	
Expected time to complete	
Availability of sufficient and relevant information regarding the change	
Cross project/system impact	
Impact on existing business processes	
Risks associated with the change	
Overall complexity	

3. Ask for additional information about the change, its objectives, or its potential impact;

4. Postpone the decision about the change;

5. Reject the proposed change altogether, providing a clear justification and ensuring the explanation satisfies the requester.

Change control committees often ask PMs for opinions on their options, which may put the PM into a dangerous position—since it is not the PM's role or authority level to make a decision. When asked what should be done, PMs should respond that they do not have a preference and it is not their decision. If pressed for an answer, PMs should avoid mixing in personal preferences and always focus on facts and project objectives. Their answers should be qualified by saying that it is not their decision to make and based on the information available, point to the option that is best for the project overall. The PM should ensure that the stakeholders involved do not try to shirk responsibility and pass decision making on to the PM, as these situations often end up with fingers pointing at PMs for promoting their own ideas in the project.

The decision made by the change control committee should be clearly and formally communicated to all involved or impacted stakeholders. If the change is accepted, the approving stakeholders should provide their signatures and the go-ahead for implementing the change. With this approval, the PM should take measures to reset the project baseline (if required), to update the project plans, and to prepare a list of action items and steps for implementing the change and incorporating it into the plan. At this point, all aspects of the change should be detailed in the change order, and in turn, the change must be treated in the same way as any of the project requirements that are part of the original plan. Any decision that is made should involve engaging the people and stakeholders who may be affected by it, so they become part of the decision, as well as notifying team members and other stakeholders about the change and the expected impact it will have on the project.

Implement, Track, and Monitor

Implementing the change is about incorporating it into the project plan and ensuring that the work it requires will be performed as part of the new plan. Once the work to implement the change begins, the PM should continue to monitor it: whether it is implemented and if it is, whether it is done according to the specifications and the plan. Similarly, the PM should monitor the project work to ensure that rejected changes are not implemented and that any additional needs are addressed as required.

Other possible issues may arise as a result of the newly-implemented changes, including: unplanned risks, misaligned work estimates, further unplanned changes, and unanticipated impacts on other areas in the project or the organization. The ongoing monitoring of the work represents an additional workload (on top of handling the CRs), making it an ongoing effort. If done properly, it may actually transform the project change control process into something that involves less risk and uncertainty.

PROJECT CHANGE MANAGEMENT CONSIDERATIONS

Beyond a proactive approach and a set of considerations for an effective change control process, there are additional considerations to keep in mind when trying to manage project change.

Change Status

Part of the effort to manage CRs effectively is to ensure that all communication around the change, and its status, is so clear that stakeholders can easily learn about the change status. For example, Figure 10.5 provides a list of status codes, which can be used to reflect options about any CR.

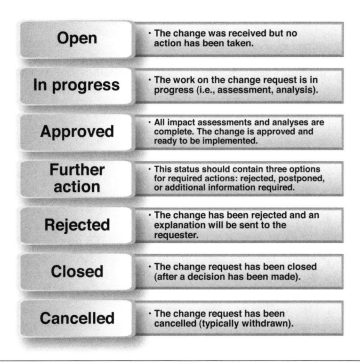

Figure 10.5 Change status codes

Change and Risk

The relationship between project change and risk is a two-way street: while changes may introduce risks, certain risks may also introduce the need to request a project change. Whether the change is related to procurement, scope and requirements, standards and quality, budgets, timelines, or resources, a CR needs to be issued, and it is highly likely to produce risks. Even if the change is intended to avoid or mitigate a risk, it may produce change-driven or secondary risks. An important part of the impact assessment is not only to measure what the change may do to the baseline but also to account for all the risks it may trigger—including downstream risks and risk dependencies, which may impact other parts of the project or the organization. Except for changes related to health and safety or to overcoming a major constraint or deficiency, changes should not be adopted when they produce more potential risks than benefits.

Risks that materialize in the project may trigger the need for CRs. Any risk event that results in changes to the project success criteria, objectives, or constraints should lead to a CR. These types of CRs are different from scope-related, "traditional" CRs, since they are submitted to capture a change in the project's conditions and reality—not for the purpose of deliberation and approval but for assessing the impact and ensuring that the baseline reflects it. These changes are submitted by the PM and can be termed "administrative CRs."

Resource Changes

The topic of "administrative CRs" relates to another type of project change: resources (particularly, human resources). When stakeholders (e.g., sponsors, functional managers, resource managers, other PMs) fail to make resources available for the project, or when resources are pulled out of the project in the middle of the work, it may introduce the need for a CR. Once again, this CR is submitted for the purpose of recording a change in the project conditions, not for approval, because as a result of this resource change, the project may lose the ability to deliver on some of its success-related commitments.

This kind of CR often causes controversy among stakeholders by its nature: it is not about changes to the project objectives, success criteria, or the work itself; rather, it is about changes to the team and the people who are supposed to perform the work. As a result of losing a skill or a level of expertise, the PM needs to reassess whether the project team has the ability to deliver on its commitments. Many stakeholders respond with various types of resistance and possible backlash, claiming it is not grounds for a CR.

To illustrate the need to submit a CR for impact assessment, PMs may use the following analogy: suppose you need to attend, in person, an event located in a city that is a one-hour highway drive away, and you plan to get there by driving your car. If, at this point, your manager decides to pull your car from the project, so it can attend to another organizational emergency, and gives you a bicycle instead, it is evident that you will not make it to the meeting on time. This is when the PM needs to submit the CR to reflect the change in project resources. Having been given the bicycle, it is still possible for you to make it to the meeting (possibly even on time), using an alternate mode of transportation. However, it will require a change in timelines, costs, and other activities—and possibly a change in the project's ability to deliver on its original commitment. Most stakeholders will immediately grasp the relevance of this analogy and release their resistance to a CR.

The "administrative change request" may also be applicable when trying to capture scope changes retroactively. When scope creep takes place and unauthorized functionality makes it into the project, as well as when a CR is not handled effectively and more work and deliverables become part of the project, there may be a need for the PM to submit this kind of CR to ensure that the project baseline and stakeholders' expectations reflect these changes.

Incremental Changes and the Salami Method

Ensuring that a realistic and up-to-date baseline is maintained helps manage stakeholders' expectations and protects the project from unauthorized or incremental changes. On many occasions, stakeholders introduce changes for various reasons and with varying impact levels and areas. Regardless of whether they are senior stakeholders, there is often an attempt to funnel these proposed changes into the project informally, with no CRs and no impact assessments. If these changes do make it in, they are likely to cause trouble later in the project—with performance issues, lack of accountability, traceability, or willingness to pay for the changes.

Many arguments may be presented for this type of case, but they are all essentially the same: an attempt to change something in the project without taking it through the proper process. The examples in Figure 10.6 are illegitimate attempts to allow changes to enter the project, unplanned and without accountability. When PMs cave and allow these changes to take place, they give these unjustified changes a stamp of "kosher" and open the door for trouble, as the project is not likely to have the time, money, resources, or capacities to successfully work on these changes.

Even the argument that these changes are small and would have no impact can easily be dismissed as a "salami method," which refers to a series of small actions or changes—each on its own does not account for much of a difference and may not justify arguing about—that when their impacts are combined accumulate to a larger and more significant impact. The analogy is to slicing a salami: when making a sandwich, we carve paper-thin slices, but a large piece of salami is missing in no time. In the project, these small changes may not appear to be worth the energy to push back and argue with the corresponding stakeholders over, but later in the

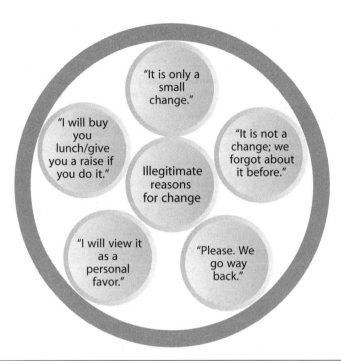

Figure 10.6 Illegitimate attempts to introduce change into the project

project, they may well spell the difference between success and performance issues, such as missing functionality or schedule and budget overruns.

Consider the Merits

When facing pressure from stakeholders to make unauthorized or informal changes, there is another item to consider, which can help PMs protect the integrity of the scope and the baseline: the project merits. One of the tactics that stakeholders try to apply is to make promises, offer incentives, or pose threats.

If for example there is a request to complete a week's worth of work in one hour, incentives, lunches, and bonuses cannot make it happen, and the PM has to stand strong and ensure that the discussion remains focused on the project merits and trade-offs. This is the time for the PM to shift the subject back to the action's impact on the constraints and the competing demands and to remind the stakeholders involved that (as they say), "you can't fit a square peg into a round hole." If something cannot physically take place, no threats or promises will make it happen. Understanding the project success criteria and the trade-off nature of the relationship between project constrains is key—not only to defining project success and managing risks but also to managing project change and measuring the potential impact of proposed changes.

The CR Form

The change control process may already be established by the organization or a project management office, but, when there is no process in place, the PM should establish one and make sure that all stakeholders are aware of it. The process should include a full set of expectations regarding the actions each involved stakeholder should take, the order of activities, the turnaround times, and any additional information that will provide transparency to the process. It should also include a CR form that once submitted by a stakeholder, kick-starts the change control process into motion.

The form should include a sufficient amount of information to allow the project team to assess the proposed change. Arguably, different project sizes and change types may require more rigor and information for consideration than others; however, the main goal of the form is to guide the requester to provide as much information as possible about the change, to allow an assessment that will produce a realistic set of expectations about the proposed project change. PMs should try to avoid overkill, where too much information is submitted about a proposed change; however, it is much more common to see changes submitted without sufficient information, resulting in unrealistic change estimates and impact assessments.

The CR form should be consistent across the project (and across the organization, where applicable) and should include all relevant information for the subsequent assessment. The following discussion serves as a guideline for the type of information to include on the form, with the level of details varying from one project to another. The PM can identify some information as mandatory and other information as optional.

Raise the Bar

While not all information may be available or even applicable for every given project, the PM should raise the bar and ask for the amount and quality of information sufficient for assessing and if required, performing the change. The goal is not to make the CR form difficult to complete, but it should contain all the information the team needs for the process. Many PMs face situations where not enough information is included in a CR, leading either to an unrealistic change assessment or to the need to circle back to the requester for additional information. Both options translate into wasted time and project resources.

Asking for full information on the CR may also reduce the number of "unjustified" requests that are submitted with insufficient information; furthermore, additional due diligence by the requester may save the need to submit the CR altogether.

It may also serve as an incentive for project stakeholders to require change quality over change quantity—that is, to focus more on meaningful CRs (quality), rather than on submitting many requests that are not quite thought through and missing significant information (quantity).

As part of the project planning process, the PM should set expectations for the change control process. While every organization has a different culture and code of conduct, it has to be established that incomplete CRs will not be further assessed until the missing information is received. PMs should not be combative about it and should try to explain, in a collaborative manner, to the stakeholders that the issue comes down to protecting the project from scope creep and other related distractions. The threshold level for the minimum required information should also be determined, in a collaborative manner, between the project team and the other stakeholders, based upon the project complexity, the nature of the CR, and the impacted areas.

In certain environments, the issuer of a CR is required to pay for the assessment and handing of the request. While once again, it may be completely inappropriate in some project settings, this can serve as an incentive for stakeholders to ensure that proposed changes really have merit and are focused on adding value to the project and its outcome. Requiring payment can also be a useful tactic with customers or other stakeholders who are quick to submit CRs but, after the impact assessment is completed, often back out after learning the overall impact of the change—especially on cost, time, and other functionalities.

In such cases, the project plan should stipulate that requested changes will be handled at no additional cost or impact until a certain number of CRs (for example, five) have been rejected by the requester. After that, the project will charge for the handling of each CR that is submitted. This approach usually triggers significant resistance from customers, but in the long run, customers learn to appreciate that this mechanism helps reduce the number of distractions in the project.

The Change Window

The task of putting a change control process in place, which works and produces realistic impact assessments, is not a simple one. However, even PMs who have an effective process in place may still face a gap in the results where, despite a thorough analysis and due diligence change control process, the impact assessment falls short of being effective and accurate. Beyond flaws in the process and difficulties in properly measuring and anticipating change impacts, the problem may be related to the timing of the requests. Since CRs are submitted on a regular basis and in no particular order, PMs may find themselves dealing with multiple CRs (greater than two) at any given point in the project, and each CR is going through the impact assessment independently.

All the CRs that are considered follow the same path of assessment and decision making at their own pace. If a request is approved and its content becomes part of the project scope, any changes it introduces to the baseline (or to any other conditions) of the project may make other in-progress assessments of later requests invalid. As a result, some CRs that go through the entire process end up being ineffective and produce impact assessments that are not realistic and do not capture the full impact of the proposed change.

Considering that it is not advisable to block the customer or other stakeholders from submitting CRs, a possible solution may be to propose windows of time to submit CRs and, once submitted, close the window until all the changes in the cycle are assessed and decisions have been made. This will not only allow proper assessment of CRs, including considering the impact they may have on each other, but it may also help slow the pace of changes submitted and in turn, cause the customer to consider each proposed change more carefully before submitting it. The ability to check CRs against an existing baseline and against each other is a more sustainable option for managing the change process than accepting changes randomly, with no consideration of their impacts on each other.

The change window should open to accommodate existing requests in the queue, then close until a decision is made about all the changes submitted. At that point, a new window will open for the next batch of CRs. There is no recommended number of allowable CRs in each window: it should be determined by the PM and the applicable stakeholders. While it is not advisable to allow too many CRs within any given window, a constant flow of CRs—regardless of how effective their assessment is—may be a sign of poor project health and an indication that there is a need to take special measures and reopen the project scope and requirements. In the event that the customer is willing to pay for each CR and absorb the risk that the impact will be determined against a stale baseline, CRs can be allowed at any time.

Too Many Changes

Despite the benefits that project changes may produce, PMs generally do not like changes in the project, since they often lead to instability and increased risk. To protect the project, there is a variety of techniques designed to cap the number of CRs to contain the risk and complexity of the project. Examples include the items already discussed (raise the bar on the amount of information required, introduce a window for submission), as well as the following techniques:

- Cap the number of requests to be handled without additional charges;
- Cap the number of rejected requests;
- Establish a freeze on requirements, or a rolling freeze on subsections of the project, to reduce the chance that CRs are made in areas that have already been built;

- Make the project iterative in nature and instead of going through changes in real time, only allow changes to be submitted during the acceptance stages between iterations.

No Excuses

It is virtually guaranteed that at some point in the project, there will be change. It arises from a variety of sources, but project change is a fact of life; it is not only important to plan for it but also crucial not to use it as an excuse for insufficient planning. The project plan must be as thorough and accurate as possible so that it contributes to reducing the future need for change as much as possible. If despite these efforts, change is introduced (i.e., through performance issues, changes of mind, overlooked or forgotten concerns, new information), the plan should be flexible and robust enough to handle the change without losing touch with reality.

With effective planning, PMs can perform one of their most important duties in the project: prevent uncontrollable changes and changes that are unaccounted for. Let's examine these two elements more closely:

- Uncontrollable changes: These changes are part of scope creep; they make it into the project without the change control process, and no time or cost estimates are made for them. These will clearly pose a problem later in the project, as schedule, budget, and testing have not taken them into account.
- Changes that are unaccounted for: These changes go through the change control process, but erroneous assumptions are made about the effort required and their overall impact. Together with other potentially negative impacts, they result in schedule and budget overruns.

Project Management

Mishandled changes not only negatively affect the project work but also cause stakeholders to express concerns about the PM's ability to manage the project. The loss of trust and belief in the PM's ability to lead the project due to mishandled changes may lead to deeper and more fundamental problems than scope issues. The PM's ability to manage project change begins with the need to maintain project procedure descriptions, as well as project decision structures, in order to properly handle project change. Other areas that need to be maintained so the change control process is effectively handled, include: the communication plan, quality plan, risk plan, and any technical plans.

FINAL THOUGHTS ON CHANGE

Change in projects is inevitable, and despite the promise change holds, it often leads to difficulties: wrong estimates, changing priorities, forgotten items, and uncertainty are only some of the major effects of project change. This chapter has presented and discussed a variety of techniques and concepts that can help in managing and containing project change so negative impacts are minimized and benefits are enhanced.

As part of the effort to reduce errors and misunderstandings, PMs should ensure that at the top of each requirements and scope document, it is stated: "if it's not explicitly in, it's implicitly out." Similar to interactions we have with service providers, where the contract specifies exactly what is included and what is not, the project documents should reflect the same spirit. When you buy a car at a dealership, the document you receive at the end of the transaction includes all the authorized signatures and all the details that will be included with the car. If you believe additional features should be on the list, you must alert the dealership staff immediately, so the contract can completely reflect your requirements. There will be no second chance to make claims for additional or implied features once you pick up the car and—even if there is—there will be an impact on what you receive as a customer. PMs are well-advised to keep this in mind as they manage project change.

11

Designing and Managing Project Communications

"Communication Plan? It Contains Who Gets What and When."

Project managers (PMs) spend 80–90% of their time communicating in various forms and settings, and, although this is a known fact, it is surprising that many do not provide sufficient focus on communication, and some do not have a communication plan altogether. Even when there is a communication plan, it often addresses only reporting lines and delivery of formal information, with little meaningful communication-related information, such as how team members and stakeholders should interact with each other, and which behavioral guidelines are expected. It seems quite simple, even trivial, to manage project communication because most of us view communication as a straightforward, routine activity; however, most PMs discount the criticality of managing communication effectively for project success. A proper communication plan should cover all communication aspects of the project, including setting boundaries; defining practices for managing expectations; facilitating the exchange of all information among all stakeholders; communicating risks, issues, changes, decisions, and updates; setting up escalation procedures and ground rules; and ultimately, fostering creativity, efficiency, and productivity.

Superb communication is the single most important attribute a PM needs to have. The PM's communication skills can make the difference between project success and failure. In most cases, it has more influence on project success than the PM's technical background, industry experience, or product knowledge. This chapter deals with what the PM needs to know in order to become an effective communicator, and what it takes to design, manage, and take control over project communications.

Project communications management "includes the processes that are required to ensure timely and appropriate planning, collection, creation, distribution, storage, retrieval, management, control, monitoring, and the ultimate disposition of project information."[1] A communication management plan is a component of the project plan that describes how, when, and by whom information about the project will be administered and disseminated.[2]

The main focus of this chapter is not on how to build a communication plan that shows which stakeholder gets what and when; rather, it is on building a meaningful team contract, as part of the communication plan, that serves as a set of ground rules and a code of conduct for the project team and stakeholders. If done right, this part of the communication plan can be an extremely valuable contributing factor to project success, since it helps with the following:

- Setting expectations for day-to-day interactions, which are often not set or clear to everyone;
- Ensuring that stakeholders and team members understand their, as well as their colleagues', roles in communications;
- Reducing unnecessary conflict from misunderstandings;
- Letting people focus on performing their work and adding value, instead of getting consumed by arguments and pursuing information that should be readily available.

According to *A Guide to the Project Management Body of Knowledge* (*PMBOK® Guide*), "PMs spend most of their time communicating with team members and other project stakeholders;"[3] as much as 80–90%. Good communication is considered critical to project success and has a hand in everything that takes place in the project, across all knowledge areas and throughout the project lifecycle. It is not complicated or difficult to understand what constitutes effective communication, but most of us (and PMs) have at least a few misconceptions about communication, including some or all of the following:

- We do not pay enough attention to the importance of communication;
- We take it for granted, thinking that being able to talk and to utilize a few tools (e.g., e-mail, texting) will make information flow in a sufficient, timely, and uninterrupted fashion;
- We are convinced that we are effective communicators and that should be enough to get everyone around us to become good communicators;
- We fail to realize that although communication is not complicated to manage, it requires effort, time, and focus to achieve success.

Misunderstandings

Project communications planning serves to reduce misunderstandings, which are common in projects, that ultimately lead to significant waste. We have different backgrounds and bring different sets of values and expectations to the table, giving us diverse ways of seeing things and unique communication needs and techniques. The saying, "it's not what you look at, it's what you see" describes the gap in communication, since we often do not understand each other and quite often do not express ourselves in the way we intend. Our beliefs and assumptions, that our communications are understood as intended, are simply not realistic and do not always match reality, as illustrated in Figure 11.1.

NOT A 50–50 EFFORT

One of the greatest problems with communications management is that we believe the responsibility for effective communication is shared, 50–50, by both sides—the sender and the receiver of a message. However, when examining the flow of communication, it is clear that this responsibility needs to be shared in a different way—100%:100%—in order to ensure the message is properly generated, transmitted, received, and understood, with an opportunity to verify information with each other, and with both parties owning the information from start to finish, as

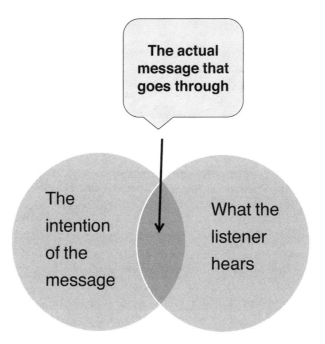

One of the core causes of miscommunication: a gap between what stakeholders intend to say and what their counterparts actually hear. It often results in only a portion of the message actually going through.

Figure 11.1 The communication gap

illustrated in Figure 11.2. The model, which is based on a basic communication model,[4] shows that each message goes through a series of potential interruptions, from the time it is generated to the time it reaches the receiver, and each of these potential interruptions is a potential failure point. The message can be distorted by any bias that the issuer has, by noises in the communication channel it goes through, and by the state of mind and the perception of the receiver. The loop the receiver of a message generates to acknowledge and provide feedback follows a similar path back to the issuer of the original message—including the three potential interruption points in the process.

The responsibility of ensuring the message is received and understood lies with both sides of the communication loop. In particular, the sender needs to ensure the following:

1. The message is generated and sent out, as and when intended;

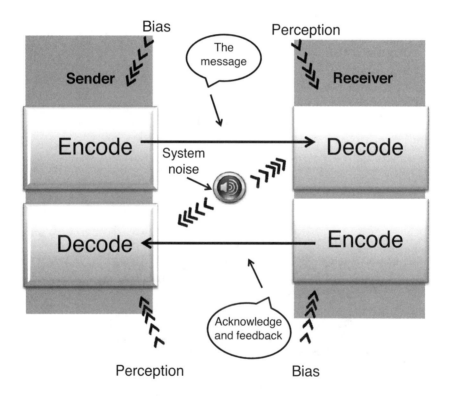

This enhanced communication model illustrates the flow of the message from its generation by the person who sends it, its journey through the system to the receiver, and the establishment of a feedback loop.

Figure 11.2   Enhanced communication model

2. It is received by the intended recipient;

3. The message is received and understood as intended by establishing a feedback mechanism and encouraging the receiver to reach out with acknowledgement and feedback.

The receiver also has a responsibility to ensure the following:

1. When expecting a message, reach out to ensure it was generated and sent. It is not enough to passively sit and wait for an expected message;

2. When a message is received, make sure it is clear and understood;

3. Reach out to confirm receipt and convey understanding of the message, by paraphrasing if needed. This will allow both sides to validate that the message was received as intended.

Many projects are plagued by incomplete communications—senders do not ensure messages are received as intended or delivered, and receivers do not reach out to confirm their understanding of the message. The completion of the communication loop, on its own, can serve to significantly reduce misunderstandings.

CHANGING PROJECT MANAGEMENT

If PMs apply the easy-to-understand concepts presented in this chapter, it can lead to a change in the way projects are managed—possibly in how project management is practiced altogether. The need to change project management as we know it is not because it is not done right: the methodologies are robust, PMs do their jobs well, and ample tools are available to help in the process. However, there are three factors that combine to make project management less effective than it can be and make projects more difficult to manage, and these factors generate the need to change how project management is done:

- A disconnect: There is usually a wide gap between various stakeholders' views and expectations and the project team's capabilities—there may also be gaps within the project team or between the team and the customer. PMs have difficulties articulating these gaps and often fail to reach out and address them.
- Lack of meaningful communication: There is a general statement that is applicable to almost all organizations and situations: "people do not listen." Most of us operate within preconceived notions and paradigms and do not make sufficient effort to pay attention to what colleagues, peers, managers, subordinates, or customers have to say. Moreover, there is little effective communication occurring within the project team or with external stakeholders. No tool can replace the human mind in engaging other

people and listening to them, and the far-reaching impact of not listening exacerbates the disconnect between stakeholders.

- As a result of these shortcomings, project results fall short of expectations. Poor expectation management, a limited ability to understand customer needs and those of other stakeholders involved in the project, along with numerous other distractions caused by poor communication, contribute to project failure more than technical difficulties and project constraints.

Changing project management does not need to involve applying new tools or enhancing technical capabilities, but rather allowing the project management profession to realize its potential and deliver higher success rates than it currently does. Change can be achieved by recognizing that the current way of managing project communications is not sufficient and that more focus needs to be given to this critical, yet overlooked area. Most organizations and PMs see communication as basic; as such, it is given a lower priority than technical knowledge.

An illustration of the gap between the need for strong communication management and the reality (i.e., the lack thereof) in most projects can be seen through the amount of time and effort PMs spend on communication planning, the loose nature and structure of communication plans, and at times, the absence of any such plans altogether. Even projects that do have a communication plan seldom address any meaningful stakeholders' needs, which underscores the need for having a communication plan and conducting meaningful communication planning.

To make project communications successful, PMs should take a few simple steps:

1. Make communication a top priority;
2. Establish a culture wherein all stakeholders and team members feel that they share responsibility for communication and fully understand their role in every interaction;
3. Match the communication channels to the needs of the project stakeholders;
4. Keep reviewing the communication processes and methods to ensure they meet the current project needs;
5. Remain open to opportunities for improvement.

Meaningful Communication

Meaningful communication is not about talking a lot or sitting in long, back-to-back meetings. It is about engaging project team members and stakeholders—reaching out to them, listening to what they have to say, and collaborating on improving the effectiveness and efficiency of working relationships. The goal is to establish working conditions that are better for everyone involved and for achieving project success. Many PMs and team members have trouble recalling when they last engaged in a meaningful conversation with their colleagues—something along the lines of "what can we do so we work better together?" or "what can I do to make things easier for you?"

There are many potential reasons that these, and similar conversations, do not take place often enough, or at all in projects, but the impact of their absence is clear: communication challenges that often translate into performance issues. These types of communication challenges in projects can often be traced back to the PM, the sponsor, and to the senior leadership of the organization and its culture. An old Turkish proverb[5] illustrates this by saying that "a fish smells from its head down," as shown in Image 11.1.

Establishing healthy project communication starts with the PM and heavily depends upon the conditions established by the sponsor. When project communication breaks down, it is the PM's responsibility to alert the sponsor and the senior leadership of the organization. Excuses, such as "it is not up to me," do not help resolve the issue and indicate a failure at the PM's level.

Across the Entire Project

Project communications is not performed in a silo—it must be integrated with all aspects of the project to ensure that information flows properly, at a sufficient pace, and in the right context within a project. Project communications management starts with performing a stakeholder analysis; goes through the planning of the stakeholder management strategy as part of the communication plan; and continues with actually

"A fish smells from its head down." When a
project fails, look up toward the leadership
(i.e. project manager, sponsor, or senior
management) in search for the root cause.

Image 11.1   The fish smells from its head down

managing and owning the project communications, setting up ground rules, establishing boundaries, and managing reporting, issues, and stakeholder expectations.

Project communication involves a wide range of formal and informal methods, as illustrated in Table 11.1. One of its main roles is to remove distractions from the project so that stakeholders and team members can focus on adding value and doing what they have been assigned to do, rather than on dealing with misunderstandings. With all the recognition that the importance of communication management is receiving, it is surprising that so many projects have no communication plans in place.

Project communications management activities, combined with stakeholder management activities, stretch across the entire project lifecycle and take place from project initiation to closure. Although the Project Management Institute (PMI) identifies project communications and stakeholder management as two separate knowledge areas, they are heavily interconnected in the sense that the stakeholder analysis identifies stakeholders' communication needs, which are fulfilled through communication planning. A combined view of the project (including communication management and stakeholder management) across its lifecycle encompasses the interactions illustrated by Figure 11.3.

COMMUNICATION PLANNING

Chapter 4 provided an extensive overview of how to conduct a stakeholder analysis, which is the gateway to planning project communications since the project

Table 11.1 Formal and informal communication

Formal Communication	Informal Communication
Meetings*	Conversations
Reports*	Phone calls
Presentation*	E-mails*
Plans*	One-on-one chats
Information gathering*	Conflict management*
Training*	Estimating*
Status updates*	Negotiations*
Changes	Assumption/issue/risk management*
	Escalation*
	Discussions related to motivation, buy-in, fact checking, clarifications

*Can be either formal or informal.

The project manager engages team members and other stakeholders via multiple communication activities; some are formal, others are informal, and most of them can be either formal or informal.

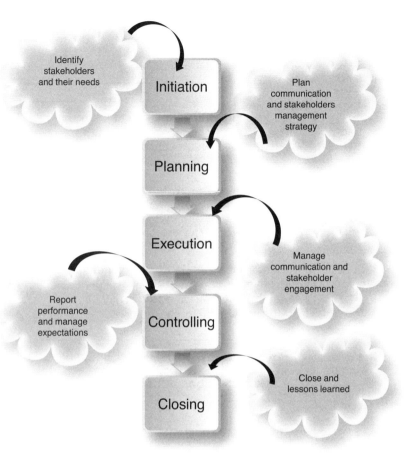

This process view captures high-level activities associated with communication and stakeholder expectations management. The activities of these two separate knowledge areas are closely related to each other.

Figure 11.3 Communication process view [in the context of the PMBOK® Guide Project Lifecycle Process Groups]

communication plan should address the stakeholders' communication needs and help manage their expectations. Effective communication planning involves the activities presented in Figure 11.4.

The goal of project communication management is to design and control project communications in such a way that it will accommodate the needs of stakeholders and, at the same time, promote collaboration and enable project success. The setup of project communications is not simply about a generic enabling

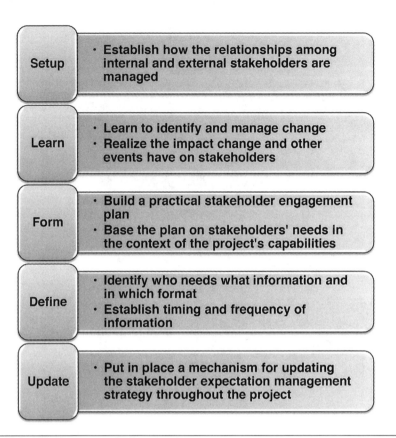

Setup	• Establish how the relationships among internal and external stakeholders are managed
Learn	• Learn to identify and manage change • Realize the impact change and other events have on stakeholders
Form	• Build a practical stakeholder engagement plan • Base the plan on stakeholders' needs in the context of the project's capabilities
Define	• Identify who needs what information and in which format • Establish timing and frequency of information
Update	• Put in place a mechanism for updating the stakeholder expectation management strategy throughout the project

Figure 11.4   Effective communication planning

of communication in a "one size fits all" format—it should proactively establish an effective and efficient flow of information within and around the project. Proactive, in this context, means to design communications in such a way that they take the needs and expectations of stakeholders into consideration and maximize the flow of information within these constraints.

It is a known fact that no two stakeholders are alike or share exactly the same needs and preferences. Therefore, project communications should take this into account and include communication formats, methods, and approaches that accommodate and address the specific needs of the stakeholders. With that said, most projects cannot afford to fully accommodate all the communication needs of all stakeholders, due to time and cost constraints. This is why the stakeholder analysis includes the process of grouping stakeholders into categories that share similar needs, thereby achieving economies of scale in project communications. It should also include a short communication needs survey, in which the PM presents stakeholders with available options for communication, allowing them to select their preferred methods.

PMs need to discuss the components of the communication plan and its options with the project stakeholders and introduce the meanings and intentions behind them. When stakeholders understand the reasoning behind certain actions, it increases the chances that they will buy-in and support the process. The discussion should also include engaging report recipients and setting expectations about reporting formats, to avoid misunderstandings and issues related to reports structures and contents.

For example, when a senior external stakeholder asks for a special report about the project, there is usually no set expectation about the format and structure of the report. The result may be a report that provides the information requested; however, there may be a gap in expectations about how the report looks in terms of its structure, format, colors used, and other technicalities. This leads to unnecessary distractions: the stakeholder is not satisfied with the quality of the report, regardless of the information presented; the PM is under scrutiny and criticism; the report may have to be reissued; and none of these add value to the project. By simply setting and managing expectations around reports, the stakeholder could have avoided the entire issue from happening. It is not a matter of pointing fingers, but the PM is part of the problem, since he/she should have asked for clarification to ensure that the report addressed the needs of the stakeholder. This is also an example of the 100:100 rule in action, which demonstrates the need for PMs to reach out and make sure they know what is expected of them in any situation, since not knowing will end up backfiring on their ability to manage the project effectively.

The Communication Plan

The communication plan consists of elements that ensure the effective flow of information, as well as establish ground rules and expectations about the daily interactions among team members and project stakeholders. Traditionally, a communication plan has two components:

1. A breakdown of ongoing team and stakeholder communication events, with focus on the deliverable description, method of delivery, frequency, owner, and audience.
2. A list of specific, one-time (e.g., milestone related) communication events. The difference from the breakdown of ongoing events is that this is aligned with the project milestones and details the communication events associated with them.

The communication plan document also contains more standard information, some of which may be available from the organization or from previous projects, that needs to be customized to the specific project requirements, including organizational structure, reporting lines, communication processes, and guidelines regarding communication for specific project matters.

TEAM CONTRACT AND GROUND RULES

The contents of most communication plans do not address the day-to-day interactions and communications among team members and with stakeholders. A team contract is a set of ground rules and behavioral guidelines that help facilitate communication between the PM and the team, among team members, and between the project team and external stakeholders. These ground rules can help narrow the gap between stakeholder expectations and the way communication and events take place in the project and by that, reduce the chances of misunderstandings and unnecessary or uncontrolled conflicts.

The nature of the guidelines and their level of detail must be based on the organizational culture, previous projects' events, and the make-up of the team. No two projects are the same, and no two organizations will require the same extent of scrutiny for those guidelines. What might be a necessity in one project may be a common practice in another, and perceived as inappropriate or even offensive in yet another project. The PM should make the decision about the style and contents of the team contract according to the stakeholder analysis and using feedback from the team members and stakeholders involved.

These days, we are so focused on tools to make life easier (e.g., web applications, instant messenger, video conferencing) that we forget that project success and customer satisfaction are really about the no-shortcuts process of establishing communication guidelines, expectations, and basic principles that should work on their own—regardless of the technology and tools used. Only when communication is set up and ready to go is it time for incorporating tools that may help make the process more efficient. The team contract can be useful to address challenges and to establish team procedures and identify expectations. The content of the team contract should be grouped into the following categories:

- Guidelines for general communication;
- E-mail code of conduct;
- Meeting expectations (including teleconferences).

General Communication

This area deals with establishing general guidelines for communication and for how team members should deal with each other and with other stakeholders. There are two parts to general communication guidelines:

1. Aspiring behaviors: these are behaviors that the team should strive to enact; they are not measurable, and therefore team members cannot be held in violation of any of these behaviors, but all team members should commit to following these principles.
2. Code of conduct and ground rules: these are "fences" that help build relationships, set expectations, and protect individual territory. They can be measured, and team members should adhere to these ground rules.

There are similarities between the two lists, in places where the aspiring behavior should become more specific. This section focuses on the communication code of conduct and ground rules, as displayed in Figure 11.5.

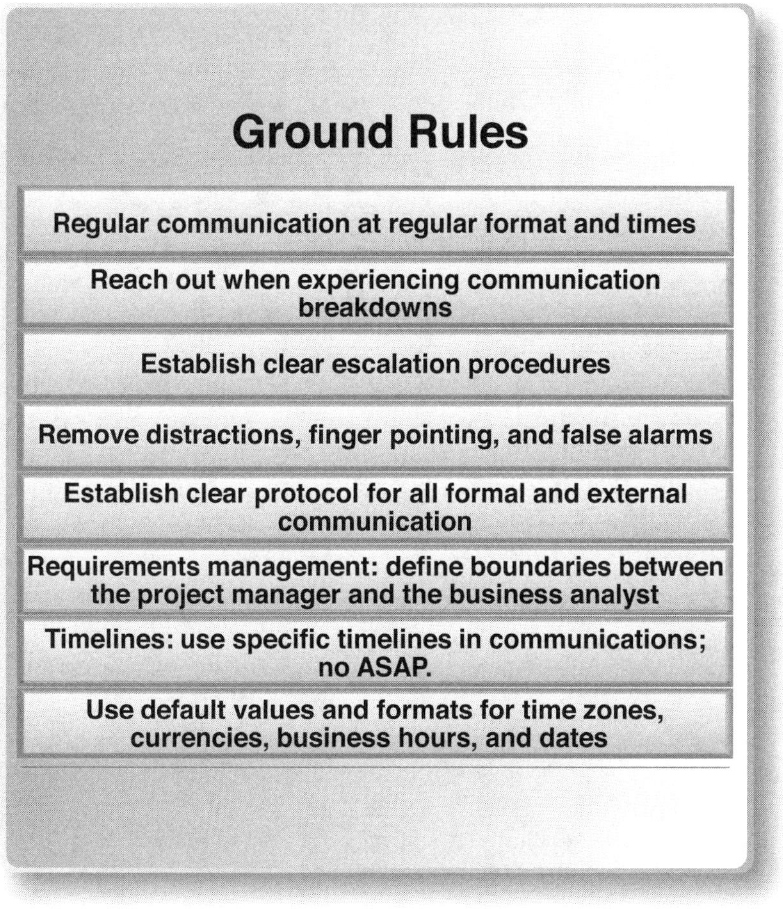

Ground Rules

Regular communication at regular format and times

Reach out when experiencing communication breakdowns

Establish clear escalation procedures

Remove distractions, finger pointing, and false alarms

Establish clear protocol for all formal and external communication

Requirements management: define boundaries between the project manager and the business analyst

Timelines: use specific timelines in communications; no ASAP.

Use default values and formats for time zones, currencies, business hours, and dates

Figure 11.5   Communication code of conduct and ground rules

E-mails

E-mail was introduced many years ago, with the great promise of streamlining communication and enabling almost real-time communication around the world. Since then, many e-mails have been sent and received, and it appears that the promise has turned into one giant load of work that consumes a significant amount of time for each and every person in the organization. Although e-mail is a basic function that can be performed and handled (on the technical side) by essentially everyone in the organization, there is a strong need for establishing some ground rules that will govern its use, reduce its volume, and ensure that e-mail actually adds value to the project and does not just consume time and energy. Figure 11.6 illustrates the guidelines for effective use of e-mail.

General
- Repeat subject line? Reach out to talk
- Conversations over email: talk and then recap in an e-mail
- Format: short and clear. Name, action, date
- Establish response time to e-mails
- Use the *out of office* message
- When someone is *out of office,* reduce e-mail sent to them and consolidate

Sending
- Subject line to reflect topic
- E-mail urgency and high priority: urgent to whom?
- Caution with CC and BCC
- Reduce group e-mails
- Read before sending
- No reply to all
- Reduce the use of read receipt
- Spell-check
- Read before sending
- If high stakes or emotional, wait and read later before sending

Figure 11.6 E-mail guidelines (Broken into general guidelines and ground rules for the sender.)

Meetings

In projects and organizations, meetings are a drag that for the most part can be summed up as dysfunctional. It does not require extensive experience for a PM to get a realistic picture of the state of the project simply by walking into a project meeting with plugged ears and looking at how the meeting is managed. Project meetings may not only serve as a reflection of the state of the project but also serve as an indication that even if the performance does not lag, there may be signs of trouble.

Well-run meetings are an asset to the project and the organization, and given that they are such a rare commodity, they may serve as a morale boost for the team and begin to be seen as a key to success of projects. To help PMs and team members run effective meetings that add value to the project and the organization, Figures 11.7(a) and 11.7(b) recommend meeting guidelines to consider. For

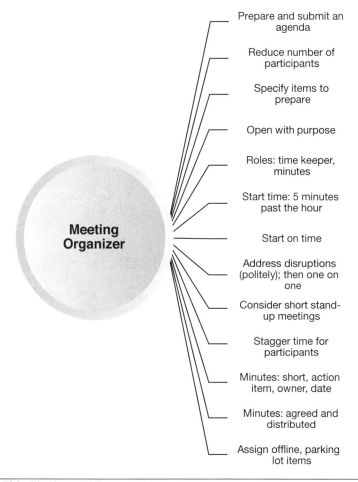

Figure 11.7(a)　Meeting guidelines: organizer

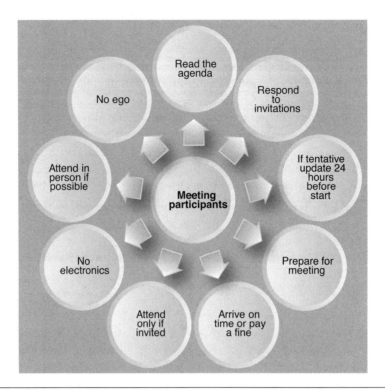

Figure 11.7(b) Meeting guidelines: participants

teleconferences, Figure 11.8 identifies guidelines for conference calls, which seem to be a growing pain in many organizations.

MORE THOUGHTS ON COMMUNICATION

This list of ground rules does not fit all situations, but it addresses the most common challenges PMs and their teams face. As an extension of the stakeholder analysis, PMs should incorporate applicable items from this list into their specific situation, and use it as a set of poka-yoke items (or error proofing, as presented in Chapter 9) to help set expectations and establish boundaries for conduct and behavior. In turn, it will enable collaboration and reduce distractions for team members and stakeholders throughout the project.

There are some additional ideas and thoughts on communication that can provide PMs with context and help them channel their efforts more effectively throughout the communication management process. These thoughts are listed in the following discussion and should be considered by PMs.

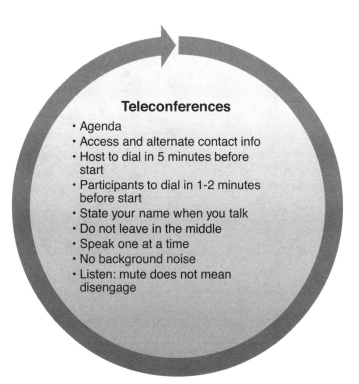

Teleconferences
- Agenda
- Access and alternate contact info
- Host to dial in 5 minutes before start
- Participants to dial in 1-2 minutes before start
- State your name when you talk
- Do not leave in the middle
- Speak one at a time
- No background noise
- Listen: mute does not mean disengage

Figure 11.8 Meeting guidelines: teleconferences

The 7% Rule

There is a well-known concept in communication that addresses people's assessment of other people's credibility. It claims that we pay 55% of our attention to the speaker's body language, another 38% to the tone of voice, and only 7% to the actual words,[6] as illustrated in Figure 11.9. However, many experts dispute this claim,[7] saying that it is applicable only in specific situations, such as when forming an opinion about a speaker or when there is a discrepancy between the speaker's words and other aspects of the communication (specifically, body language and tone).

The Value of a Good Relationship

Effective communication, which addresses the needs of project stakeholders, can serve as a framework for stronger and better relationships with them. It also enhances the team's ability to leverage relationships and improves both creativity and performance. In the event that project performance does not meet expectations, effective communication can buy the project team more time to improve performance and can help manage expectations more effectively. By contrast, even

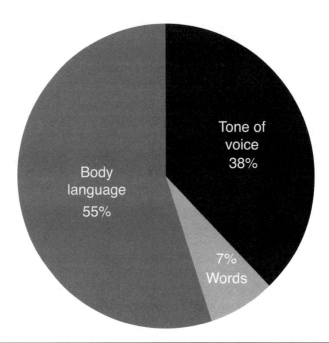

Figure 11.9 Verbal and nonverbal communication analysis (Source: The nonverbal communication analysis by Albert Mehrabian.)

projects that are performing well can suffer from weak relationship management and ineffective communication, since the customer will not be able to properly recognize progress and achievements and will be distracted by breakdowns in communication.

Beware of Making Exceptions

Exceptions should not be allowed in handling conflicts or any other behavioral issues. Nor should special treatment and excuses be allowed because they will open the door for others to follow the precedent of these inappropriate behaviors and will set a new (lower) standard moving forward. If these behaviors are permitted, it will be easy to lose control over the team's behaviors and over the development of negative sentiments and attitudes.

Communication Failure

Failing to own and manage project communications effectively leads to loss of trust, damaged stakeholder motivation, a reduction in people's faith in the process, confusion in understanding roles and responsibilities, and inevitably, hampered relationships. When team members and stakeholders treat each other as enemies, rather than as partners, the goal of winning prevails: we no longer seek the win-win resolution, and we allow emotions and egos to dictate our decision making.

Quality, Not Quantity

Effective communication does not mean communicating all the time. It is about the effective and efficient use of our time and constantly looking to improve communication—with less effort. Adding new tools to the arsenal of options does not necessarily add value, unless those tools address needs that stakeholders have and that directly contribute to project results. From excessive use of tools and too much communication comes the desire to disallow, or at least limit, the use of electronics in meetings.

Drama

Drama distracts stakeholders from the main issues at stake, often resulting in conflict and leading to a "cry wolf" syndrome, where people become deaf to indications of alarm. Drama forces team members to adjust their priorities, to attend to the matter under consideration, and may derail their in-progress efforts to add value to the project. It often triggers escalations, which consume more resources and time than when conflicts are handled without drama. Furthermore, drama adds to team members' frustration.

Like most other behavioral challenges, dealing with drama needs to take place on a one-on-one basis and without putting the producer of the drama on the spot. One successful approach is to explain that the drama may well be justified but misinterpreted by many. This approach appears to shift the blame from the producer of the drama to other stakeholders without naming names or pointing fingers. It does not question the motives or behavior of the producer of the drama, and the change in behavior is more about style than blame.

Conflict Management Plan

The communication plan can include a conflict management plan that provides processes, escalation procedures, and roles and responsibilities for conflict management and resolution. It can help maintain order in the project team and maintain focus on the problem, when conflict takes place, by providing a clear process for its resolution. This then saves the need for stakeholders to think about how to approach the conflict and helps them concentrate on working toward a resolution.

A simple conflict management process should include the following generic stages:

1. Recognize that conflict is taking place;

2. Articulate the shared goals to ensure that the conflict is framed within the context of the project;

3. Focus on a win-win approach for a resolution by separating the people from the problem and working jointly toward a resolution;

4. Determine whether further escalation is required;

5. Come up with options for evaluation and present their context and reasoning;

6. Decide on a solution that reflects the project needs, while addressing the needs of both sides within it, so the solution is not disconnected from the project's or stakeholders' needs;

7. Communicate the solution and take appropriate action.

Give People What They Want

When presenting a range of potential communication methods, list all available options (to remain cost effective, do not ask an open-ended question) and allow stakeholders to select their preferred approach to communication that addresses their needs. Establish all the details of communication in advance, to ensure that expectations are set and that the team has the ability to deliver on these expectations.

Double Standard

No one wants to admit it, but most of us apply some level of double standard when dealing with others. One of the important benefits of effective communication is in creating the reality in which everyone gets a fair chance to communicate and contribute to the project and the decision making. When we do not feel we are getting a fair chance to communicate our thoughts and be heard, we often "check out" of the process, with negative attitudes, conflict, trust issues, and performance problems to follow. Fairness involves judging ourselves by the same standards with which we judge others. Giving everyone a fair chance and establishing transparency starts with communication by ensuring that we do not judge ourselves by our intentions while judging others by the results of their actions.

FINAL THOUGHT: OWN THE COMMUNICATIONS

If there is an area that all PMs should excel at, it is communication. Owning project communications is the key to success for everything else in the project. Communication not only consumes most of the PM's time but is also the most important factor in managing attitudes and impressions. Ultimately, communication affects every single aspect of the project: from scope and change management to schedule and budget, risk, quality, resources, expectations, and procurement.

REFERENCES

1. Project Management Institute (PMI), *A Guide to the Project Management Body of Knowledge*, (*PMBOK® Guide—Fifth Edition*), 533, (Sylva: PMI, 2013).
2. Based on the *PMBOK® Guide,* 532.
3. Ibid., 252.
4. Based in the "Basic Communication Model," in the *PMBOK® Guide*, 294.
5. Based on: http://www.phrases.org.uk/meanings/fish-rot-from-the-head-down .html.
6. Based on: Albert Mehrabian, *Silent Messages: Implicit Communication of Emotions and Attitudes* (Belmont: Wadsworth, 1971).
7. Based on: Phillip Yaffe, "The 7% Rule—Fact, Fiction, or Misunderstanding," *Ubiquity*, Volume 2011, October 2011, 1–5, at http://ubiquity.acm.org/article .cfm?id=2043156.

12

Organizational Influences

Projects do not take place in a vacuum. They are part of organizations, which go through changes of their own—reorganizations; changing priorities; and shifting and varying resources, areas of focus, and directions. The changes that projects represent need to be incorporated into the wider context of the overall strategy of the organization, and the projects' outcomes need to turn into meaningful benefits. This book tries to instill in PMs the notion that every project action should be considered within the broader organizational context to ensure that every activity adds value to the organization.

CHAPTER STRUCTURE: 3 IN 1

This chapter deals with three distinct matters that all have one common denominator: they have a direct impact on the organization, and therefore PMs need to take them into consideration. The three topics are:

1. **Organizational influences:** This section contains a review of concepts to safeguard the alignment between the project and the organizational goals, thoughts around the critical chain, and how to leverage it for collaboration through cross-project dependencies, and a discussion about the two-way relationship between risks and change requests (CRs).

2. **Lessons learned and post implementation review:** This includes the specific roles in improving the organization's capabilities, from both a project performance perspective and a product perspective. This section also provides details on how to perform these two activities effectively.

3. **Project rescue and recovery:** This is about projects that fail to deliver on significant success criteria and projects that outright fail, requiring specific action beyond "business as usual." It discusses the recovery effort, which is about specifying new objectives, working with the organization for more resources, and at times, appointing a recovery manager to lead the project to meet its newly defined success criteria.

ALIGNMENT

Project alignment is not about checking the project performance against its own objectives (i.e., scope, time, and cost); rather, it is about measuring how the project is doing in relation to organizational objectives. Even when projects are on track to deliver on their internal success criteria, they may not fulfill the reasons the organization decided to undertake the initiative. On a regular basis, PMs should keep their eyes on the organizational objectives, on the project's alignment with them, and on the project sponsor's needs. In the event of a misalignment between the value the project delivers and the organizational needs, it is only a matter of time before the project is either terminated or required to go through a major overhaul, in the form of a recovery, to redefine its objectives.

The project charter can be viewed as the vision statement of the project, and it is where the project mandate is defined and articulated. The need to maintain alignment between the project and the organization is yet another reason for a clear, concise, and short charter. Going back to this document at various points allows the organization and the PM to review the reasons for certain things being done, and whether they are performed in certain ways. If the value is not realized by the project activities as intended, the review can help articulate the need for recovery, along with the nature and extent of that recovery.

CRITICAL CHAIN

With limited abilities to deliver success without the organization's active support in priorities and resources, PMs need to resort to cross-project collaboration to manage resources and dependencies more effectively. The concept of the *critical chain* is related to project portfolio management and attempts to identify inter-dependencies between projects within the organization. These interdependencies involve multiple factors, which may be interrelated and may involve resources and deliverables. There are a limited number of techniques for managing cross-project dependencies,[1] and they include: effective cross-project communication and sched-ule optimization methods, led by the critical chain.

The critical chain[2] provides effective risk-focused approaches that can help mini-mize cross-project impacts. Operating within multiple project environments, most projects do not have the ability to focus on risks and issues in other projects, and—even though they may be carefully planned and run effective risk management—they may be subject to cross-project risks, particularly the availability of resources. The critical chain identifies critical resources for multiple projects and ensures their effective utilization by staggering projects around their availability and protecting each project with schedule buffers. Effective cross-project communication and col-laboration among PMs, through regular interactions, may provide opportunities for establishing early alert systems for cross-project impact areas. The critical chain is difficult to apply in most project environments because it requires organizational change, such as more candid estimates and permission to include schedule buffers. Despite these challenges, it can serve as a platform for the improvement areas in the following discussion.

Collaboration and Early Detection

Cross-project resource dependencies can be discussed and determined among the PMs who share resources. Coordination meetings should take place at intervals, which depend upon the projects' velocity, and they should focus on reaching agree-ments on how to allocate resources that are shared among multiple projects. It helps shift PMs away from the current, inefficient way of fighting and arguing over resources—typically after the fact, when problems have already caused resource scheduling conflicts (as seen in the culture of alligators from Chapter 1).

Instead, PMs can proactively create an early detection system and figure out which project has the greater need for resource allocation. This mechanism can help PMs and resource managers proactively agree upon resource allocation and avoid scrambling as crises happen and events unfold. This approach also helps to improve working relations, as PMs become less focused on fighting with each other and more focused on doing their jobs. It also helps create momentum in productivity and an environment that other PMs endeavour to become part of.

Resource Management and Organizational Considerations

This joint effort between project and resource managers (and among PMs) to manage resource contentions establishes best practices related to building a problem alert system. Typically, when there are problems that cause resources to extend their stay on a project instead of moving on to report to the next project on their schedules, there is no early detection system to give the next PM a heads-up, as illustrated in Figure 12.1.

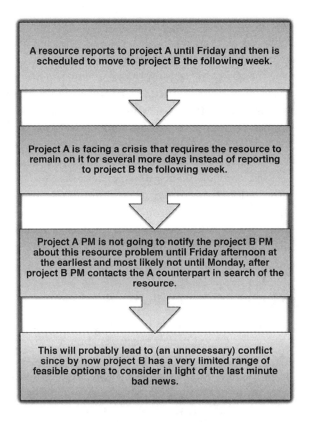

A resource reports to project A until Friday and then is scheduled to move to project B the following week.

Project A is facing a crisis that requires the resource to remain on it for several more days instead of reporting to project B the following week.

Project A PM is not going to notify the project B PM about this resource problem until Friday afternoon at the earliest and most likely not until Monday, after project B PM contacts the A counterpart in search of the resource.

This will probably lead to (an unnecessary) conflict since by now project B has a very limited range of feasible options to consider in light of the last minute bad news.

This inefficient chain of events contains no consideration for the overall organizational benefits. The ensued conflict between the project managers adds no value.

Figure 12.1   A typical scenario that represents challenges with shared resources

The decision by PM A to keep the resource is right for project A, but it does not take into consideration the organization's needs. While the decision may save project A's performance, it may cause project B significant damage, which may have an overall greater negative impact on the organization as a whole. PM A should contact PM B earlier in the week (Wednesday or Thursday at the latest), when it is apparent that the resource will need to remain on the project. This will alert PM B to the situation, at which point, both PMs can collaborate to ensure that the decision will be best for the organization. In the event that they are unable to make a decision, they should escalate the matter to their sponsor(s) for a more focused view of the conflicting priorities in order to optimize its handling and ultimately, add value to the organization. Once again, the key to resolution is communication, managing expectations, and establishing ground rules.

Cross-project Urgency

PMs are consumed by extensive volumes of work in managing their own projects, and they lack the perspective and/or capacity to look for and worry about problems and challenges in other projects. Chapter 7 offers a project urgency assessment that allows PMs to compare the urgency of their own projects with other projects that compete for the same resources. This can help direct and reallocate resources to where they will add the most value, rather than being driven by considerations that may be unrelated to the merits of the situation (for example, political considerations, PMs who scream louder, or those who have more influence on decision makers). The main objective of this process is to ensure PMs do not make decisions, to give priority to one project over another, that are disconnected from organizational considerations and do not add value to the organization.

RISK AND CHANGE REQUESTS

Chapters 8 and 9 dealt with project risks and project changes; however, there is an area where they overlap in a two-way fashion—project changes may produce risks, and risks may produce the need to go through a formal project change.

The Impact of Change on Risk

The objective of the project change control mechanism is to support the decision-making process on CRs and assess the impact each change will have (if implemented) on the other project constraints and success criteria. Part of the assessment needs to take into consideration any risks that may be introduced as a result of implementing the change and the work associated with it. This side of risk management is often overlooked (or forgotten altogether) and results in CRs being accepted and implemented without proper risk assessment. PMs cannot rely on tools in this case—they must ensure that each CR goes through a full risk assessment process, including cross-project risks, to ensure there is no negative organizational impact.

The Impact of Risk on Change

The subject of risk impact on project change is related to project recovery because, under certain conditions, it leads to one or both of the following:

1. When the risk impact is significant and causes a change in any of the project's constraints and success criteria, it requires a CR to be submitted. The purpose of this kind of request is less for approval, as the event already took place, than to ensure that the change is captured and properly reflected in the baseline.
2. In the event that risk impacts are severe and major project objectives are no longer within reach, it may require the project to enter into a recovery mode. This is when the PM and the sponsor realize that business cannot continue as usual, since the project objectives have been (or are on track to be) compromised in such a way that success criteria and stakeholders' expectations need to be redefined.

In the event that a risk impacts the project to the extent that it cannot be absorbed without changing the baseline, the PM needs to submit a CR. This kind of CR often faces resistance, since stakeholders do not view it as a good enough reason to justify a change, but if the PM fails to submit the CR, the impact will not be captured in the baseline. Failing to change the plan and expectations will result in a gap between the project plan and the reality and will inevitably lead to performance issues down the road. It may also lead to underestimating the need for resources to recover from the risk, which will have a cascading effect on the organization and its ability to allocate resources to its various projects.

LESSONS LEARNED AND POST IMPLEMENTATION REVIEW

Anything the PMs and the organization manage to learn from previous projects is valuable. To maximize the benefits, it is important to share the lessons and implement them moving forward. No one questions the value of capturing and implementing lessons learned; however, in practice, relatively few PMs and organizations go through the effort of doing this, mainly due to cost, time, and resource constraints, as well as from a belief that lessons will be captured without going through the process. The gap between PMs who recognize the value in lessons learned and the low number of PMs who conduct it is typically driven by one (or more) of the reasons listed in Figure 12.2.

There is an underlying theme behind these reasons (or excuses): they are all driven by organizational priorities and by a failure, at the upper levels of the

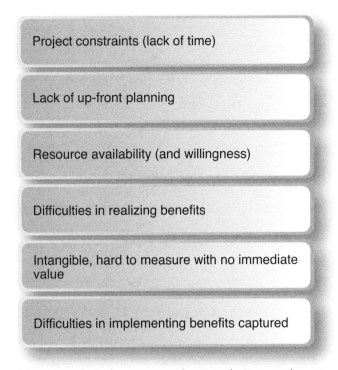

Project constraints (lack of time)

Lack of up-front planning

Resource availability (and willingness)

Difficulties in realizing benefits

Intangible, hard to measure with no immediate value

Difficulties in implementing benefits captured

It is unclear why project managers do not conduct a proper lessons learned process despite its proven importance and value.

Figure 12.2   The gap

organization, to realize the value of capturing and implementing lessons learned. Capturing lessons learned is related to quality management, and starts with awareness by the senior leadership of the organization of their roles in creating the right conditions for project success.

In addition, this process almost exclusively concerns future, long-term organizational benefits and often has little or nothing to do with improving the performance of the existing project. Sponsors, senior management, and PMs may not have a strong incentive to expend existing project resources on, or the capacity for, an undertaking that aims at capturing and implementing potential benefits for future projects.

LESSONS LEARNED ARE NOT ONLY ABOUT LESSONS

The process of capturing lessons learned however, goes beyond learning from mistakes—it has far-reaching benefits for the organization.

Team Building

The process of capturing lessons from the project brings the team together and helps team members reframe how they view the way things took place in the project. It involves a series of activities that even if they yield no tangible ways to improve processes, get the team to take a second look and identify areas for personal improvement.

Collaboration and Confidence

The effort to learn from mistakes helps build confidence among team members that the organization cares about how projects are performed and genuine effort is being made to improve things. It also helps achieve stakeholders' buy-in by delivering actions oriented toward continuous improvement and growth. It sends a positive message to all stakeholders involved (including the customer), and may help improve participation in the process and enhance confidence and faith in future capabilities and performances.

Not Only at the End of the Project

Most projects conduct their lessons learned exercises at the end of the project. While this is the best time to look at the project in hindsight, the inherent problem with the timing is that many resources may no longer be available or involved in the project—they may have moved on, left the organization, or been promoted. This limits the ability to properly capture lessons and takes away most of the benefits of the process, since the people who were involved are not providing the feedback.

A simple way to overcome this problem was suggested in Chapter 11: the effort to capture lessons learned and significant events in the project should not begin at the end of the project; rather, it should take place at regular intervals throughout the project. At the end of every status meeting, the team should engage in a quick round of capturing lessons for that week. The effort should only take a couple of minutes and include the following steps and ground rules:

- The PM asks all participants in the meeting to provide feedback about what took place in the past week;
- Feedback should be one sentence that capture the essence of that week, with focus on what went right/wrong, surprises, unplanned successes, or anything worth noting;
- No feedback or further discussion is allowed;
- The PM will create a lessons learned feedback form (illustrated in Table 12.1) to capture the feedback, by recording each participant's comments for the appropriate date.

Table 12.1 Lessons learned feedback form

Date \ Team Member	Lori	Leah	Whitney	Evan	Sam
Week 1: Feb 13th	Requirements not finalized	Unclear role of new consultant	Too many arguments about features	No assumptions in charter	No reference for effort estimates

The information collected will serve as a starting point for the lessons learned process to take place at the end of the project. Many of the comments and observations may not add much value, but feedback that is collected continuously will give the PM material and context to start the actual task of capturing the lessons for the project.

From Lessons Learned to Best Practices

After observing and understanding the project's events, the team will come up with lessons learned and make recommendations for the organization to implement in future projects. Once proven, these captured lessons learned can turn into future best practices.

How To Do It

A lessons learned exercise is the process of gathering, documenting, and analyzing feedback on events that happened during a project, which may be beneficial for future projects. It gives the team and the organization a chance to reflect on events and activities during the project, and it helps bring closure to the project. Specific areas to discuss and reflect upon are listed in Figure 12.3.

The main point of this exercise is to check how things took place (as opposed to the "what") in the project and with the team. The findings should be captured and articulated in such a way that the organization and team members will be able to apply the lessons learned in an effort to not repeat the same types of mistakes in the future.

The Purpose

All attempts to identify and apply lessons learned in projects are driven by a generic set of goals, which are essentially aimed at getting better at performing project work. At times, organizations go through the process without a specific goal in mind, or with no clear idea of the type of benefits they are trying to realize. When organizations face specific types of challenges or problems that linger across projects and

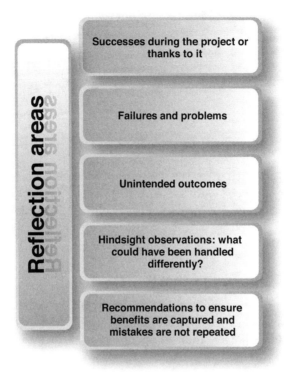

Figure 12.3 Areas that should be discussed and reflected upon

over time, they conduct the lessons learned process with specific objectives in mind and with a clear idea of the value it is intended to add to the organization.

The Process

Although the concept is straightforward, many organizations lack focus on what they are trying to get out of a lessons learned process, or the rigor and discipline to do it in a meaningful way. The implementation of lessons learned has to take place in the short term, to ensure that the value gained from it does not turn stale. It also includes taking steps to ensure that the lesson is documented and captured across the organization. The best value is achieved if the lessons are incorporated into ongoing procedures in order to reduce the need to revisit the lessons learned database in the future. The implementation should involve one or more of the following: creating a cheat-sheet, creating a list of new guidelines, updating related processes and procedures, or getting the project management office to distribute the captured lessons across the organization—to maximize the benefits from it and to reduce the chance that other PMs stumble onto a similar problem. The steps of this process are illustrated in Figure 12.4.

Figure 12.4   The lessons learned process

What to Ask

There are two types of questions to ask about the project in the lessons learned process: general and phase-driven. The general questions inquire about various areas of the project in an effort to check the team's effectiveness, interaction, and communication with its surroundings—for example: processes; decision making; sign-offs; interactions with the organization, customers, vendors, and other stakeholders; team dynamic; conflict management and morale; and how effectively it handled the knowledge areas, the issues it was facing, and the changes that took place.

There are over three dozen general questions that could be asked, but not all projects require all areas to be investigated. However, there are five questions that should be included in all lessons learned exercises:

1. What went right in this project? Why?
2. What went wrong in the project? Why?
3. What was a surprise? What ended up being okay, despite a lack of planning? Was luck a factor in achieving success? If so, where did luck replace good planning?

4. Did the project significantly differ, in any way, from others you have worked on? In what way? What was the impact of this?
5. Did the project events and outcomes significantly differ from the plans? What was expected to be straightforward and ended up being straightforward? What was expected to be difficult and ended up being difficult?

In addition to the general questions, some lessons learned questions should focus on stages or phases of the project and on events and activities that took place in each of these phases (e.g., initiation, planning, implementation and control, closure, and handover and transition). These questions should be asked about each phase to determine whether processes and activities took place as required and how effective they were, check if the goals of each of the phases were achieved as intended, and examine whether there were any events that are worth mentioning (i.e., both good and bad).

Keep in Mind

Additional items to keep in mind about the lessons learned process include the need to ensure that relevant team members and stakeholders participate in it, and that it involves an attempt to gain access to previously gathered lessons learned material and quality assurance plans and reports for a better understanding of issues, challenges, and successes that took place in the project.

The person conducting the lessons learned process must keep it from being perceived as a finger pointing, or blaming process so that people are not afraid to express their views and opinions. It should be done in a setting that guarantees confidentiality, while addressing the issues at stake, and provides confidence that the process will not backfire and jeopardize their careers or relationships. Lastly, it is important to note that effective planning involves a communication plan and setting up ground rules, timelines, and expectations.

POST IMPLEMENTATION REVIEW

A post implementation review (PIR) takes place sometime after the project is completed (often 3–6 months later). The reason it is not conducted immediately after the implementation is to allow time for things to settle and performance to revert to normal, in order to measure how successful the integration of the project's product into the business was.

Unlike the lessons learned exercise, which checks how the project work was performed, the PIR deals with checking how successfully the project's benefits are realized and objectives are met. Conducting a PIR requires planning in advance—including allocating time, money, and resources to conduct the work—along with granting permissions for access by the users of the project's product (often the customer). The value the PIR produces is about helping future projects with setting objectives; planning, setting and managing expectations; managing the project overall; and delivering value.

Where to Look for Information

Those who perform the PIR should seek input from the PM and selected members of the team, key stakeholders, and the customer. A variety of project documents need to be reviewed as part of this process, with focus on those listed in Figure 12.5.

How to Do It

The PIR may include observations and conversations with the customer to check for feedback about the success of the project's products and benefits. This can also be done through a structured customer survey to collect specific and honest information from the customer and the users of the product about their expectations, perception of its success, and overall feedback. The survey should strive to

Project charter

- Helps to determine the intended project objectives and measure the variance between the original and actual results.

Project plans

- Helps check for gaps between the intended and actual performance of the project's major success criteria, including scope and requirements, schedules, budgets, and quality and performance standards.

Findings from the lessons learned exercise

- Serve as inputs to the PIR since they may have been influencing factors that impacted the realized project benefits.

Figure 12.5 Project documents to focus on

be objective and future-focused. Due to resource availability and to the need for objectivity and openness, it may be required to obtain the services of a third party to conduct the PIR.

PROJECT RESCUE AND RECOVERY

Projects that face major risks or performance issues that pose significant negative impacts on their success criteria may reach the point that the original, intended, objectives are no longer within reach. At that point, a choice needs to be made between terminating the project or attempting to fix it. When the performance falls below a certain level, it is reflected on the status report in red; however, there may be a variety of potential responses to a red status color:

- The PM needs to determine whether the color actually represents a major performance issue. It is possible that budget or time status may fall in the red zone, but it does not mean that the project is in immediate or urgent need of repair.
- In more extreme cases, a major decision needs to be made about whether and how the project is going to proceed:
  - The sponsor, customer, or steering committee may realize that the project is not salvageable. At that point, preparation needs to take place for terminating and closing the project. Even if the project does not proceed, it needs to be closed properly.
  - When "critical to success" areas suffer from major performance issues and it becomes clear that the project will not be able to meet its intended targets and produce its desired objectives, but there is a need to continue the project, a decision needs to be made to shift gears. This involves treating the project differently from this point forward—that is, resetting expectations for an adjusted set of benefits and performance, and kick-starting a project recovery or rescue effort.

What Recovery Is NOT About

When talking about project rescue and recovery, one of the first and most important things to clarify to stakeholders is that it does not mean restoring the original intended performance and bringing the project back to the previously desired level. When projects enter a recovery stage, it is about re-juggling priorities and adjusting performance expectations so work efforts can be planned for *new* targets. If a project enters a recovery stage, it is no longer business as usual—it is about cutting losses and redefining expectations and success criteria.

What Is a Failing Project?

At some point in their lifecycles, many projects reach the point when a recovery effort needs to take place due to performance issues that if they continue, will lead to project failure. A failing project is one that either does not make the journey from conception through to a successful implementation and closeout or will not make it to a successful end at the current performance level. In either case, a recovery or rescue operation is needed.

There is usually more than one factor to be highlighted as the cause of project failure, and it is often difficult to define or trace back to where the seeds of failure were planted. That said, there are a few factors, listed in Figure 12.6, that if present are likely to signal potential project failure. These factors are, in part, environmental and in part, under the control of the PMs, but they are all indications that the project might be mismanaged and/or out of control.

Things that if present may signal elevated potential for problems and project failure

Figure 12.6 High risk factors

WHAT IS RECOVERY ABOUT?

Once the go-ahead is given for a recovery and rescue operation, the project enters a new phase, which often starts by installing a recovery manager in place of the PM. While it is common to have the PM leading the recovery efforts, having a different person leading the recovery may help signal a change in momentum.

Once it is acknowledged that the project is failing to meet its targets and cannot continue in the same direction, the recovery begins and should consist of five steps:

1. Assign a recovery manager: Whether the recovery manager is the current PM or someone else, the sponsor should make an announcement that the recovery is under way and formally introduce the recovery manager to the project stakeholders.

2. Develop a recovery charter and conduct a recovery kickoff meeting: This will set the tone and the expectations for the recovery and redefine the goals and objectives of the project.

3. Conduct a current state assessment: Any recovery effort starts with understanding the current state of the project—where it is failing and the extent of its problems. The findings from this assessment will determine not only the nature of the effort moving forward but also the end result of the recovery. One of the goals of the assessment is to gain understanding of the nature and severity of the problems and challenges the project is facing, so that the plan addresses actual problems and root causes, rather than merely trying to fix symptoms.

4. Recovery plan development: Before the plan is formed, there may be a need to present recovery options to the sponsor and senior management and wait for them to decide on their preferred option. Creating a plan expands on the objectives set forth in the charter and factors in the current state assessment to create a roadmap and a set of actions to perform the recovery.

5. Lead the recovery operation: Execute the recovery plan, monitor the progress, and control the outputs, outcomes, and results as they are realized.

Once the stakeholders recognize that the project is failing, a decision to recover and rescue it has to be made promptly to allow for a quick start of the recovery process. Any time lost at this stage may make the recovery more risky, costly, or even no longer feasible.

Recovery Charter

The recovery charter is slightly different in nature from a regular project charter in the sense that one of its first orders of business is to mandate and authorize conducting a current state assessment of the failing project. Beyond ordering the assessment, the charter is a written document that captures the agreement between the project sponsor and senior management, on one hand, and the recovery manager, on the other. It specifies the expected deliverables the recovery must produce, and in a similar fashion to a regular project charter, it provides approximate time and cost estimates of the recovery effort.

The recovery charter should provide the context and set the stage for the assessment of the current state of the project and the recovery effort. Once the assessment is complete, the charter will serve as the guiding foundation for the recovery plan, where specific details and estimates will be made. For context and high-level objectives, the charter should include the components listed in Table 12.2.

The Recovery Team

Whether the recovery team is made up of the project team members or is a newly formed team, an important activity to be performed early on in the process by the project recovery manager is to build trust and reduce the level of anxiety among team members and other stakeholders. This anxiety is usually driven by uncertainty about the state of the project, frustration about the events that have led the project to its current state, and concerns about post recovery career implications.

Although it is understandable that team members feel anxious and uncertain under these conditions, it may hinder the recovery effort and hurt the team's effectiveness. To alleviate these concerns, the recovery manager must demonstrate leadership by providing transparency and instilling confidence in the process. Throughout the process, the recovery leader should also encourage members and promote a results-driven attitude, rather than a "shoot the messenger" one.

TIPS FOR RECOVERY

The recovery effort is essentially a project on its own, but with the potential for a greater level of intensity and even higher stakes. A successful recovery will require

Table 12.2 Recovery charter components

Project recovery manager and team members
Detailed project information
Assessment scope and considerations
Assessment deliverables
Assessment methodology
Recovery major milestones and target timelines
Organizational influences
Approvals

the recovery manager and the team to use the list in Figure 12.7 and review the details in the following checklist:

- **Keep your composure:** The damage is already done. It is now time to focus on moving forward with the recovery efforts. Staying calm helps you focus on the target and sends a message of leadership to the stakeholders.
- **Be methodical:** For a chance to achieve the new objectives, the effort must follow a preset methodology. Beyond consistency and direction, it is also a demonstration of leadership by the recovery manager.
- **Review project documentation thoroughly:** This is usually done as part of the current state assessment that precedes the recovery effort, but it is important to ensure that all relevant documents, plans, and artifacts from the project are reviewed, to maximize the context and information on the state of the project and how it got to where it is today.

✔ **Keep your composure**

✔ **Be methodical**

✔ **Review project documentation thoroughly**

✔ **Benchmark**

✔ **Momentum**

✔ **Focus on communication**

✔ **Define and follow the new objectives**

Figure 12.7 Recovery tips

- **Benchmark:** Make sure to cross reference information against independent sources for context and validity. The fact that the project has gotten to its failing point may serve as an indication that its plans and records-keeping were also flawed.
- **Momentum:** Installing a new recovery manager symbolizes a change in leadership, in the processes, and hopefully in momentum. At times, it may add credibility to have a recovery manager coming from outside the organization. Another contributor is to build momentum, starting with smaller deliverables and shorter timeframes, to create a sense of success. Having an easier time achieving those smaller targets, it will likely get easier to cope with the more challenging aspects of the recovery.
- **Focus on communication:** This is a key success factor for every project—especially for recovery efforts. Review the project's communication practices and use them as a starting point for enhancement across the board.
- **Define and follow the new objectives:** Do not drift away from the newly set success criteria and objectives. The recovery is not about fixing everything that is broken in the project, but about delivering the new expectations.

Ask Yourself

At the start of the recovery, as well as throughout the process, a few questions need to be asked, in order to check whether the recovery can be successful and to avoid repeating the mistakes that led to the project failure in the first place. These questions are listed in Figure 12.8.

THOUGHTS ON RECOVERY

Although the recovery is a project in itself, it is not a regular "business as usual" one. Monitoring the status, controlling the results, and recalibrating the process must occur in shorter intervals than in a regular project to ensure quick response and adjustments when needed. It may also require adjusting the timelines, milestones, deliverables, and expectations so they reflect reality and still deliver on the objectives. With frequent changes, there is also an increased need for more frequent reporting on the success criteria and the constraints, and for an increased focus on timely and realistic reporting. Keeping stakeholders informed is absolutely crucial to success, since any sense of uncertainty may derail the recovery effort.

The frequent changes and adjustments in project recovery, combined with the higher stakes and the newly defined objectives, translate into higher levels of risk. The recovery manager should manage risk rigorously and thoroughly, which

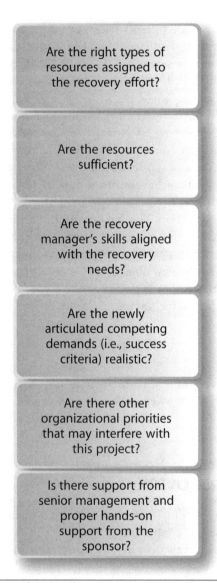

Figure 12.8 Recovery questions to ask

may call for more frequent meetings and assessments than the project team is accustomed to (at times, it may need to be daily). It is important to have all team members and stakeholders thinking about risks, and the reward system should have prevention activities built into it so there are tangible rewards for team members who manage risk properly, proactively, and preventatively.

ORGANIZATIONAL INFLUENCES FINAL THOUGHTS

Projects must be aligned with their environments and are heavily impacted by events in the organization. A significant portion of the project's fate is determined, even before a PM is assigned to it, and it is important for any PM to understand the organizational forces, since the project is going to be influenced by them.

To improve the chances for delivering project success, projects need to be aligned with the organizational objectives. While it is not up to PMs to establish such alignment, they need to know the reason for their projects and alert the sponsors, in the event that their projects do not seem to deliver value to the organization, or when the project expectations appear unrealistic.

Collaboration with stakeholders from outside the project and with other PMs is also critical for success, since it enables early detection and alert systems that streamline communication, help address problems before they escalate, or even avoids the problems altogether. Lessons learned and a PIR are easy wins for capturing success and noting failures in an effort to improve performance moving forward and reduce the need for future project rescue and recovery operations.

Project recovery gives the project a second chance: both the recovery team and the recovery manager must realize that there is only one chance to do the recovery right, and therefore the recovery plan needs to be robust and realistic enough that the recovery gets done right the first time. There is no room for error, and stakeholders, who may already be frustrated and disappointed with the project, will not give it another second chance. The concepts discussed in this chapter share a dual set of goals: one is to fix problems that already occur in existing projects (corrective action), and the second is to avoid making the same mistakes moving forward (preventive action).

REFERENCES

1. Adapted from H. Eilat, B. Golany, and A. Shtub, "Constructing and evaluating balanced portfolios of R & D projects with interactions: A deal based methodology," *European Journal of Operational Research*, Vol. 172, Issue 2006, 1018–1039 (2006).
2. Based on Eliyahu M. Goldratt, *Critical Chain* (Great Barrington: North River Press, 1997).

13

Integration: Putting It All Together

"But We Have Spent So Much Money On It, We Can't Stop Now."

In investments, an attempt to "catch" a stock on its way down is considered a mistake; however, this knowledge is not always properly applied by organizations in relation to projects. For various reasons, many organizations continue to invest money in failing causes and projects, ignoring all the warning signs. While it is not the project manager's (PM's) decision to make, the ability to say "no" to sponsors is necessary. As long as it is done in a professional manner and supported by empirical evidence, it is possible to survive the consequences. Yet, despite the need to warn stakeholders, PMs often remain oblivious to reality and refuse to recommend pulling the plug on failing endeavors.

This book has discussed and articulated ways to manage projects better, focusing on shifting the reader's mindset toward performing transformational project activities, rather than on how to do things. It does not take the route of reiterating methodologies or mechanics, such as how to build schedules, but rather tries to help you focus on what you need to look for, know, ask, or explore in an effort to perform your ongoing project chores and activities better. The role of this chapter is to tie up any loose ends around the concepts introduced in the book and to add a few pointers, anecdotes, and thoughts that may further help you focus on the areas you need in order to draft an action plan for improving the way you manage projects.

NOT A PERFECT WORLD

Project management is not perfect, and no one can make it perfect because it involves people, cultures, and forces that are much stronger than the abilities of any individual PM. With that said, there are still many ways to improve individual project environments by identifying and managing those things that PMs do have control over.

Most of the principles critical to project management success are well-known and quite simple; the challenge, then, is to ensure that PMs get the time and capacity to pay attention to these principles. Most PMs find themselves in similar situations throughout their projects, regardless of the environments or organizations they work in, and they can be summarized by concepts presented early in the book: the vortex of events that suck the PM's energy and attention to attend to urgent problems, and the "culture of alligators" that causes further waste and frustration due to an almost consistent lack of collaboration. Such conditions cause PMs to focus on short-term goals and prevent them from pursuing benefits for the organization and the business as a whole.

Leadership

In Chapter 3, the discussion of leadership reiterates that PMs must not only pay attention to their leadership skills and develop them but also ensure their leadership styles are appropriate for the organizations and the environments in which they operate. Leadership is not only about demonstrating leadership skills, such as charisma; it is also about leading by example and sending the right message, day in and day out. A genuine leader is not a seeker of consensus, but rather the person who builds and achieves consensus.

The following are some leadership principles to pay special attention to:

Lead By Example—Our actions transmit loud and clear messages to the environment, whether intended or not. "Walking the walk" is a test that does not receive a sufficient amount of focus, but it sends a strong message: "do as I do, not as I say." Project team members and other stakeholders carefully observe the meaning and context of the PM's actions, and they often reciprocate with similar actions. For example, it is not enough to make the right decision; it is also critical to follow a decision-making process that meets stakeholders' needs for transparency and style.

Leading by example starts with following processes, while sending a message that no double standard will be tolerated in the project. Leading by example is about building trust and ensuring that when team members look to the PM, they see a person who inspires them, connects with them, and is there to address their needs. It is also about stepping up and taking a leadership role.

One-on-One—PMs need to work one-on-one with team members and stakeholders and give them enough attention to make them feel comfortable. An agitated stakeholder, who does not feel sufficiently informed, may single-handedly derail a good project. The task of working one-on-one is not only time consuming but also challenging and draining; however, the return on this investment is proven and significant. Working one-on-one also involves managing stakeholders' expectations on an ongoing basis and focusing on achieving win-win resolutions.

When dealing with conflicts, or any other challenging situations, such as having to deal with difficult people, PMs need to realize the importance of resolving these situations in a timely manner and in such a way that stakeholders will feel that their needs have been addressed. At times, it may require playing up to team members' or stakeholders' egos. Owning the project communication, setting and managing expectations, managing conflict effectively, following and enforcing processes, making timely decisions, showing transparency and consistency, managing risks effectively, and focusing on values that are meaningful for stakeholders are all building blocks of leadership and show stakeholders that there is a leader in the house.

Brownouts: Everything Matters, Even the M&Ms

The PM needs to establish performance standards that aim high, and ensure that project quality is never compromised. This starts with ensuring that the small things are performed as they should be, since problems with small things often translate into trouble with big things. Team members should not shirk responsibility, or discount the importance of performing every single activity right and as required.

An excellent example of focusing on the need to pay attention to detail comes from a story concerning the rock group Van Halen. Legend has it that Van Halen's standard performance contract contained a provision, specifying that they be provided a bowl of M&Ms backstage, but with all brown M&Ms removed.[1] As part of their contracts, they listed and detailed hundreds of items to be provided, from luxurious accommodations, backstage food, and high-end transportation details to security, lights, and sound equipment specifications. The story goes that Van Halen was known for the "no brown M&Ms contract clause" (near the middle of the contract), and it was rumoured that even a single brown M&M was sufficient legal cause for cancelling a concert.

The motivation behind including this clause was not a quirk or a whim, but because this was an easy way for them to determine whether the technical specifications of their contracts had been thoroughly read and complied with. Van Halen's goal was to avoid technical errors with their equipment and entourage; when they walked backstage, one of the first things they did was check the bowl of M&Ms. If there was even one brown M&M, they knew they were going to run into technical errors, and Van Halen reasoned that if the organizers did not comply with such a simple request, they obviously did not read the contract thoroughly, and inevitably other technical errors were likely to take place. We can also term this "the cockroach principle:" if you see one, there are hundreds more.

DOING IT RIGHT

Prevention activities need to take place during project initiation and continue throughout its lifecycle. They do not magically guarantee that things will get done the right way, but they ensure things do not fall off the rails—the project starts right and stays on track. Prevention starts with the project charter, readiness and complexity assessments, and continues with the risk management process. Beyond these foundations of problem prevention, there are more specific items to focus on to guarantee the project remains on track.

The areas of focus in this section can serve as a checklist and be viewed as part of the prevention efforts. For each area the PM needs to define, the desired standard and the amount of information required is based on the project environment and type of organization, and items for which it is not done properly may signal potential trouble. Part of the list recapitulates and articulates information already mentioned in the book; for other items, additional context and perspectives are provided so PMs can gain a better understanding of them.

Conflict

While conflict is inevitable, PMs need to identify how much of the conflict actually adds value and deals with substance, in comparison with how many of the disagreements become personal. It is the PM's job to reduce personal conflicts and ensure that issues and disagreements are resolved in a timely manner—before they escalate further and compromise the team's performance. The goal is not to suppress conflict, but to ensure that it remains constructive and focused on the project goals. A focus on egos and personal agendas should not be part of dealing with conflicts.

PMs must remember that while project management is not a popularity contest, the ultimate goal is to reduce unnecessary conflicts. However, with limited time and capacity for handling conflicts, the urge to accommodate stakeholders in conflicting situations may backfire in the long run. Beyond sending a message of weak leadership to other stakeholders, accommodating stakeholders teaches them that demanding more yields better results for them, which causes them to push their advantage and ask for even more—as the old proverb says: "with the food comes the appetite."

Although conflict is a necessity and should be embraced—when it is about the subject matter and is constructive for team performance—it should not turn into a power struggle or a distraction. It is legitimate to have differences in opinion, but PMs must always consider the project success criteria and the project mandate, as provided by the sponsor. When the conflict becomes about ego, it does not help the cause and should be resolved quickly—with minimal damage to those involved.

Stakeholder Analysis and Long-Term Thinking

In the stakeholder analysis, PMs must take into consideration the account managers and the need to maintain good relations with the client. The goal is to create a mechanism to provide transparency, so customers have timely and relevant information available, and so that they view the project as a success, throughout the project lifecycle, and especially at its end and after the project is completed.

In addition to its measureable performance criteria, success also involves keeping customers informed and managing their expectations. Transparency and candid communication should follow the notion of "argue now, or fight later;" hence, the PM needs to establish an environment that fosters and encourages stakeholders to address problems and issues early on, with no fear of backlash. In most cases, customers will be more open to challenges, even bad news, if it is communicated early rather than at the last minute. Beyond the resulting sense of transparency, addressing problems immediately provides more options for fixing them, possibly at a lower cost.

Communication

The PM must own the communications in the project. Communication is not only about leading meetings and sending out reports but also about establishing behavioral guidelines; controlling the tone, style, and content of messages within the project organization and with stakeholders; setting expectations; addressing individuals' concerns; developing rapport with people; and addressing morale issues before they are reflected in project performance. PMs should not be glued to their desks; rather, they should listen, observe, engage in one-on-one conversations, be visible in a supporting role, and work behind the scenes to ensure expectations are met, issues are resolved, personal concerns are addressed, appropriate senses of urgency are in place, and value is produced.

Owning the project communication is not about building an ideal world; rather, it is a low-hanging fruit that allows the PM to gain control over critical success factors in an environment where the PM has little control over most constraints and variables. In addition to managing formal communications, PMs must also stay connected with stakeholders and manage by walking around,[2] to ensure they are tuned in to stakeholders' needs and feelings. PMs must conduct themselves with transparency and honesty, and foster the need for honesty and transparency among all stakeholders at all times.

Processes

Ensure that processes are defined and articulated, so team members follow them as required. Working by shortcuts and/or cutting corners almost guarantees performance issues downstream. Despite the fear that most PMs have of pointing at process problems (since they will be required to fix these problems on their own time), and their lack of control over or visibility into many of the processes, PMs need to confirm whether the activities and processes they need to do are aligned with their project needs and to alert the appropriate stakeholders of any gaps. The price to be paid later is much greater than the short-term effort and inconvenience involved.

On the topic of processes and procedures, it is important to keep in mind that these are all tools and means that are intended to help deliver success and value to project stakeholders. PMs need to protect the team from being consumed by ceremonial aspects of the work or focusing too heavily on following procedures, rather than on adding value to the project. As an example, consider parents, who are busy taking pictures of their children performing in a class, dance, recital, or show: they forget to live the experience and enjoy it.

Sponsor

The support of the sponsor is critical to project success. This support involves both the promotion of the project's needs, high up in the organization, as well as the appropriate level of hands-on support and involvement. Specifically, it serves as an escalation point, provides leadership and exception-handling procedures, allows a parallel line of communication with other stakeholders and the customer, provides a sense of security to the team that there is backing for the project, and serves as a decision-making point. Absentee or micromanaging sponsors often illustrate leadership gaps and spell project problems.

The PM should identify the level and nature of the sponsor's involvement as part of the stakeholder analysis and define boundaries and expectations. In the event that setting boundaries and expectations raises issues, the PM must alert the sponsor and the organization about the situation. Unclear objectives and unrealistic expectations need to be identified up front, and these gaps need to be addressed with the sponsor. Failing to rectify these situations should be reflected in the risk log and quantified for overall impact on project and organizational success.

When the sponsor does not provide sufficient support or direction, the PM should ensure that reaching out, asking questions, and making assumptions is done without compromising the relationship with the sponsor. It requires PMs to quickly learn to know their sponsors by performing a due diligence process, in order to position themselves as part of the solution—despite posing difficult questions and pointing at areas of concern to the sponsors. Even when a project has more than one sponsor, and they pursue conflicting priorities, the onus is on PMs to align the sponsors with each other, to alert them to discrepancies, and to maintain positive relationships with them. When decision makers (often sponsors) stall and do not provide timely approvals and sign-offs, the PM must articulate to them the costs of not making sound and timely decisions in order to ensure they understand the impacts of inaction.

Requirements and Priorities

Conflicting and changing requirements and priorities will take place, and there is a need to proactively manage them. This includes establishing and enforcing a formal and effective change control process, and ensuring the project moves in a direction that reflects the latest objectives mandated by the organization. It involves conducting an ongoing review of the success criteria and the trade-off relationships between project constraints, and timely performance adjustments to reflect them.

These adjustments are about understanding stakeholders' needs, comparing them to the state of the project, and ensuring requirements and functionality are prioritized, deferring or removing lower priority items from project scope. The more control the PM has over this process, the better the stakeholders' relationships will be, and the easier it will be to handle looming challenges.

Resources

Even though PMs usually do not own the resources on their project, they need to understand the reporting mechanism and what other projects and initiatives resources are involved in. For shared resources that are critical to project success, PMs need to work together with other PMs to maximize the utilization of those resources based on the priority and urgency of all projects involved. Scheduling and resource allocation should take into consideration any potential operational interruptions based on historical information.

Resources should not be over-assigned because it almost always leads to performance problems. When there is a push by resource managers, senior management, the customer, or the sponsor to over-assign resources or to assign unsuitable resources, PMs should spell out the impact up front, the options available, and the most suitable alternative.

Matching resources to activities and deliverables through the responsibility assignment matrix (RAM), or a RACI/RASCI chart (i.e., responsible, accountable, support, consulted, informed), helps ensure that activities are accounted for and have a resource to perform them. When PMs do not have a suitable resource to perform an activity, the RAM can help qualify the shortage as an assumption, a potential risk, or as an action item to confirm later. The main benefits of building a meaningful RAM are that it shows PMs areas of missing information and helps them focus on rectifying the shortfalls or notifying stakeholders of their expected impacts.

Risks

Some risks do not result from a negative event, rather, they arise from pressure to deliver on time, even when it is unrealistic, an attempt to assign an unsuitable resource to a task, or an attempt to save money. The PM must be able to realize and to articulate when requests are unrealistic, identify their associated assumptions and, if applicable, their impact. The impact must be quantifiable and articulated within the context of the success criteria.

Project Risk vs. Business Risk

There is a difference between project risk and business risk. While it is not the responsibility of PMs to manage business risks, PMs must take business risks into consideration. Project risks are threats and opportunities that may affect the project deliverables and success; business risks are about post-project considerations and long-term impact areas, such as risks that organizational objectives will not be met (including product lifecycle costs, service levels, profitability, and customer satisfaction) or operational issues that may arise as a result of the project results.

Issue Management

Issues include anything the project needs to deal with. They are not necessarily negative, especially if they are recorded and managed effectively. Issues have a tendency to accumulate at a faster pace than they are resolved, and this trend usually continues to various degrees until some point in the project execution when the issue resolution rate outpaces issue creation. The PM needs to identify trends in the current project's issue resolution rate and compare it to previous, similar rates. While no two projects are alike, if issues are raised at an alarmingly high rate, or their resolution rate is low when compared with similar projects, the PM needs to take action and address the issue of issues management, as it often signals deeper project problems.

Project Change Control

Most discussion of project change management deals with ensuring that the scope is managed and contained, and that there is no scope creep or "gold plating" (doing more than the customer asked for). However, PMs must also make sure that the human aspect of the change is attended to satisfactorily. When project scope, or any other conditions change, PMs need to check how the team and other stakeholders respond to and deal with the change, and to measure their buy-in and abilities to cope with it.

Project changes, by nature, require team members to do different things, perform them in different ways than they have so far, or work under different conditions (timelines, environments, relationships). These changes take people out of their comfort zones, create uncertainty, and may lead to resistance from stakeholders—who object to the change, or are conservers, wanting to maintain the old ways. The resistance may have far-reaching impacts on the change itself, the team, stakeholder expectations, and project performance; PMs need to measure stakeholders' reactions to change, monitor the ways they deal with it, and manage their levels of buy-in and their performances moving forward. Unfortunately in most projects, an insufficient amount of focus is given to the human side of project change management, which is a contributor to project change failures.

Estimating and Scheduling

This book has not discussed transactional activities—the mechanics of day-to-day project performance, such as collecting requirements, building schedules, and managing budgets. Instead, it has focused on transformational activities that channel the PM's focus into doing the right things and doing them in such a way that they manage stakeholder expectations and ensure project success. Beyond the techniques required to build project schedules, there is a series of considerations that PMs must take into account in order to compose a realistic schedule. In the following discussion, these considerations are identified, as part of the effort to equip PMs with the right information about what to focus on while building the project schedule.

Procrastination

Many people are procrastinators by nature, and it is the PM's job to set up realistic expectations for the team, and to build mechanisms that help people performing the work deliver on time. When a university professor gives students a deadline for submitting an assignment, students often immediately ask, "is there an extension?" The professor's answer should be: "yes, there is an extension, and it is already built into the specified deadline." In many ways, project team members tend to act in a similar fashion, and the sense of urgency only arises shortly before the deadline.

The solution involves educating the team, so the elevated sense of urgency does not appear at the last minute. Alternatively, under tight deadlines, and when the relationship with the customer allows, PMs should try to run two schedules: one for the customer and another for the team, which depending on the situation, should be several days or a few weeks earlier. This will buy the PM a buffer; however, it will work only for situations in which the PM has a strong relationship with the customer and the later deadline can be safely guarded. If the team finds out about the two dates, all trust between the team and the PM will be lost.

Language

One aspect of estimating that is closely linked to communications is the terms and measurements used in the estimating process. PMs must ensure that when asking for estimates from team members and other stakeholders, these estimates are expressed in measures of *effort,* which the PM will translate into **duration**. Effort is like "ideal time:" get the resources to estimate how long it will take them to perform a task uninterrupted—when they are fully dedicated to doing it.

These estimates will be translated by the PM into calendar times, which take all loss factors into account (availability, productivity, utilization, distractions, emergencies, and interruptions). It is important to set these expectations straight from the start, so resources do not provide delivery dates but effort estimates. These estimates should be as objective as possible, free of bias and with no regard to any of loss factors. The rationale is that just as PMs do not tell resources how to perform the work, resources should not be telling PMs how to manage the schedules.

Microsoft Project

Microsoft Project, and other project management applications, should not be viewed as more than what they actually are. They are resource and schedule management tools that can be very helpful for PMs—if utilized properly. It is important to keep in mind that an application cannot think for a PM. *Microsoft Project* will view all resources assigned to a task as equivalent, unless specified by the PM. For example, if two resources are allocated for two similar tasks, *Microsoft Project* will allocate the same duration for them—even when one resource is an experienced and skilled person, and the other is an intern. In addition, the software will not think about risks, assumptions, and constraints unless the PM builds them into the plan.

Delays

One of the most elusive aspects of project estimating is the impact of project delays. It is very difficult to accurately and realistically measure project delays and the schedule impact of various project events, but to make the process easier, it is important to understand that project delays are nonlinear. When PMs notice resources are working on activities that are not specified in their plans, the resources often dismiss the impact by saying, "it will only take me an hour to finish this before I go back to do my part of the plan." What the resources fail to understand is that the resulting delay may be much longer than one hour because of the nonlinear nature of project delays. While it is difficult to measure the full magnitude of delays on the project as a whole, PMs need to ensure that the people performing the work are focused on doing the work—as planned—and are not distracted by non-value-adding activities.

Contingency

One of the most common battles PMs engage in is asking stakeholders for sufficient time to perform the work. With the most thoughtful of schedules, taking into account all aspects of the project, there are elements completely outside the PM's control, such as sudden illnesses, organizational changes, professional development, and other events. These losses may use over 20% of total resource availability—which does not take sign-offs and customer-driven delays into consideration.

Depending upon the nature of the organization, the customer, and historical project information, PMs need to build these time impacts into the project schedule and as required, stipulate them in assumptions, constraints, and risks. Historical information may also be helpful in providing an indication of how much additional time is sufficient to request, depending on similar previous situations. For example, if senior stakeholders tend to arbitrarily reduce the amount of extra time requested, then PMs should ask for more time than they need—hoping it will be reduced back toward their (more realistic) original estimate.

The Starbucks Delay

One of the most interesting ways to illustrate that every action we take has an impact on the schedule, including the order in which we perform these actions, can be done through the following example: When a team member enters a morning project meeting late, with a cup of coffee (not with coffee for everyone), the PM mentions that he should have not stopped for coffee and by that, would have saved the 5–10 minutes that caused him to be late. In response, he says he got the coffee after leaving home earlier in the morning and not before the meeting.

To address the situation effectively, the PM should discuss the matter with the team member after the meeting. Effective communication starts with addressing issues and challenges with people on a one-on-one basis, rather than in front of the entire team. In addition, the PM needs to explain to the team member how his reasoning for being late makes no sense. By picking up the coffee earlier, he locked in a block of time (the time spent at the coffee shop), which was added to the critical path. The better thing to do would have been to wait to get coffee until the end of the commute, making it conditional on arriving at work on time—"if there is enough time, then I can buy coffee." In the event of a slower-than-usual commute, he would not have had time to stop for coffee. Picking up the coffee at the start of the commute removed his flexibility.

Moving Targets

Estimates should be viewed as moving targets until the other side fulfills their part (e.g., the customer provides input for requirements). As illustrated in Figure 13.1: If a task needs to start this Monday morning and is scheduled to take 10 days, but it depends upon a prior task that has not yet been completed, the clock should not start ticking on the subsequent task until the previous task is completed. The duration of the succeeding activity will remain the same, and there should be no expectation that the next task can be performed faster than planned. An attempt to perform the task faster is likely to compromise quality.

In these situations, the onus is on the PM to ensure that all stakeholders are aware of the following:

1. The total delay from the preceding activity being completed late;
2. The subsequent activity requires the original amount of time planned, and it will start when the previous activity is completed;
3. The overall impact of the delay on the project schedule.

Most projects are likely to face various types of performance issues, interruptions, resource contentions, dependencies, and risks—all of which contribute to schedule delays. However, this discussion is meant to direct the PM's focus toward a series of simple concepts that will help to avoid making scheduling mistakes before the work has even started. In the event that such mistakes make it into the project schedule, it is almost guaranteed that at some point, the project will suffer delays.

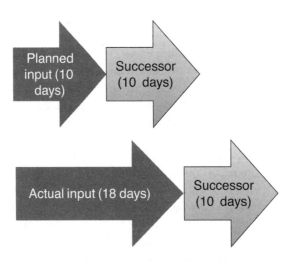

The duration of the successor remains the same (or even gets longer) regardless of how long the predecessor is.

Figure 13.1 Moving target

No Backwards Estimates

When stakeholders present PMs with deadlines and target dates, PMs must ask for time to come up with plans and when planning, put the target dates aside and realistically plan how long it should take to complete the work. When completing an estimate, there should be two sets of dates: the target date and the actual date. If they are not the same, the PM needs to present the findings and perform a gap analysis on the date variance, in order to come up with options for addressing the gap. The options should illustrate the findings and demonstrate the impact of each action.

Planning backwards from the target dates practically guarantees building shortcuts into the schedule, which (practically) guarantees subsequent schedule, resource, and cost overruns, as well as quality issues. PMs should illustrate the available options in such a way that puts themselves and the stakeholders on the same side, dealing with the challenges together. PMs are not the problem—and stakeholders should not view them as such—just because they come up with realistic plans, which question the validity of original target dates.

Estimates for Unknown Conditions

When trying to plan for something that has not been done before, PMs and team members face significant uncertainty—since they do not have the ability to know what might happen and which risks are even possible. For these situations, there are three things to keep in mind:

1. Identify and articulate the conditions necessary for the work. Get buy-in for these conditions;
2. Identify the assumptions that support the premise, and the conditions that are believed to be in place, for the purpose of planning;
3. Identify risks associated with the plan. These are known-unknowns that can be identified up front.

Based on the level of confidence in the estimates, price the potential impact of what might happen due to risks that have not been considered. This will serve as the basis for contingency planning and for requesting additional time, money, or resources to accommodate unexpected events, if needed.

Non-critical Path Delays

In addition to managing activities on the critical path and ensuring they are completed on time, PMs need to pay attention to activities that are off the critical path. While delays with non-critical path activities may appear harmless, especially early in the project, they can be damaging to the project. Most delays in a project, even early ones, are hard to overcome and should be accounted for, even if they are not on the critical path.

Non-critical path delays will cause these activities to take longer to complete and to finish later than planned. Even if they have no direct impact or dependencies that affect the critical path, they will cause trouble later in the project, since all the non-critical path activities that are currently staggered along the project will start piling up toward the end. At that point, the team is likely to have problems coping with the extra work volumes, and these activities will be subject to further delays. On top of the capacity issues they may cause, additional delays may push one or more of these non-critical path activities far enough to match the critical path, or even to surpass the critical path and redefine it, by delaying the end date of the entire project.

Status Reporting and Success Criteria

One of the components of project communication is status reporting. In sports, when referees are hardly noticed and the game flows, it means they are managing the game well. Similarly, a good, effective, and flowing status meeting is a result of behind-the-scenes leg work, due diligence, and effort by the PM to ensure the meeting flows properly. This leg work includes sending an agenda, ensuring ground rules are in place and that participants are prepared, confirming the quality and timeliness of information, and educating all participants about escalation procedures and exception reporting. An important part of running effective meetings is to ensure that people provide the PM with updates, especially exceptions and surprises, prior to the meeting. It reduces the element of surprise in the meeting and gives the PM time and opportunity to organize an action or escalation plan. It gives the PM more control, helps demonstrate this control to participants, and allows the surprise-free meeting to be managed in a composed manner.

Incorporating earned value principles into the reporting enables the PM to examine the progress, status, and forecast reports presented in the meeting and question their validity, as appropriate. When team members and stakeholders make promises about future performance, earned value principles can help the PM distinguish between realistic and unrealistic promises and estimates. The earned value principles can even be applied toward projects in which the PM does not directly manage or control the budget. Using historical information and simple estimating techniques, the PM can create estimates that are based on percentages of scope progress, relative to a timeline and a budget line. Time and money lines show the anticipated progress as a percentage of the entire project, and—when the plan shows that a phase should be complete, or its budget limit is reached, but it has not actually achieved its objectives to date—it is a sign that the project is underperforming and action is required.

Status reporting needs to take place in the context of the success criteria to allow the PM to focus on what matters most. When PMs know the success criteria (which one, two, or three constraints are critical for success), a red status for any one constraint may not necessarily be a bad thing. For example, if the project's mandate is to deliver on time, running over budget may not be damaging to project success.

Keep Them Thinking but Maintain Focus

It is important for the PM to engage team members and stakeholders in a way that encourages them to channel their thinking from the "what" to the "how." They will focus on how to do their work better, leaving the "what" to the PM, yet still notice when it is inconsistent with the plan, with their understanding of the technical aspects of the project work, with stated stakeholders' needs, or with historical performance levels. It is important that people do not operate on auto-pilot, constantly pay attention to how they perform their work, and keep an eye open for improvement opportunities.

This idea is contrary to what many PMs and service providers try to do: get people to stop thinking and have machines and tools do the thinking for them. This is becoming a common theme in cars, with technology and features gradually replacing the driver's need to think: tire pressure gauges, rear-facing side-mirror cameras, auto-applied breaks when backing up, bumper-proximity sensors, and lane shifting alarms are safety features (poka-yokes i.e., error proofing) that although important and convenient, are replacing the need for the driver to pay attention, apply judgment, and think. With too many of these gadgets, their marginal benefits may be negative—they may, at times, lead to distractions and misunderstandings. The real benefit of poka-yoke items is not to replace people's need to think, but to make things safer and more user friendly. The goal in project management is to avoid crossing that line by establishing measures to achieve success while keeping the team engaged.

Productivity, Utilization, and Efficiency

Squeezing out more work from people in the form of overtime and over-working them can yield benefits and improve performance, but only to a certain degree and only in the short term. At some point, we need a break from constant intensity in order to recharge since we cannot keep running at full steam over an extended period of time. In many organizations, the culture for project team members is about overtime, over-utilization, and doing more with less. While PMs have little or no control over these conditions, it is important for them to recognize when they exist, try to warn senior stakeholders about their potential consequences, and identify related assumptions and potential risks when needed. These conditions often lead to reduced productivity, less innovation, team morale issues, and overall inferior performance in the long run. Over-doing overtime and over-squeezing project resources ignore the principle of staying tuned in to people's needs and will likely lead to a disconnect with team members and other stakeholders.

During peak periods and before deadlines, it is normal and legitimate to squeeze more hours from team members, but after every peak, there has to be a valley—a lull that allows them to regroup and look for ways to improve their performances toward the next peak. When team members are expected to produce more with fewer resources on a constant basis, the focus is no longer on productivity, and the PM needs to alert senior management of the challenges it may lead to.

False Alarms

Many stakeholders and team members tend to overreact when they face challenging situations by declaring an emergency or by trying to get the PM to make an exception, break a process, or redirect resources to their causes. These false alarms have over-reaching negative impacts that go beyond the waste of resources on efforts that add no value. False alarms also lead to:

- Distractions: The team's focus shifts from value-adding activities to the "emergency;"
- Attracting the attention of multiple stakeholders and requiring valuable time to refocus;
- "Crying-wolf" sets a precedent for other stakeholders to raise false alarms of their own since they will get the attention they seek;
- The "culture of alligators:" team members and stakeholders placing themselves ahead of the needs of others derails the project effort.

When projects are plagued by false alarms, it is often a signal of problems and challenges with the team, the PM's leadership, and a lack of team cohesiveness. It often comes from the absence of a clear set of expectations and ground rules and a misalignment between stakeholders' expectations and objectives. PMs should perform the following actions to combat these problems:

- Define what constitutes an emergency and ensure it is communicated to all stakeholders and team members;
- Educate stakeholders on escalation procedures in the event of an emergency. This will reduce distractions and ensure the emergency is real and addressed appropriately;
- Ensure that the communications plan is in place and that ground rules are communicated and enforced.

Lessons Learned

Learning from project events, successes, and mistakes needs to take place on an ongoing basis and in real time whenever possible. This will ensure that the team grows and improves and does not repeat its own mistakes. Over time, the PM should build a repository of lessons learned and areas for improvement.

When trying to implement lessons learned, it is important to focus first on "low hanging fruit" that are fairly quick and easy to fix and on issues with lower risks (in the event of a failure to fix them). This will create positive momentum and allow the project team to seek more significant improvement opportunities. It is also important to focus on improving no more than a few areas at any given time so the team does not get overwhelmed with multiple changing variables that can create confusion and uncertainty.

One of the challenges to learning from previous project mistakes is the limited access to historical information and dated, incomplete, or low quality information in historical records. Organizations should consider mandating the way lessons learned processes are conducted and documented for every project since it is highly likely to provide future savings and improvements that justify the extra effort and costs of doing it. Lessons learned exercises help organizations improve their project performances over time and can serve as team building exercises that improve communication, processes, and accountability through constructive feedback. In addition, applying the lessons learned from previous projects and updating best practices to reflect these improvements in future projects reduces the need to resort to historical information and to records from former projects.

Cost Savings

When PMs notice that cost saving efforts by the organization may lead to project challenges and problems (most commonly with resources), they must alert the sponsor and identify these concerns as assumptions and risks. However, it is not enough to raise concerns; PMs also need to identify and specify the impact of the cost savings on the project, the customer, and the organization as a whole. Specifying the impact will not only raise the PM's credibility but also, if supported by evidence, will increase the likelihood that senior management will take it into consideration.

The PM's due diligence involves both investigating the anticipated impact and building a business case by demonstrating the impact in values and currencies that resonate with the stakeholders involved. It requires an understanding of the impact areas, as well as an understanding of the stakeholders' drivers and interests. The business case should also include evidence that demonstrates the true long-term costs of the short-term savings. Unfortunately, in many cases, under-spent money early in the project leads to more costly problems later on. For example, savings at the design stage may lead to subsequent problems with the product, or eliminating training to cut costs will likely lead to performance issues down the road.

Financial Management

Every PM should be trained in financial management. Even though PMs do not usually manage project budgets, they must be able to understand financial management basics, so they do not take actions and make decisions that are out of touch with cost and budgetary considerations. For example, in many large projects, people feel they have more room to play because there is more time and money involved, not realizing that any time and budget overrun that takes place early in the project will have to be paid for later. Although processes and methodologies are, quite often, better enforced in large projects because of the sheer magnitude, amount of money at stake, and time span, many stakeholders and PMs feel that small slippages "here and there" will not impact the big picture. This misconception often plagues projects, and financial management training will help PMs realize that every action and decision has a cost, which someone has to pay for and has to be accounted for financially.

Rewards and Recognition

The need to properly reward team members and recognize achievements is often mentioned in the context of project communications, stakeholder management, and leadership. However, rewards and recognition should include incentives that are tangible and meaningful. Even in an era of significant cost savings, making incentives tangible and meaningful for those who perform the work is fundamental to making team members feel appreciated and ensuring that they continue delivering results and value. It is part of understanding people's needs and realizing that monetary rewards are the most effective type of incentive. Although most PMs have neither the authority nor the means to provide monetary incentives to team members, it is important to illustrate to senior management the value of creating a more meaningful incentive system and the benefits it will yield in maintaining and sustaining team member conformity, support, loyalty, and performance.

INTEGRATION, FOR REAL

Most of the concepts and ideas of project management are straightforward on their own, but one of the main challenges PMs face is to put everything together. Figure 13.2 helps demonstrate what project integration is about. The integration effort—putting it all together—is at the core of what project management is about. It involves balancing the project objectives with those of the organization, ensuring that they do not conflict with each other and that whatever the project produces is beneficial to the organization. Since circumstances force PMs to be reactive (e.g., the vortex, illustrated in Chapter 1), PMs need to demonstrate emotional resilience,

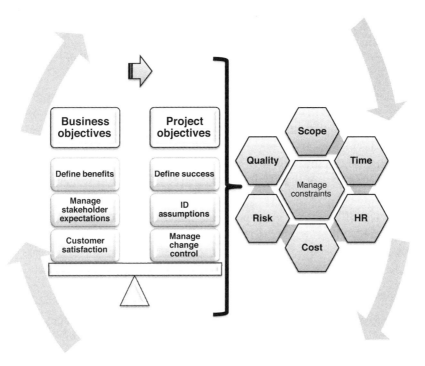

Project integration is about making all the knowledge areas work together toward achieving the project goals and integrating the project's results as a whole into the organization. It all starts with the business objectives (on the left), which drive the project objectives and cycles through the project's competing demands.

Figure 13.2   Integration, for real

which is about managing what matters and not caving in to distractions and pressures that are misaligned with the project objectives—all the while maintaining relationships and ensuring stakeholders save face (i.e., maintaining their dignity, credibility, and egos).

WHO IS MORE IMPORTANT?

Every project (and in fact, life in general) is plagued by people who, for some reason, believe they are more important than everyone else. This sense of self-importance materializes in all sorts of ways, but the most noticeable ones are:

1. Delaying: Some people have no regard or respect for others' time. Many people are consistently late in producing deliverables, reports, or results but do not have the courtesy to alert recipients in a timely manner. Others

are late to meetings, leaving colleagues waiting for them, or extending meetings beyond their original posted timeframes—both with no consideration or respect for people's time or for the fact that there are other things to do.

2. Talking: Most people have a need to be heard and to say what is on their minds, even if the listeners don't agree with them, or if they are out of time to complete their thoughts—hence, the need for tight meeting agendas to prevent participants from hijacking the meetings. In any team setting, communication involves listening and needs to go both ways; an important part of that is allowing other people to express themselves as well.

3. Behavior/Resources: Some people conduct themselves under a double standard, allowing themselves actions, privileges, and behaviors they would not tolerate from others. In projects, this commonly appears in the form of holding resources beyond their original timeframes and by that, preventing them from attending to their next projects, or stealing resources from other projects with no regard for the crisis levels or needs of those projects. The result appears in the form of performance issues, unnecessary conflicts, frustration, attitude problems, and shifts of team focus away from the actual work.

Driving and Project Management

This self-importance syndrome (SIS) is noticeable in other aspects of day-to-day life, specifically with cutting in line and in driving. In fact, it is likely that these behaviors in day-to-day life are performed by the same people depicted in the project examples here. When we are driving on a main street and realize we are heading in the wrong direction, most of us will go around the block to correct the route. However, people with SIS will block traffic, making a U-turn in the middle of the street, because they feel more important than others. In doing so, they inconvenience others (which may cause an accident or a delay), putting their own personal needs ahead of those of others.

In the context of projects, these kinds of double standards impose direct costs to the organization (delays, wastes of resources, conflicts), do not add value (diverting resources from where they should add value to other self-declared priorities), and are simply frustrating (lack of team work, setting the wrong example, needing to engage in unnecessary conflict). If it were possible, it would be helpful for sponsors to include a driving test for PM job candidates because it could serve as a strong indication of how they will conduct themselves in the project and with other stakeholders, especially when there are conflicting priorities.

HOW TO SAY NO WHEN YOU NEED TO (AND STILL KEEP YOUR JOB)

Saying no is one of the toughest challenges PMs need to deal with. The "no" is not intended to refuse doing work but to avoid committing to unrealistic or impossible conditions.

"No" Does Not Stand Alone

Before looking further into how to say no, it is critical to ensure that the "no" is said in context and is supported by evidence. Whenever someone says no (refusing to do something, rejecting an idea, disagreeing) it must not come as a stand-alone response and must be qualified by asking the following:

1. Why not?
2. What would be better?

If these two stipulations are not included in their responses, they should not be allowed to voice their opinions. These stipulations must be established as part of the communications management plan, and agreeing to them will improve communications, reduce bias and conflict, and help the team focus on the issues at stake rather than rejecting each others' ideas. All these benefits will be achieved by ensuring that people do not reject each other's ideas for ulterior motives or without supporting evidence.

These two stipulations will also reduce to a minimum the number of instances where a conversation involves someone saying no, and when asked why not, the response is "there must be a better way." When people disagree with each other, it is legitimate to voice opinions—but not in a vacuum, with no supporting evidence. Explaining "why not" is the first thing to do, to provide context and reasoning to the rejection, and then proposing a better way is the next requirement. There are times in which an offered option will not necessarily be the best idea, but will propose the "lesser of two evils;" dismissing an idea with "there must be a better way" is simply not conducive to a constructive discussion.

Why It Is Difficult to Say No

For various reasons, stakeholders often apply pressure on PMs to make commitments that may be beyond the project team's capabilities. Many PMs make commitments to deliver on unrealistic requests, mainly because they have difficulty saying no when they need to, for reasons illustrated in Figure 13.3. In most cases, the pressure on PMs is not malicious, nor is it designed to force them to fail, but rather it is a result of stakeholders' desires to achieve something—together with a

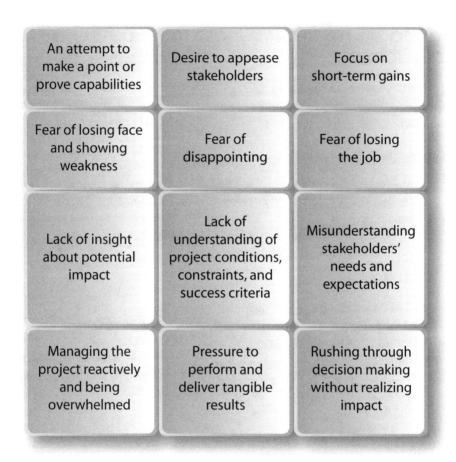

An attempt to make a point or prove capabilities	Desire to appease stakeholders	Focus on short-term gains
Fear of losing face and showing weakness	Fear of disappointing	Fear of losing the job
Lack of insight about potential impact	Lack of understanding of project conditions, constraints, and success criteria	Misunderstanding stakeholders' needs and expectations
Managing the project reactively and being overwhelmed	Pressure to perform and deliver tangible results	Rushing through decision making without realizing impact

Figure 13.3 Common reasons why PMs have a hard time saying no.

lack of understanding of project conditions and constraints. This is, in fact, one of the most foundational components of the PM's role—to ensure that stakeholders' requests are addressed appropriately and in the context of the project conditions and team capabilities. Failing to say no misleads stakeholders into believe that the project team can deliver something it cannot, and it is the first step in mismanaging stakeholder expectations.

Variations to a "No:" When Facing Unrealistic Expectations

The balloon theory (Chapter 7), which helps in considering the trade-offs between demands, illustrates the conditions the project has to contend with, but it needs to be taken up a notch: While in theory PMs can propose a variety of trade-off options for competing demands, in practice there are few feasible and acceptable options, which involve making time and scope trade-offs in most cases. When stakeholders make an unrealistic request that cannot be delivered on time or to specifications, the available options are:

1. Deliver late: This is often an unacceptable option since there is already a commitment to deliver on time. In this case, something (or someone) else has to pay the price for trying to meet timelines.

2. A hybrid solution, or a phased approach: Deliver a portion of the scope on time and have the rest delivered in stages at later dates. This option requires significant due diligence to sort out functionality priorities and may not be practical for all products and environments.

3. Deliver on time but with less functionality: Similar to a hybrid solution, reducing the scope in order to deliver on time requires time to perform due diligence and may not be possible in all environments.

4. Add money and/or resources: If there is a real need for the product to be delivered in its full scope and on time, it is likely that additional funds will be required. However, in the following three conditions, a trade-off for additional money and resources will not be applicable:

    a. If the PM does not directly manage the project's budget, negotiating an increase in the budget is not an option;

    b. Additional money and/or resources may not be available. In fact, in most organizations, there is no extra money or resources that could be allocated to the project;

    c. In many situations, adding money or resources will not make things better, and—due to the learning curve, training needs, and the law of diminishing returns—it may hinder the effort and lead to additional delays and problems.

5. Assume more risk: PMs must keep in mind and articulate that the risk component of the competing demands balloon is not a stand-alone item; rather, it is fully driven by the result of balancing constraints with each other. It is not an option to say "let's just increase the risk level in the project" instead of balancing constraints. The risk is a reflection of the actions taken in the project, and more risk means higher probability for quality problems downstream.

The Process of Saying No

To ensure that any need to say no is not taken out of context and is qualified by sufficient information, the following steps should be taken:

1. Go back to the stakeholder analysis and identify the stakeholder's drivers and values;

2. Ask for time to review the request, consider it, and consult with subject matter experts (SMEs). No commitments should be made on the spot as there has been no opportunity to make realistic estimates;

3. If it is unrealistic to deliver the request, identify other options, which are feasible alternatives that comply with the success criteria. For example, if it is important to deliver on time, propose a scope reduction or, if applicable, request additional resources;

4. Build a business case that illustrates to the relevant stakeholders the available options—in the context of values that resonate with the stakeholders and in language that appeals to their success criteria. The business case should articulate the consequences of agreeing to perform the work—even if its objectives are unrealistic—and pricing agreeing to the work in a currency the stakeholders understand and care about;

5. Make sure to state assumptions, existing conditions, the stakes involved, and the price to pay. It is possible that one side or the other is missing information.

Relationship Management

When saying no to stakeholders, PMs must keep a close eye on their relationships with these stakeholders, including paying special attention to the needs and feelings of the stakeholders involved. For the message to be delivered effectively and as intended, PMs must price decisions and impacts in terms and values that address the stakeholders' points of view, and they must ensure that the information provided addresses the stakeholders' true needs.

Even in the absence of due diligence about what is at stake and what the options are, there are a few approaches that PMs should resort to:

- Additional time to come up with a set of options;
- Stakeholder analysis in order to understand their needs;
- Prioritized lists of requirements to remove less critical items, with few dependencies connecting them;
- Access to SMEs for situational assessment and for specification of the impact of each option.

FINAL THOUGHTS

The Romans used to say: "*Amat victoria curam*"—"victory loves preparation in advance." This book provides a series of insights, thoughts, ideas, and concepts that serve as a foundation to managing projects in ways that deliver the required results.

Special emphasis is given to planning and other activities that take place early in the project, to build a foundation for focus, resolve, and success.

From stakeholder identification, analysis and expectations management, through to project communication planning and management, to giving PMs the means to focus on what matters and on what adds value, this book performs the same role the PM is supposed to perform: to ensure that every stakeholder and team member focuses on what they are required to do and are not being distracted by non-value-adding activities.

Without getting into the mechanics of managing the day-to-day aspects of the project, such as schedules, budget, and requirements, this book helps PMs build an infrastructure of control and a concept of success by focusing on what really matters in projects: understanding stakeholders' needs, communicating with them effectively, focusing on what matters to them, articulating and pursuing success criteria, making assumptions, managing risks proactively, defining quality, handling conflict effectively, and navigating the organizational political landscape.

This book emphasizes areas on which PMs need to focus to effectively utilize their time and differentiates between being busy and being productive. Many PMs believe that attending multiple meetings and responding to dozens of e-mails is productive and do not realize that it is just being busy. Being productive is about adding value and focusing on what matters to stakeholders and managing their expectations.

All the activities, thoughts, concepts, and ideas presented and articulated here are about getting the PM to do the right things, and integrating all of the available information so that stakeholders' expectations are managed and customer satisfaction is achieved. They are also about adopting a long-term, sustainable approach that focuses on balancing stakeholders' considerations and integrating all the factors surrounding the project so value is created both for the project and for the organization—in the short term and the long term—and in such a way that the project effort addresses and delivers project success, business needs, operational considerations, organizational goals, and strategic objectives.

MOVING FORWARD

Contrary to popular belief, change cannot be sweeping or imminent, and it takes an ongoing and continuous effort to change the way things are done and to achieve results. PMs and practitioners should take any ideas from this book and apply them to their environments as part of action plans to improve the ways they perform their work. Such an action plan should include the following stages:

1. List ideas that are applicable to your environment.

2. Identify one or two things as "easy wins" or "low hanging fruit." These are concepts that are fairly easy to apply and that are believed to yield benefits. Start small, with something that has lower risk and can be implemented in conjunction with a close colleague, which can reduce the stakes and negative impacts of failure. Picking an easy win will not only deliver success but also help create a momentum of success that will increase the appetite of those involved in improvement efforts in other areas.

3. Set up an action plan for achieving the goal, along with a realistic timeline with checkpoints.

4. Evaluate your progress and the degree of success at the end of the period. Even if the desired result is not delivered, do not despair. There may be a need to adjust timelines, objectives, or even to focus on a new area for improvement.

5. Management expert Peter Drucker said, "unless commitment is made, there are only promises and hopes . . . but no plans." Therefore, do not stop after one improvement area—continue on to the next, reinforcing and building on the newly created value.

At the end of the day, project success is not about any one single competing demand, but rather about identifying which success criteria matter for stakeholders and delivering on these areas. The goal is not to deliver the full scope, on time, on budget, or a fully working product, but to meet stakeholders' and customers' expectations by delivering what they asked for, what was promised to them, what they needed, and what was agreed upon.

REFERENCES

1. Based on: http://www.snopes.com/music/artists/vanhalen.asp.
2. The origin is traced to executives at Hewlett-Packard in the 1970's. Mike Mears, *Leadership Elements: A Guide to Building Trust*, 51 (Bloomington: iUniverse, 2009).

Index

Assumption log
cost–benefit considerations, 146
placeholder, 146
Assumptions and monitor
baseline set, 148
performance measurement, 148
Avoidance and acceptance, 199, 201. *See also* Risks

Balloon theory, 322–323. *See also* Integration and organization

Change control
agile methodologies, 236
assess and analyze, 244
change request (CR), 242, 244
control flow, 242
decision making, 245–246
due diligence, 241
implement and track, 246–247
and monitor, 246–247
preliminary impact assessment, 243
process, goal, 244
scale review, 244–245
understanding process, 242–243
Change request (CR), 242
analysis, 244
Communications
management, 159
project, designing and managing (*see* Project communications)
and risks, 176–177
Complexity categories, 31

Conflict in organization, 62
causes, 70
managing expectations, 67
misconceptions about, 77
personalities' impacts, 68
resolution techniques, 73–76
sources, 65–71
steps to manage, 69
Conflict management, 159–160
plan, 275–276
Constraints face-off matrix (CFM)
needs, 119
project delivery, 118
stakeholder analysis, 117
success criteria, 118
Contingency planning, 202–203
Controlling risks, 206–208
Cost
components, 221
consists, 221
Critical chain
collaboration and detection, 281–282
coordination meeting, 281
cross-project urgency, 283
organizational considerations, 282–283
resource management, 282–283
Cross-project urgency face-off, 171
Cross risk paired analysis, 195. *See also* Urgency, risk in
Culture in organization. *See* Politics in organization
Customer relationship management, 161–162

Day planning. *See also* Prioritization; Time
management
activities and deliverables, 155
daily, 154–155
emergencies, 155–157
improvement, 155–156
unexpected events and risks, 155
Detectability. *See also* Risks
importance, 198

Effective risk management, 175. *See also*
Risks
Efficiency, 175. *See also* Risks
80–20 Rule. *See* Pareto principle
Emergencies in day planning, 155–157
Enhance measurements, 131
project failures, 132
project success, 130
Enhancing, 201. *See also* Risk response
planning
Environmental complexity, 34
Expectations management, 162–163
gaps in, 125–126
PM options, 124–125
stakeholders, 124
Exploiting, 202. *See also* Risk response
planning

Identification process for risks
categories, 186
data quality, 184–185
missing information, 184
RBS, 185
steps, 186–187
Influences in organizations, 279
alignment, 280–281
collaboration and confidence, 286
critical chain, 281–283
feedback form, 287
lessons learned, 284–285, 287
post implementation review (PIR),
290–292
process for lessons learned, 288–289
project rescue and recovery, 292–295
questions for lessons learned, 289–290
recovery tips, 295–297
risk and change request, 283–284

Integration and organization
backwards estimates, 313
balloon theory, 322–323
communication, 305–306
conflict, 304–305
contingency, 311
cost savings, 317
delay impact, 310–311
financial, 318
issue, 308
job retaining, 321–324
lessons learned, 316–317
moving targets, 312
noncritical path delay, 313
prevention activities, 304
processes, 306
productivity and utilization, 315–316
project change control, 308–309
project management, 301–304
relationship management, 324
requirements and priorities, 307
resources, 307–308
rewards and recognition, 318
risks, 308
self-importance syndrome (SIS), 320
sponsor, 306–307
stakeholder analysis, 305
status reporting and success criteria,
314–315
transformational activities, 309
unknown conditions, 313
unrealistic expectations, 322–323

Kickoff meeting, 37
benefits, 39
key ingredients, 38
plan and conduct, 40
Known-unknowns risks, 174–175. *See also*
Risks

Leadership
different views, 59–60
styles, 60–62

Management responsibility, project quality
customer, 216
offshoring, 217
waste, 217

Micromanagement, 153
Mitigation, 173, 199–200
MoSCoW method, 92

Non-value-adding items, 164
Non-work-related activities, 164–165

Organizational/management complexity, 33
Organizational success, 130. *See also* Success and constraints

Pareto principle, 153–154
Planning Poker, 192. *See also* Risks analysis
Poka-yoke technique, 225–226
Politics in organization, 43
    conflict, 62, 71–72 (*see also* Conflict in organization)
    escalation, 76–77
    influence, 44, 47–51
    leadership, 59–62
    meetings management, 56
    personal power measure, 45–46
    politically-driven behaviors, 45
    relationships, 51
    soft rewards, 45
    team building, 57–58
    team development, 62–65
    values, 47
    win-win resolution, 54–56
    ways to reduce negative politics, 77–79
Post-implementation review (PIR), 161, 290–292
Prioritization, 154. *See also* Pareto principle
    types of activities, 157
Priority and urgency, in project, 168–171. *See also* Transformational focus
Proactive risk management, 175–176
Probability. *See also* Risks analysis
    and impact matrix, 193–195
    Planning Poker, 192
    tolerance level, 194–195
    values for measures, 193
Probability-impact formula, 188
Project assumptions

    categories, 140
    conditions, 137
    consequences, 140
    flow diagram, 144
    manageable, 150
    maturity date, 139
    organizational capabilities, 138
    planning around, 140
    possible sources for, 145
    probability-impact assessment, 142
    process flow, 143
    progressive elaboration, 142
    project plan, 139
    project risk, 136
    risk analysis process, 140, 141
    specify and record, 136
    stakeholders, 139
    taking actions, 141
    technical, 147
Project attributes, 35, 37
    list, 36
    table headings, 36
Project change management, 235
    change control, 236
    communication planning, 240
    complexity assessment, 237–238
    considerations, 247–254
    objectives and scope, 237
    planning activities, 237–238
    proactive, 237–241
    process for change control, 241–247
    readiness assessment, 237
    requirements management process assessment, 238–241
    requirements quality criteria, 240
    stakeholder analysis, 238
Project change management considerations
    change and risk, 248
    change window, 252–253
    CR form, 251
    incremental changes and salami method, 249–250
    merits, 250–251
    mishandled changes, 254
    quality maintenance, 251–252
    resource, 248–249
    uncontrollable changes, 254

Project charter, 128, 166–167
  as foundation and mandate, 127
  importance, 127
Project communications
  changing project management, 261–264
  conflict management plan, 275–276
  double standard, 276
  goals, 265
  good relationship values, 273–274
  management plan, 258
  misunderstanding, 258–259
  model, 260
  plan, 267–268
  process view, 265
  responsibilities, 260
  setups, 265–266
  team contract and ground rules, 268–
    272
Project complexity assessment
  breakdowns, 30
  categorize and measure, 30
  levels, 33
  measurement, 33–35
  project attributes, 35–37
  technical, 33
Project history milestones, 8
Project management
  communication, 13–14
  leadership, 302–303
  meaningful conversations, 5
  more with less, 10–12
  overreliance on tools, 13
  performance standards, 303
  poor risk management, 14
  products lifecycles compression, 10
  project outcomes, 9
  team performance, 14–15
  "two layers" concept, 13
*Project Management Body of Knowledge
  (PMBOK® Guide)*, 84
Project management, changing, 261
  entire project, 263–264
  meaningful communication, 262–263
Project Management Institute (PMI), 84,
  219
Project objectives triangle, 120

Project quality, 160–161. *See also* Quality
    and customer satisfaction; Quality
    in project
Project readiness assessments, 21
  areas, 25
  categories, 29
  considerations, 26–29
  goals, 23
  hard to implement, 24
  integration, 24
  preparedness scale, 28
  proprietary readiness measure, 28
  results, 29–30
Project rescue and recovery
  charter, 294–295
  current state assessment, 294
  high risk factors, 293
  performance issues, 292
  team, 295

Qualitative risk analysis, 188
Quality and customer satisfaction, 160–161
Quality assurance, 219–220
Quality control
  technical aspect, 220
Quality in project
  benefits, 228
  considerations, 224–225
  cost, 220–223
  customer satisfaction, 230
  defects and change, 230–231
  estimating and scheduling, 229
  human factors, 232
  management plan, 223–224
  management responsibility (*see*
    Management responsibility, project
    quality)
  mistake proofing, 225
  philosophy, 218–219
  plan guidelines, 226
  planning, 218–219
  poka-yoke technique, 225–226
  quality assurance, 219–220
  results, 219
  scope and requirements, 230–231
  way to measure, 215
Quantitative risk analysis, 188

RACI (or RASCI) Chart
  capacities, 103
  elements, 105
  enhanced into, 105–106
Readiness and complexity, 40–41
Recovery tips
  charter component, 295
  efforts, 295–297
Relationship management, 324
Requirements for stakeholders
  complexity, 93–94
  MoSCoW method, 92
  prioritization, 92
  value and benefits, 94–95
Residual risks, 205–206. *See also* Risks
Responsibility assignment matrix (RAM)
  four steps, 106–107
  RACI (or RASCI) Chart, 103–106
  stakeholder analysis, 103
Risk and change request, 283
  impact of, 284
Risk breakdown structure (RBS), 185
Risk impact breakdown table (RIBT), 190, 192
  risk impact areas and context, 191
Risk response planning, 198
  part, 202
  response strategies, 199
  steps, 199
  threats and opportunities, 201
Risks
  approaches and methodologies, 176
  assessment, 196–197
  characteristics, 174–175
  and communication, 176–177
  dependencies, 208
  elements in, 179
  emotional resilience and, 177–178
  escalation procedures and, 212
  identification process, 184–185 (*see also* Identification process for risks)
  management, 160, 175–176
  meetings, 212
  planning and approach, 178–179
  and politics, 212
  positive and negative solutions, 211–212
  proactive risk management and communication, 209–210

RBS, 185
  register, 179–180
  response planning, 173
  terminology, 174
  trigger, 197
Risks analysis
  measure of impact, 189–190
  probability and impact matrix, 188–189, 192–195
  qualitative and quantitative, 188
  RIBT, 190–192
  use range, 193
Secondary risks, 204–205. *See also* Risks
Sharing, 201. *See also* Risk response planning
Soft rewards, 45–46
Stakeholders, 83
  according to PMI, 84
  analysis, 84, 87–91, 101
  assessment tool, 95
  attitudes, 102–103
  categories, 86–87
  engagement and expectations management, 108–109
  engagement review, 111
  engagement strategy, 95
  expectations management, 162–163
  identification, 84–87
  influence-interest grid, 88–91
  interests and success criteria, 97
  internal and external, 85
  MosCoW method, 92
  requirements (*see* Requirements for stakeholders)
  responsibility assignment matrix (*see* Responsibility assignment matrix [RAM])
  risk attitudes, 99
  support vs. activity levels, 96–97
  transaction vs. transformational, 99
Success and constraints, 113–114
  acceptance criteria, 126
  actions to avert project failures, 132
  alignment, 133
  approval criteria, 126–127
  constraints face-off matrix (CFM), 117–119
  criteria table, 128

customer satisfaction, 133
defects, changes, and accuracy, 133
expectations setting (*see* Expectations management)
factors, 129–130
possible options, 122
project charter, 127–128
project criteria, 115–117
project objectives triangle, 120
quality attributes, 133
scope, time, and cost, 128–129
stakeholders criteria, 115
trade-off relationship, 117
trade-offs, 119, 122–123
triple constraint/competing demands, 117
utility, 133
Success criteria expectation gaps, 125
Success criteria table, 128
SWOT analysis
guidelines, 181–182
strengths and opportunities, 182–183
strengths and threats, 183–184
team, 203
weaknesses and opportunities, 183
weaknesses and threats, 184

Team and process success, 130. *See also* Success and constraints
Team building
blocks, 50
stages, 63–65
time and budget constraints, 57
Team contract and ground rules, 270
aspiring behaviors, 269
guidelines, nature of, 268
meetings, 271–272
Technical complexity, 33
Timely risk analysis, 175. *See also* Risks
Time management, 154. *See also* Pareto principle

PM's role, 158
types of activities, 157–158
Transactional activities, 157
Transference, 200–201
Transformational activities, 157–158
Transformational focus
alignment to business objectives, 167–168
communication, 159
conflict, 159–160
control change, 158–159
customer relationship management, 161–162
deliverables and, 161
expectations management, 162–163
lessons learned, 161
merits and trade-offs, 171–172
out of scope activities, 168
people management, 166
priority and urgency, 168–171
project charter, 166–167
quality and customer satisfaction, 160–161
risks, 160
work on objectives, 165–166
Trigger, 197. *See also* Risks
importance, 198
Triple constraint/competing demands, 117
Trust
destroyers, 49
ingredients, 49

Unknown-unknowns risks, 174–175. *See also* Risks
Urgency, risk in
cross risk paired analysis, 195
expected monetary value (EMV), 196

Wasting time, 163
types, 164